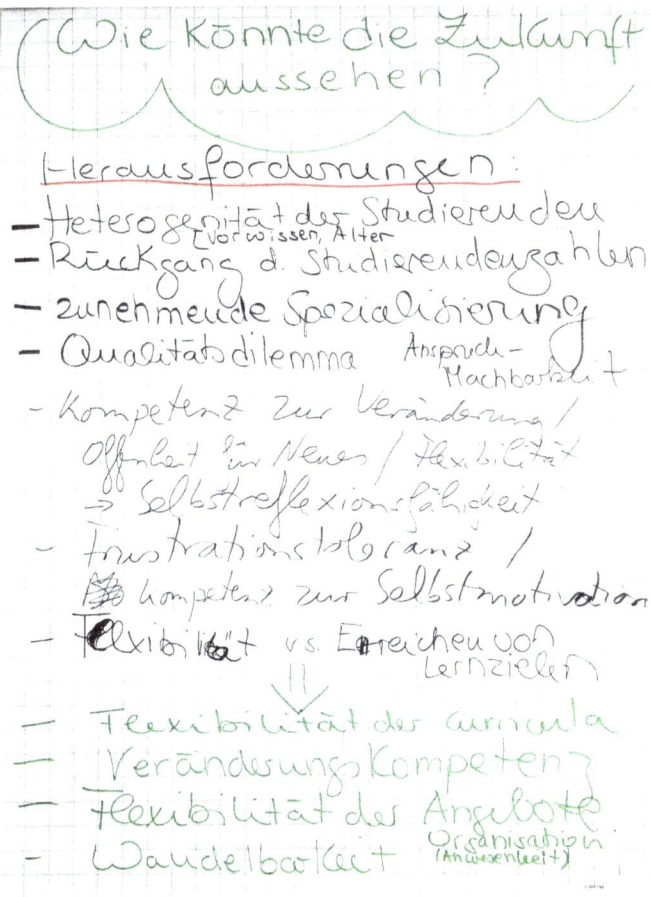

Abb. 2: Ergebnis der Arbeitsgruppe: Wie könnte die Zukunft aussehen?

Die Anforderungen an die Hochschulen, die Hochschulsprachenzentren bzw. die Lehrenden wurden von den Teilnehmerinnen und Teilnehmern des Panels mit folgenden drei Sätzen zusammengefasst:
- Wir brauchen in verschiedener Hinsicht mehr Flexibilität.
- Wir müssen an den (neuen) Kompetenzen der Studierenden anknüpfen.
- D. h. Lehrende müssen ebenfalls wandelbar sein, brauchen andererseits aber auch eine gewisse Gelassenheit.

Literaturverzeichnis

ALONSO, G. (2009). *Kompetenzförderung an der Hochschule. Eine hochschuldidaktische Konzeption von Lernszenarien zur integrativen Vermittlung von Schlüsselkompetenzen.* Göttingen: Sierke Verlag.

BOOS, M. / MIOSGE, N. / FISCHER, J. / BÖGEL, S. / ABBASI, A. (2016). *Integrationstandems und Supervised Networking mit geflüchteten Menschen in studentischen Gruppen durch Service Learning.* In: Gruppe. Interaktion. Organisation. Zeitschrift für Angewandte Organisationspsychologie (GIO), October 2016, Volume 47, Issue 3, 225-230.

CARÉ, J.-M. / DEBYSER, F. (1995). *Simulations globales.* Sèvres: CIEP.

COUNCIL OF EUROPE (2009). *Relating Language Examinations to the Common European Framework of Reference for Languages: Learning, Teaching, Assessment (CEFR). A Manual;* abrufbar unter: http://www.coe.int/t/dg4/linguistic/Manuel1_EN.asp#Manual (letzter Zugriff: 24.04.2017).

DEBYSER, F. (1996). *L'immeuble.* Paris: Hachette.

EUROPARAT (2001). *Gemeinsamer europäischer Referenzrahmen für Sprachen: lernen, lehren, beurteilen.* Straßburg: Europarat / Berlin et al.: Langenscheidt.

FISCHER, J. / CASEY, E. (2005). *Der Einsatz von Fallstudien im Fremdsprachenunterricht an Hochschulen.* In: Gebert, D. (Hrsg.). Innovation aus Tradition. Dokumentation der 23. Arbeitstagung 2004. Bochum: AKS-Verlag, 175–184.

FISCHER, J. / CASEY, E. / ABRANTES, A. M. / GIGL, E. / LEŠNIK, M. (Hrsg.) (2008). *LCaS: Language Case Studies. Teacher training modules on the use of case studies in language teaching at secondary and university level. A handbook.* Strasbourg: Council of Europe.

FISCHER, J. / CHOUISSA, C. / DUGOVIČOVÁ, S. / VIRKKUNEN-FULLENWIDER, A. (2011). *Guidelines for task-based university language testing,* Strasbourg / Graz: Council of Europe.

FISCHER, J. / MUSACCHIO, M. T. / STANDRING, A. (Hrsg.) (2009). *EXPLICS – Exploiting Internet Case Studies and Simulation Templates for Language Teaching and Learning. A Handbook.* Göttingen: Cuvillier Verlag.

KAISER, F. J. (Hrsg.) (1983). *Die Fallstudien. Theorie und Praxis der Fallstudiendidaktik.* Bad Heilbrunn: Klinkhardt.

KIEFER, K.-H. (2004). *Fallstudien – zum Umgang mit einer erfolgreichen Lernmethode im Fachsprachenunterricht Wirtschaftsdeutsch.* In: Info DaF 1, 68–98.

Modulkatalog der ZESS. In: Amtliche Mitteilungen II der Georg-August-Universität Göttingen vom 07.03.2017/Nr. 4, 1353–1888; abrufbar z. B. unter: http://www.uni-goettingen.de/de/modulkatalog-der-zess/476097.html (letzter Zugriff: 25.04.2017).

Rahmenordnung UNIcert® von März 2014, S. 13, abrufbar unter: http://www.unicert-online.org/de/dokumente/unicert%C2%AE-rahmenordnung (letzter Zugriff: 25.04.2017).

RIBÉ, R. / VIDAL, N. (1993). *Project Work.* Oxford: Heinemann.

SCHART, M. (2003). *Projektunterricht – subjektiv betrachtet. Eine qualitative Studie mit Lehrenden für Deutsch als Fremdsprache.* Hohengehren: Schneider Verlag.

WIGGLESWORTH, G. (2008). *Task and Performance Based Assessment.* In: *Shohamy, E. / Hornberger, N. H. (Hrsg).* Encyclopedia of Language and Education, 2ndEdition, Volume 7: Language Testing and Assessment. 111–122.

YAICHE, F. (1996). *Les simulations globales – moded'emploi.* Paris: Hachette.

Zentrale Einrichtung für Sprachen und Schlüsselqualifikationen der Georg-August-Universität Göttingen (2016). Projekt „Integrationstandems und Supervised Networking", http://www.uni-goettingen.de/de/de/551743.html (letzter Zugriff: 25.04.2017).

Panels A5, B4

Dominique Brasseur / Holger Ehlert
Praxis- und Berufsorientierung an Hochschulen (Panel I und II)

Die Panels „Praxis- und Berufsorientierung an Hochschulen I und II" waren im Rahmen der Tagung als aufeinander aufbauende Arbeitskreise konzipiert und die Ergebnisse werden daher hier auch in einem Beitrag zusammenfassend dargestellt.

Vertreterinnen und Vertreter der praxis- und berufsorientierenden Programme, der Career Services und der Hochschulforschung waren eingeladen, gemeinsam die Situation an deutschsprachigen Hochschulen vor der Folie des nunmehr fünfzehnjährigen Bologna-Prozesses sowie die Perspektiven und zukünftigen Herausforderungen der Praxis- und Berufsorientierung im Wissenschaftskontext zu diskutieren.

Wohl kaum ein anderes Handlungsfeld innerhalb der deutschen Hochschullandschaft ist bis heute so heterogen ausgeprägt wie das der Praxis- und Berufsorientierung. An dieser Tatsache hat sich auch fast zwei Jahrzehnte nach Erscheinen der ersten umfassenden Bestandsaufnahme im deutschsprachigen Raum wenig geändert.[1] Umso interessanter und wichtiger ist es, wenn die verantwortlichen Akteure von verschiedenen Hochschulstandorten zusammen treffen, um sich gegenseitig über ihre Arbeit vor Ort auszutauschen, Probleme gemeinsam zu diskutieren und sich schlussendlich zukunftsorientiert weiter vernetzen.

Entsprechend intensiv wurden im Rahmen beider Panels zunächst ausführliche Vorstellungsrunden durchgeführt, die seitens der Moderation bereits mit Fragen zu aktuellen zentralen Problemen und den konkreten jeweiligen Zielsetzungen für das Jahr 2017 verknüpft wurden.

---

[1] Vgl. Ehlert, Holger / Welbers, Ulrich (Hrsg.): Handbuch Praxisinitiativen an Hochschulen : berufsorientierende Angebote für Studierende an Universitäten. Luchterhand. Hochschulwesen – Wissenschaft und Praxis. 1999.

Der wachsende Bedarf an praxis- und berufsorientierenden Angeboten war in den Vor-Bologna-Studiengängen nicht in den Studienstrukturen berücksichtigt. Dies gilt insbesondere für die Geistes- und Kulturwissenschaften. Bereits seit den 90er Jahren wurden daher an einzelnen Hochschulen diverse Programme entwickelt, um Studierenden bereits studienbegleitend besser auf den Übergang in den Beruf vorzubereiten. Die Ausrichtung, Finanzierung und institutionelle Verortung dieser Programme an den Hochschulen ist bislang weiterhin sehr unterschiedlich organisiert: So zum Beispiel auf Fachbereichs- oder Institutsebene, im Rektorat oder als eigene Zentrale Einrichtung. Career Services sind in der Regel in der Verwaltung angesiedelt. Die Finanzierung erfolgt aus Dritt- oder/und Haushaltsmitteln, Studienbeiträgen, Sonderprogrammen, über die Bundesagentur für Arbeit, durch Spenden, mit sonstigen Mitteln oder auch über Teilnahmebeiträge.

Die Mehrheit der vertretenen Programme klagt über ungenügende Planungssicherheit und circa ein Viertel über eine schlechte personelle Ausstattung. Weiterhin werden ein häufiger Personalwechsel aufgrund befristeter Arbeitsverträge und eine unpassende Seminarraumausstattung als Herausforderung benannt.

Trotz hohem Interesse bei der Anmeldung zu den Veranstaltungen wurde einhellig die generell schlechte Teilnahmedisziplin der Studierenden beklagt sowie deren mangelnde Motivation, sobald Lehrveranstaltungen nicht kreditiert werden.

Großen Wert legten die Vertreterinnen und Vertreter einhellig auf die enge Zusammenarbeit mit regionalen und überregionalen Arbeitgebern. Über die Hälfte der Programme kooperiert mit der Bundesagentur für Arbeit, nahezu die Hälfte unterstützt die Studierenden bei der Suche nach geeigneten Praktika.

Als Ziele im Sinne einer Weiterentwicklung wurden dann auch benannt: personelle Stabilisierung, Angebots- und Qualitätssicherung, Positionierung/Etablierung in der Hochschule, neue Modulkonzepte, Ausbau individueller Beratung, Ausbau/Zusammenarbeit mit Unternehmen/Unternehmerkontakte, Entrepreneurship, kontinuierliche Weiterentwicklung und Halten des qualitativen und quantitativen Niveaus, Ausbau der Vermittlung von Praktika, Vernetzung innerhalb der Hochschulen, Multimedialität, sowie die Entwicklung neuer Formate.

Intensiv und kontrovers wurden insbesondere die Themen „Campusmessen" und die Rolle und Funktion der Bundesagentur für die eigene Arbeit an den Hochschulen diskutiert. Dabei waren die Diskutantinnen und Diskutanten stets bestrebt, sowohl die Perspektiven der Hochschulen, als auch die der Unternehmen, die der Bundesagentur – vor allem aber die der Studierenden in den Blick zu nehmen.

Panel A6

Elke Muddemann-Pulla

Selbstpräsentation im Web 2.0 – welche Schlüsselqualifikationen sind hier wichtig?

Zusammenfassung

Selbstpräsentation im Web 2.0 stellt für Studierende und AbsolventInnen einen modernen Weg der Suche nach Praktika, Jobs und Stellen dar.[1] Der Fokus liegt dabei auf sozialen Business-Netzwerken wie XING oder LinkedIn, die sich auf die Darstellung der Berufspersönlichkeit spezialisiert haben. Diese Art der Selbstdarstellung verlangt jedoch mehr als den Status des „digital native" oder die klassische implizite Vermittlung von Schlüsselkompetenzen im (Fach-)Studium – es handelt sich vielmehr um eine Schlüsselkompetenz, die explizit vermittelt werden muss. Auf Hochschulen kommt die Aufgabe zu, MitarbeiterInnen von Serviceeinrichtungen entsprechend zu qualifizieren, damit sie Studierende und AbsolventInnen für Chancen und Risiken der virtuellen Selbstpräsentation sensibilisieren und bei der Erstellung eines aussagekräftigen professionellen Profils unterstützen und beraten können.

1. Selbstpräsentation im Web 2.0: Chancen und Risiken für Studierende/AbsolventInnen

Fast alle Studierenden und AbsolventInnen kennen die mediale Selbstpräsentation in Form von Netzwerken wie Facebook, Twitter & Co. und nutzen sie zur Darstellung ihrer Person im privaten Bereich.[2] Fast alle wissen aber auch, dass die sehr persönliche Selbstdarstellung in reinen Kontakt-Netzwerken sich

---

1 Vgl. Hesse/Schrader 2014, S. 46.
2 Vgl. Hesse/Schrader 2014, S. 11.

nicht unbedingt für die Suche nach Praktikumsstellen, Jobs oder einer festen Anstellung eignet. Sie sind sich der Risiken durchaus bewusst, die bei einem unreflektierten, ungeschickt angelegten Profil für Jobfindung und Karriere entstehen könnten:
- (ungeschickte) Netzwerk-Aktivitäten hinterlassen dauerhafte Spuren im Internet und sind lange auffindbar,
- Brüche im Lebenslauf werden sichtbar,
- Schwächen und Unzulänglichkeiten offenbaren sich ungewollt,
- Berufschancen werden nachhaltig eingeschränkt.

Trotz aller Gefahren wäre jedoch in fast allen Branchen das größte Risiko, aus Sorge vor Fehlern erst gar kein Profil anzulegen – offenbart sich darin doch eine mangelhafte oder fehlende Medienkompetenz, die in den meisten Berufen heute nicht fehlen darf. Daher sollten die Chancen eines durchdachten Profils in Business-Netzwerken den Studierenden/ AbsolventInnen verdeutlicht werden:
- systematischer Aufbau einer virtuellen Reputation,
- Finden und Pflegen entscheidender Kontakte im Business-Bereich,
- gezielte Praktikums- und Jobsuche,
- Gewinnen von Aufmerksamkeit und Vertrauen durch überlegte, planvolle Datenpreisgabe,
- wirksame Platzierung des individuellen Kompetenzprofils und fachlicher Spezialisierungen.

2. Anforderungen an aussagekräftige Profile in Business-Netzwerken

Welche konkreten Anforderungen eine Selbstpräsentation in Business-Netzwerken stellt und was ein Personalverantwortlicher „zwischen den Zeilen" daraus entnehmen kann, ist nur wenigen (Neu-)Nutzern klar. Für die Gestaltung der Profile in sozialen Netzwerken gibt es einige Grundregeln, die auf jeden Fall beachtet werden sollten:[3]

---

3 Vgl. Bärmann 2014, S. 20 ff.; Hesse/Schrader 2014, S. 69 ff.

- mit Übersichtlichkeit und gutem Gesamteindruck punkten,
- durchdachte, authentische Angaben machen,
- eigene Kompetenzen und Stärken in den Mittelpunkt der Selbstdarstellung stellen,
- Brüche und Ungereimtheiten im Lebenslauf geschickt verarbeiten,
- ein ansprechendes, professionelles Foto wählen,
- proaktiv an qualitativ hochwertigen Kontakten arbeiten,
- bei Bewerbungen AnsprechpartnerInnen im Wunsch-Unternehmen finden und direkt kontaktieren,
- per Aktivitätsindex das individuelle Engagement zeigen,
- praktische Erfahrungen herausstellen (Jobs, Praktika, geleistete freiwillige Dienste, Ehrenämter etc.),
- spezielles Wissen, Projekterfahrung und Soft Skills benennen,
- erworbene Fremdsprachen erwähnen – auch Basiskenntnisse,
- Hobbys/Interessen angeben: authentisch ja, exzentrisch nein,
- möglichst präzise formulieren, was genau wo gesucht wird: Branche, Position, Region,
- Keywords (= Schlüssel-Suchwörter von Personalverantwortlichen) geschickt platzieren.

Daneben ist es wichtig, über die Unterschiede und Spezialisierungen der diversen Business-Netzwerke Bescheid zu wissen. Die hierzulande meist genutzten Business-Netzwerke sind XING und LinkedIn; neben aktueller Fachliteratur gibt es Online-Quellen wie z. B. LinkedInsider[4], die ein gutes Bild von Funktionalität und Nutzen der Netzwerke geben. Generell gilt: XING eignet sich eher für den deutschsprachigen Raum (D-A-CH) und ist in der kostenpflichtigen Premium-Variante deutlich besser nutzbar; LinkedIn gilt als größtes internationales Business-Netzwerk und bietet bereits in der Basis-Version gute Funktionalität.

---

[4] Siehe Literaturverzeichnis.

3. Selbstpräsentation im Web 2.0 als Herausforderung an die Vermittlung von Schlüsselkompetenzen in der Hochschule

Studierende und AbsolventInnen benötigen für einen gelungenen Berufseinstieg mithilfe ihres Netzwerk-Profils zunächst generelles Wissen zu aktuellen Entwicklungen auf dem Arbeitsmarkt und den Anforderungen von Arbeitgebern. Außerdem brauchen sie aber ein Bewusstsein ihrer eigenen Stärken und vor allem auch ihrer vorhandenen Schlüsselkompetenzen. Diese sind definiert als „erwerbbare allgemeine Fähigkeiten, Einstellungen, Strategien und Wissenselemente, die bei der Lösung von Problemen und beim Erwerb neuer Kompetenzen in möglichst vielen Inhaltsbereichen von Nutzen sind, so dass eine Handlungsfähigkeit entsteht, die es ermöglicht, sowohl individuellen Bedürfnissen als auch gesellschaftlichen Anforderungen gerecht zu werden."[5]

Gefragt sind also solche Kompetenzen, die nicht (nur) im Fachstudium als fachbezogenes Wissen, sondern quasi „nebenbei" erworben werden. Klassischerweise werden diese Kompetenzen in vier Bereiche eingeteilt:[6]

1. Sozialkompetenz
    - Teamfähigkeit
    - Einfühlungsvermögen (Empathie)
    - Kommunikationsfähigkeit
    - Integrationsbereitschaft
    - Kritikfähigkeit
    - Umgangsstil
    - Menschenkenntnis

2. Selbstkompetenz
    - Selbstvertrauen
    - Selbstdisziplin
    - Selbstreflexion
    - Belastbarkeit
    - Engagement
    - Motivation
    - Neugier
    - Eigenverantwortung

---

5 Orth 1999, S. 107.
6 Vgl. Schaeper 2005, Schaeper/Briedis 2005.

3. Methodenkompetenz
    - Präsentationstechniken
    - Umgang mit neuen Medien
    - Strukturierte Arbeitsweise
    - Zeitmanagement
    - Analytische Fähigkeiten
    - Problemlösungskompetenz
    - Stressresistenz
    - Organisationstalent

4. Sachkompetenz
    - Spezielles Fachwissen
    - Breites Grundlagenwissen
    - Kenntnis wissenschaftlicher Methoden
    - Fächerübergreifendes Denken
    - Fremdsprachen
    - Allgemeinbildung
    - Kenntnisse in EDV
    - Wissen aus Rechts- und Wirtschaftswissenschaften

Studierende und AbsolventInnen haben zwar häufig ein hohes Bewusstsein über ihre Sachkompetenzen, da diese meist in Papier-Form als Zertifikate und Bescheinigungen „greifbar" sind. Es fehlt jedoch meist eine klare Vorstellung ihrer konkreten Sozial-, Selbst- und Methodenkompetenzen. Diese zu identifizieren, zu inventarisieren sowie konkret und griffig für das Online-Profil zu formulieren, gelingt häufig nur mit Unterstützung durch erfahrene BeraterInnen. Bislang gehört diese Form der Beratung an vielen Hochschulen in das Portfolio der Career Services. Während fast 20 % der Career Services Bewerbungsmappen-Checks anbieten, wird jedoch nur bei 10,5 % eine Profilanalyse durchgeführt.[7] Von Beratung oder Workshops für das Erstellen von Online-Profilen in sozialen Netzwerken wird nicht ausdrücklich berichtet. Hier scheint also noch eine Lücke zu klaffen, die die Hochschulen im Interesse des erfolgreichen Berufseinstiegs ihrer AbsolventInnen mit entsprechenden Angeboten füllen sollten.

---

7   Vgl. CSND 2015.

4. Ideen und Anregungen zur Implementierung der Schlüsselkompetenz „Selbstpräsentation im Web 2.0" in die Beratung an Hochschulen

Eine wesentliche Rolle bei der Analyse und Identifikation von Schlüsselkompetenzen kommt dem Abgleich von Selbst- und Fremdwahrnehmung zu, wie zu Beginn des Workshops anhand eines klassischen Partnerinterviews deutlich gemacht wurde. Darüber hinaus sind biografische Methoden hervorragend geeignet, Schlüsselkompetenzen sichtbar zu machen; hier sind etwa narrative Methoden in Beratungsgesprächen als nützliche Instrumente einsetzbar. Ein systematisches Heranführen an das Erarbeiten der vorhandenen Schlüsselkompetenzen geschieht mit dem ProfilPASS®, der seit 2004 als Kondensat vieler verschiedener Kompetenzerfassungsinstrumente in Deutschland als entwicklungsorientierter Ansatz konstruiert und implementiert wird. Kernelement der ProfilPASS®-Arbeit ist eine Annäherung an vorhandene Kompetenzen über die Erfassung von Tätigkeiten, aus denen schrittweise zunächst Fähigkeiten und dann Kompetenzen herausgearbeitet werden.[8] Die so ermittelten Kompetenzen werden anschließend auf verschiedenen Kompetenzstufen (A-B-C1-C2) bewertet und bilden in ihrer individuellen, einmaligen Zusammenstellung einen Profil-Baustein, der gut für die Selbstpräsentation im Web 2.0 nutzbar gemacht werden kann. Im Workshop wurde in Kleingruppen auf diese Weise exemplarisch an authentischen Beispielen von zwei Teilnehmenden gearbeitet. In der Auswertung wurde betont, dass die Konzentration auf ausschließlich positive Aspekte sowie die intensive Auseinandersetzung mit den eigenen Fähigkeiten und Kompetenzen die Selbstwahrnehmung und die Selbst-Wertschätzung deutlich verbessert. Damit ist eine gute Basis für ein durchdachtes Netzwerk-Profil gegeben. Beim Transfer von Kompetenzen in das Online-Profil sollte darauf geachtet werden, dass eine frische, griffige Formulierung der Schlüsselkompetenzen jenseits von Schlagwörtern (wie z. B. „Teamfähigkeit") gewählt wird. Auch dabei ist kompetente Beratung hilfreich.

---

8   Vgl. Harp, Sigrid u. a. (Hrsg.), 2011.

5. Fazit: Selbstpräsentation im Web 2.0 – Herausforderung an Hochschulen

Moderne Medien erobern neben dem Arbeitsmarkt längst auch die Hochschulen. Studierende/AbsolventInnen der aktuellen Generation Z als „digital natives" nutzen Soziale Netzwerke längst mit großer Selbstverständlichkeit, jedoch nicht immer mit der nötigen Professionalität und dem notwendigen Feingefühl. Sehr junge Studierende/AbsolventInnen mit relativ wenig Selbstreflexionskompetenz und (noch) wenig Lebenserfahrung, aber einem großen Bedürfnis nach Selbstdarstellung stellen die Hochschulen vor neue Herausforderungen. Mediale Kompetenz – auch und gerade für die Erstellung von Selbstpräsentation im Web 2.0 –muss als fester Bestandteil der Vermittlung von Schlüsselkompetenzen an Hochschulen integriert und eine qualifizierte Beratung bei der Analyse und Verwendung von Schlüsselkompetenzen vorgehalten werden. Die Ziele eines solchen Angebots sind:

- Studierende/AbsolventInnen zu sensibilisieren für Chancen und Risiken der Selbstpräsentation in beruflichen Online-Netzwerken,
- Profilanalysen für Studierende/AbsolventInnen in größerem Umfang anzubieten,
- Selbstreflexionsfähigkeit und Formulierungsvermögen der Studierenden/AbsolventInnen zu fördern.

Um das leisten zu können, müssen Hochschulen ihre MitarbeiterInnen
- umfassend medial zur Nutzung professioneller Netzwerke aus- und fortbilden,
- für die Analyse und Identifikation von Schlüsselkompetenzen schulen und
- bei der Kontaktpflege zu und dem Informationsaustausch mit Unternehmen – vor allem Personalverantwortlichen! – unterstützen und fördern.

Literaturverzeichnis

BÄRMANN, FRANK (2014): XING: Erfolgreich Netzwerken im Beruf (mitp/Die kleinen Schwarzen). Bonn.

HARP, SIGRID / PIELORZ, MONA/SEIDEL, SABINE/SEUSING, BEATE (Hrsg.) (2011): Praxisbuch ProfilPASS – Ressourcenorientierte Beratung für Bildung und Beschäftigung. Bielefeld.

HESSE, JÜRGEN / SCHRADER, HANS CHRISTIAN (2014): Beruf & Karriere: Die überzeugende Selbstpräsentation im WWW: So nutzen Sie Social Networks, Blogs & Co. für Ihre erfolgreiche Online-Reputation. Freising.

KOSS, STEPHAN (2014): LinkedIn für Dummies. Weinheim.

LUTZ, ANDREAS/RUMOHR, JOACHIM (2013): Xing optimal nutzen: Geschäftskontakte – Aufträge – Jobs. So zahlt sich Networking im Internet aus. Wien.

ORTH, HELEN (1999): Schlüsselqualifikationen an deutschen Hochschulen. Konzepte, Standpunkte und Perspektiven. Neuwied.

SHAH, MICHAEL RAJIV (2014): Karrierebeschleunigung mit Linkedin. Freising.

WARNEMANN, HEINZ W. (2014): XING für Einsteiger: Social Media Minis. Freising.

WOLFF, CONSTANZE (2014): XING für Dummies. Weinheim.

LINKEDINSIDER: https://linkedinsiders.wordpress.com/category/statistik, zuletzt geprüft am 12.07.2016.

CSND (2015): Bericht zur Umfrage des Career Service Netzwerk Deutschland e.V.: Ausgangslage der Career Services an deutschen Hochschulen, http://www.csnd.de/fileadmin/user_upload/Presse-News/Offizielle_Dokumente/Ausgangslage_web.pdf, zuletzt geprüft am 12.07.2016.

SCHAEPER, DR. HILDEGARD (2005): Präsentation zur AKC-Jahrestagung 2005, http://www.dzhw.eu/pdf/pub_vt/22/2005_06_04_Vortrag_SQ_Giessen.pdf, zuletzt geprüft am 12.07.2016.

SCHAEPER, HILDE/ BRIEDIS, KOLJA (2004): Kompetenzen von Hochschulabsolventinnen und Hochschulabsolventen, berufliche Anforderungen und Folgerungen für die Hochschulreform. HIS Projektbericht https://www.bmbf.de/pub/his_projektbericht_08_04.pdf, zuletzt geprüft am 12.07.2016.

Panel B2

Bernd F. W. Springer
Ohne Kulturwissenschaften kein Europa. Vom Nutzen sprachlich-kulturellen Wissens für die Verständigung mit unseren Nachbarn

Das Projekt eines gemeinsamen Europas steckt in der schwersten Krise der letzten Jahrzehnte. Überall sind starke nationalistische Bewegungen auf dem Vormarsch, die Flüchtlingskrise hat in allen Ländern rechtspopulistische Ideen salonfähig gemacht, in Osteuropa sind teilweise der Rechtsstaat und die Pressefreiheit in Gefahr, das Schengen-Abkommen ist partiell außer Kraft gesetzt, Großbritannien tritt aus der EU aus und auch aus anderen Ländern werden Forderungen nach Volksabstimmungen über einen Verbleib in der EU laut.

Zwar wissen wir alle, dass die großen Herausforderungen des 21. Jahrhunderts globaler Art sind, vor denen einzelstaatliches Handeln an Sinn verliert, doch wir sehen zunehmend, dass rationale Argumente gegen die Ängste der Menschen nichts mehr ausrichten können. Obwohl weder die Sicherheitsbedürfnisse, noch die Bedrohung des Lebensstandards, noch der Umgang mit massiver Zuwanderung sich einzelstaatlich lösen lassen, ist überall eine Rückbesinnung auf nationale Interessen zu beobachten.

Diese Rückbesinnung auf die eigene nationale Identität ist nicht verwunderlich. Über Jahrhunderte haben alle europäischen Staaten eine Generation nach der Generation dem Prozess des *nation-making* ausgesetzt. In Kriegssituationen, in denen Staaten gegen Staaten kämpften, dominierten in der Regel nationalstaatliche Identitäten und an diesen orientieren sich in Krisen- oder Angstsituationen die Menschen bis heute zuallererst.

Bernd F. W. Springer

Es ist das größte Versäumnis Europas, dass man keinen dem *nation-making* vergleichbaren Prozess der Schaffung europäischer Identität in den Schulen und Medien verankert hat. Die meisten Europäer fühlen sich nicht in gleich starkem Maße als Europäer, wie sie sich als Italiener, Franzosen oder Polen fühlen. Bei allen Vorteilen, die die europäische Einigung den Menschen gebracht hat – emotional ist Europa nur bei wenigen angekommen. Und so kommt es, dass wir heute ein Europa ohne Europäer haben.

Dennoch hat es immer schon, auch lange vor der EU, solche Europäer gegeben. Dazu zählten viele Künstler und Schriftsteller wie Heinrich Mann, Stefan Zweig oder Lion Feuchtwanger. Was zeichnete solche Leute aus, die sich schon vor hundert Jahren als Europäer fühlten?

Zuallererst: Sie beherrschen mehrere europäische Sprachen, nicht nur eine einzige. *In diesem Sinne* ist die *lingua franca* der Tod Europas. Weil die Menschen glauben, mit Englisch kämen sie überall durch, was de facto nur für zeitlich und inhaltlich begrenzte Kommunikationssituationen stimmt. Zweitens haben jene frühen Europäer sich eifrigst in die Geschichte und Kultur anderer Länder eingelesen. Drittens haben sie andere Länder bereist und dort gelebt, Freunde gefunden und sich eingelebt, sei es auch nur für einen begrenzten Zeitraum. Sie haben am Leben, an der Kultur und am kollektiven Imaginarium anderer Länder teilgenommen – das alles hat dazu geführt, dass sie sich dort auch ein bisschen zu Hause fühlten und sie so die eigene Identität weiten, bereichern konnten. Und so wurden sie zu Europäern. Teilweise auch zu großen Vermittlern zwischen den europäischen Nationen und Kulturen.

Noch einmal also die Frage: Wie wird man Europäer? Erstens durch Fremdsprachen, zweitens durch kulturelles Wissen, drittens durch lebendige Auslandserfahrungen.

Die wichtigste Grundlage für eine europäische Identitätsbildung sind also gute bis sehr gute Fremdsprachenkenntnisse, und zwar nicht nur in der *lingua franca*. Aber Sprachunterricht mit etwas Landeskunde ist bei weitem nicht genug. Man braucht auch profunde *kulturelle* Kenntnisse. Was geschieht, wenn diese zu kurz kommen, zeigt das Beispiel eines Tests, der Aufschluss über den Wissensstand von Studenten der deutschen Sprache in Spanien geben sollte. Auf einer Karte Mitteleuropas sollten die Studenten einige Städte in Deutschland, Österreich und der Schweiz identifizieren. Die Namen der Städte standen neben der Karte, auf der Karte selber gab es weiße Flecken, in die diese Namen einzutragen waren. Gut 35 % verorteten Berlin dort, wo Wien liegt, Hamburg in der Schweiz, Wien an der Nordsee, Zürich in Ostdeutschland, und Wien am Rhein. Bei den historischen Kenntnissen gaben über 30 % an, dass der 2. Weltkrieg mit dem Fall der Mauer endete, Hitler 1989 in der Schlacht um Stalingrad starb und der erste Kanzler der Bundesrepublik Deutschland Bismarck hieß. Was die Einwohnerzahl Deutschlands angeht, glaubten 25 %, dass sie über 200 Millionen liege. Schloss Neuschwanstein wurde als Wohnort von Angela Merkel identifiziert, der Austragungsort des Oktoberfests nach Berlin verlegt, Goethe wurde zum Komponisten des Rings der Nibelungen erklärt und Fritz Lang soll den Faust geschrieben haben.

Bei einer solch grundlegenden Orientierungslosigkeit in Bezug auf das Grundwissen über ein anderes Land ist es schwer vorstellbar, dass selbst noch so gute grammatische Kenntnisse den Sprecher zur Kommunikation mit Einheimischen befähigen.

Dieses Beispiel soll an die heute nur allzu gerne ignorierte Tatsache erinnern, dass Sprachkenntnisse ohne kulturelle Grundkenntnisse nicht zur Kommunikation befähigen. Daran zu erinnern ist deshalb wichtig, weil in vielen europäischen Wissenschaftsministerien die Auffassung kursiert, Philologien seien altmodisches Zeug, das heute überflüssig ist. Diese Auffassung scheint nämlich einen beliebten nächsten Schritt zu legitimieren, der im Zuge europäischer Sparmaßnahmen die Philologien ganz abschaffen und die Vermittlung von Fremdsprachenkenntnissen in Sprachschulen auslagern will. Diese Entwicklung ist in einigen Ländern bereits in vollem Gang. Dies wäre – unbemerkt von der Öffentlichkeit – ein folgenschwerer weiterer Schritt zur Demontage Europas.

Nicht die Abschaffung der Philologien ist sinnvoll, sondern ihre Modernisierung und Umwandlung in Kulturstudien, oder Cultural Studies, wie es meistens heißt. Damit ist Folgendes gemeint: Nicht nur Sprache und Literatur, als die beiden traditionellen Gegenstände der Philologien, sondern auch Film, Musik, Kunst, Geografie, Geschichte und Politik sind mit einzubeziehen, wenn es um die Frage geht: Welches Wissen müssen wir vermitteln, um Studenten in die Lage zu versetzen, ein anderes Land, eine andere Kultur, eine andere Mentalität zu verstehen?

Dazu bedarf es eines erweiterten Kulturbegriffs, wie er in der Forschung zur Interkulturellen Kommunikation schon seit Jahrzehnten zugrunde gelegt wird. Und man muss hinzufügen: Auch Kenntnisse in Interkultureller Kommunikation gehören zu modernen spanischen, französischen, italienischen oder deutschen Kulturstudien.

In dem Buch „Das kommt mir spanisch vor", 2012 im iudicium Verlag München erschienen, werden auf gut 300 Seiten die klassischen *critical incidents* versammelt, analysiert und kommentiert, die dafür sorgen, dass es – in diesem Fall zwischen Spaniern und Deutschen – trotz bester Sprachkenntnisse und guten Willens immer wieder zu atmosphärischen Störungen kommt.

Aus diesem Buch stellte der Vortrag in seinem Hauptteil einige solcher *critical incidents* vor. Dabei ging es um folgende Bereiche, die in traditionellen Philologien und auch in modernen Sprachlehrbüchern oft nicht vorkommen.

1. *Begrüßungs- und Abschiedsrituale:* Vor allem zwischen Menschen verschiedenen Geschlechts können kulturell unterschiedliche Begrüßungsrituale Unsicherheiten verursachen. Die in romanischen Ländern üblichen Küsse auf die Wangen würde etwa gegenüber einer moslemischen oder japanischen Frau Empörung verursachen. Beim Verabschieden sollte man z. B. darauf achten, wie viel Zeit man diesem Vorgang in einer Kultur einräumt. In Spanien dauert das Verabschieden in der Regel mehr als doppelt so lange wie in Deutschland, es ist ein eigenes Ritual.
2. *Verhaltensnormen und Etikette:* Gewohnheiten des Schlange-Stehens oder das Verkehrsverhalten jenseits der eigentlichen Verkehrsregeln, wie z. B. das konkrete Aushandeln der Vorfahrt zwischen Autofahrern und Fußgängern, sind ungeschriebene Regeln, die selten in einem Reiseführer zu finden sind. Am einfachsten sind noch die Regeln der Etikette zu erlernen, z. B. die Tischsitten, denn hierfür gibt es oft einschlägige Ratgeber.
3. Ähnliches gilt für *Essgewohnheiten:* Dass die Bedeutung des Brotes und auch des Kaffees (z. B. Kaffee und Kuchen) in der spanischen und in der deutschen Kultur sehr unterschiedlich sein können, sieht bzw. erlebt man

relativ leicht, so dass man hier versuchen kann, sich den Ess- und Trinkgewohnheiten des Gastlandes anzupassen, wenn man dies möchte.
4. *Fragen des Geschmacks* (Wasser mit oder ohne Kohlensäure) und der Mode (Krawattenfarbe) sind deutlich sichtbar bzw. schmeckbar, treten daher relativ leicht ins Bewusstsein und können, mit toleranter Einstellung, ohne größere Schwierigkeiten als kulturelle Unterschiede akzeptiert werden.
5. *Unterschiedliche Geräuschpegel* werden zwar in der Regel auch sofort wahrgenommen, aber der andere Umgang mit lauten Geräuschen wird trotzdem nicht ohne weiteres verstanden, so dass es schwerlich zu einer toleranten Einstellung gegenüber einem anderen Umgang mit ‚Krach' bzw. ‚ruido' kommt.
6. *Gesten und Körpersprache* sind zwar leicht wahrnehmbar, was aber noch nicht bedeutet, dass sie auch richtig gedeutet werden (z. B. das Wippen mit dem Bein).
7. *Polychrones bzw. monochrones* Verhalten (d. h. man macht mehrere Dinge gleichzeitig oder eins nach dem andern) ist zwar prinzipiell auch wahrnehmbar, bleibt aber meistens unbewusst und kann zu einer negativen Gesprächsatmosphäre beitragen. Wenn ein Angestellter in einer Bank einen Kunden bedient, gleichzeitig am Telefon spricht, im Computer etwas sucht und einem Kollegen durch Gesten etwas zu verstehen geben will, dann kann ein solches Verhalten, wenn es andauert, auf einen Angehörigen einer monochron orientierten Kultur äußerst unhöflich wirken.
8. Die *Trennung von Privatsphäre und Arbeitswelt* ist seltener wahrnehmbar, sie gehört zu den kulturellen Grundeinstellungen einer Gesellschaft, die oft unbewusst bleiben. Man kann sie nur durch Interpretation konkreter Indizien erschließen. Ich kann nur schwer abschätzen, ob die Tatsache, dass mich ein Geschäftspartner vom Flughafen abholt, ein Signal außergewöhnlicher Zuvorkommenheit ist, oder eher zu einer in dieser Kultur verbreiteten Form der Vorbereitung einer angenehmen Verhandlungsatmosphäre gehört.
9. *Sprechhandlungen* sind einer der wenigen linguistischen Aspekte im Bereich dieser Kommunikationsstörungen. Und dennoch geht es hier

nicht so sehr um grammatische oder lexikalische Fragen, sondern um die unterschiedlichen kulturellen Kodierungen einer Aussage. „Wie geht's? – Qué tal?" ist in Spanien oft als Begrüßungsformel (ähnlich wie das englische „How are you?") gemeint, wird aber von einem Deutschen in der Regel als Frage verstanden und natürlich wirkt es in dieser Perspektive dann irrtümlicherweise oberflächlich, wenn der andere sich an einer Antwort gar nicht interessiert zeigt.

10. Noch viel schwieriger zu durchschauen ist das Thema von *expliziten oder weniger expliziten Äußerungen*. Etwa die Frage, wie man in einer bestimmten Kultur Kritik übt, ob man die Kritikpunkte direkt ansprechen darf oder besser nur andeutet, ist ein hochkomplexes und wenig erforschtes, aber für die Kommunikation sehr wichtiges Thema.

11. Das gleiche gilt für *Gesprächsorganisation und Gesprächsstrategien*. Beides sind Aufgaben für eine kulturspezifische Diskursanalyse. Man weiß, dass die Gesprächsorganisation z. B. zwischen Franzosen und Deutschen oder auch Chinesen und Deutschen völlig unterschiedlich, ja fast inkompatibel ist – und zwar unabhängig von der Sprache, in der die Unterhaltung stattfindet.

12. Schließlich ein Thema, dass so wichtig ist wie die Luft zum Atmen: Sie ist immer da, man sieht sie nicht, man denkt fast nie explizit an sie, aber ohne sie geht gar nichts. Das ist das Thema von *Zeit und Raum*. Hierbei geht es weniger um unterschiedliche Essenszeiten oder die Frage, ob man am Restauranttisch mehr oder weniger Platz hat als in einem anderen Land. Das sind nur die Spitzen des Eisberges. Zeit und Raum sind die beiden wichtigsten Grundkategorien unserer Wahrnehmung. Sie bestimmen wesentlich unsere Gefühle und Urteile, aber sie bleiben meistens unbewusst. Was ist Pünktlichkeit in einer bestimmten Kultur? Was bedeutet *lange warten*? Was bedeutet *schnell sprechen*? Wie viele Menschen pro Quadratmeter prägen unsere Vorstellung von *leer* oder *überfüllt*? Was sind *weite Entfernungen*?

Wenn wir diese kulturellen Besonderheiten einmal danach ordnen, wie leicht oder schwer wir sie wahrnehmen und uns auf sie einstellen können, dann ergibt sich das Bild einer Pyramide oder die in ähnlichen Zusammenhängen so oft benutzte Metapher eines Eisberges. Sie hat den Vorteil, dass jedes Kind weiß, dass die Gefahr für einen Schiffbruch bzw. für ein Auflaufen nicht da am größten ist, wo der Eisberg sichtbar ist, sondern an seinen vielfach größeren, unter der Wasseroberfläche verborgenen Teilen. Das Gleiche gilt auch für den Kontakt mit anderen Kulturen.

Die sichtbaren Phänomene können wahrgenommen und bewusst verarbeitet werden: Architektur, Mode, Literatur, Ikonen und Symbole, Berühmtheiten etc.

Verhaltensweisen sind zwar auch sichtbar, aber nicht immer in ihrer Bedeutung verstehbar: ein formelles, korrektes und höfliches Verhalten oder ein lockeres, informelles, entspannteres Auftreten, ein autoritärer oder ein partizipativer Führungsstil, Strategien der Unsicherheitsvermeidung, Formen der Äußerung von Kritik, Umgang zwischen den Geschlechtern und Generationen, umweltbewusstes Verhalten etc.

Noch schwieriger wird es bei Meinungen und Urteilen, die aufgrund von oft unbewussten, auf jeden Fall aber unsichtbaren Werten zustande kommen: der Wert der Arbeit, die Bedeutung von Sicherheit bzw. persönlicher Absicherung, Individualismus versus Kollektivismus, Fragen der Geschlechter(un)gleichheit, Einstellungen zur Demokratie etc.

Und schließlich die kulturellen Grundeinstellungen. Sie sind nicht nur unsichtbar, sondern in der Regel auch gänzlich unbewusst: Raum- und Zeitgefühl, das Verhältnis des Menschen zur Natur, Auffassungen von der Natur des Menschen als grundsätzlich gut oder böse, Glücksvorstellungen, religiöse Grundmuster, die Verteilung von Reichtum und Macht. Natürlich können diese Grundeinstellungen bewusst gemacht werden, aber im Alltag steuern sie unser Denken und Fühlen doch meistens in unbewusster Weise, da wir sie durch unsere Sozialisation verinnerlicht haben und nicht täglich neu hinterfragen.

Alles das spiegelt sich wider in unseren Muttersprachen. Für alles das hält die Sprache Redemittel, Sprichwörter und verschiedene Register bereit, die *genau so* in einer anderen Sprache vielleicht gar nicht existieren. Oder um es anders zu formulieren: Jede Sprache ist eine eigene Welt. Jede Sprache ist *die* ganze Welt, mit ihrer Geologie und ihrer Botanik, mit dem kompletten Katalog menschlicher Leidenschaften, den Tiernamen und ihren Namen für

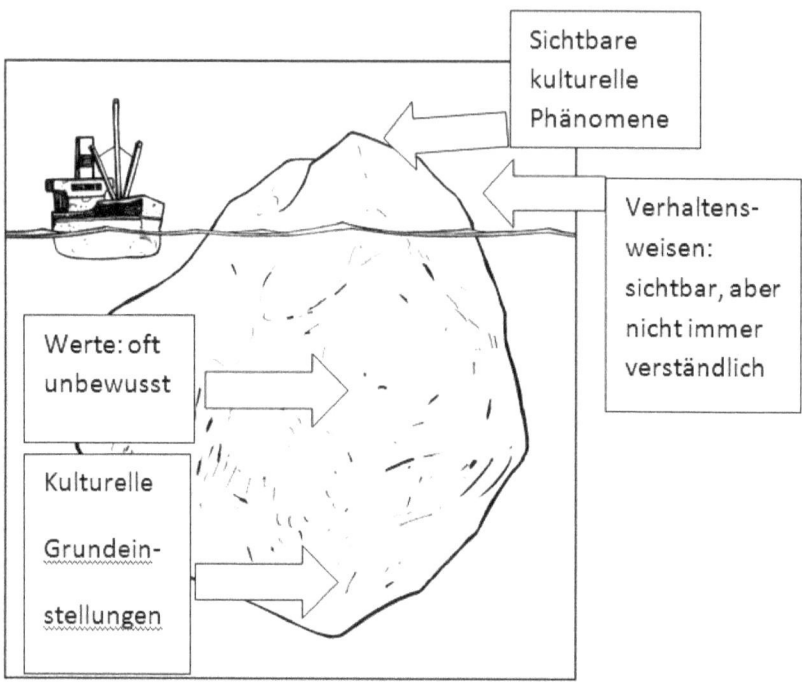

Abb. 1: Bewusste und unbewusste Wahrnehmung kultureller Phänomene

das, was gar nicht existiert. Jede Sprache hat ihre eigene Perspektive auf die Welt. Dies ist ihre Kultur.

Wer glaubt, dass wir weltweit problemlos kommunizieren können, nur weil wir vielleicht sehr gut Englisch sprechen, versteht nicht, dass ein Chinese, ein Deutscher und ein Spanier, auch wenn sie sich in ausgezeichnetem Englisch unterhalten, nach verschiedenen kulturellen Codes agieren, denn sie hören auch beim Gebrauch einer *lingua franca* nicht auf, wie ein Chinese, ein Deutscher und ein Spanier zu denken und zu fühlen.

In einer anderen Sprache kommunizieren bedeutet in einem anderen kulturellen Kontext handeln. Jenseits grammatischer und syntaktischer Aspekte hat jede Sprache eigene kulturelle Register, ihre eigenen kulturellen Codes.

Diese zu dechiffrieren ist eine Aufgabe, die jenseits des konventionellen Spracherlernens liegt. Kulturelles Wissen hilft uns
- zu verstehen, dass Sprache und menschliche Kommunikation essenziell kulturell kodiert sind,
- uns selber und unsere eigene Kultur besser zu verstehen,
- andere Kulturen und Menschen besser zu verstehen,
- Vorurteile zu revidieren,
- uns im Kontakt mit Ausländern sicherer zu fühlen,
- im privaten und beruflichen Kontakt mit Ausländern mehr Erfolg zu haben.

Bei der im Kontakt mit anderen Kulturen geforderten Anpassungsleistung geht es weder um eine kulturelle Selbstaufgabe oder völlige Assimilation an die fremde Kultur, noch um eine Separation von ihren Einflüssen, wie dies der Fall ist, wenn man in einem fremden Land strikt nach den Gewohnheiten der eigenen Kultur weiterlebt und jegliche Anpassung verweigert. Die Balance zwischen der Wahrung eigener und der Offenheit für fremde Kulturstandards, die einem sinnvoll, gut oder nützlich erscheinen (man muss sich nicht alles zu eigen machen!), bereichert die eigene Persönlichkeit: Man überprüft eigene Werte, behält sie bei, wenn dies wünschenswert erscheint, und ergänzt sie durch andere Werte. Diese Balance führt auch zu ‚Toleranz' im besten Sinne des Wortes: zu eigenen Positionen und Werten stehen und gleichzeitig andere Auffassungen verstehen und als gleichberechtigt akzeptieren.

Es ist also wichtig, vor kulturellen Unterschieden nicht die Augen zu verschließen, auch wenn es lange Zeit politisch nicht korrekt war, kulturelle Unterschiede zu betonen. Dazu bedarf es eines besonderen kulturanalytischen Wissens; es reicht nicht, ein paar unterhaltsame Anekdoten über meine Begegnungen mit Franzosen, Polen oder Chinesen zum Besten geben zu können. Kulturelles Wissen bereichert uns persönlich und versetzt uns in die Lage, andere Mentalitäten zu verstehen. Gute Sprach- und Landeskenntnisse, gegenseitiges Verstehen und Respekt sind die Grundlage für ein friedliches Miteinander, für Anpassung und Integration. Ohne ein kulturelles Grundwissen über unsere Nachbarn gibt es kein Europa, ohne kulturelle Fremderfahrungen keine Europäer.

Literaturverzeichnis

BERND F. W. SPRINGER: *Das kommt mir spanisch vor,* iudicium: München, 2012, S. 277.

BERND F. W. SPRINGER (Hrsg.): *La comunicación hispano-alemana. Por qué no nos entendemos y cómo conseguirlo,* Edition Reichenberger: Kassel, 2015, S. 304. (In beiden Büchern findet sich weitere Literatur zum Thema)

Panel B3

Gardenia Alonso / Johann Fischer

Handlungs- und Kompetenzorientierung im Bereich des Lehrens, Lernens und Überprüfens von Fremdsprachenkompetenzen?

1. Ziele des Panels

Ziel des Panels war es, zunächst Konzepte des handlungsorientierten Unterrichts und Prüfungsansatzes zu erläutern, abzugrenzen und zu reflektieren, bevor in einem zweiten Schritt eine Bestandsaufnahme hinsichtlich der bereits erfolgten Umsetzung an den vertretenen Einrichtungen vorgenommen und abschließend die Frage nach zukünftigen Weiterentwicklungen und Bedarfen bearbeitet wurden.

2. Handlungsorientierung und Kompetenzorientierung – Definition und Abgrenzung

Das Lernen von Fremdsprachen gestaltet sich in Beziehung auf konkretes *Handeln* sowie in vielfältigen gedanklichen Operationen. Der Kompetenzaufbau entwickelt sich dabei durch Problemlösen, Handeln und die Reflexion des Handelns. Aber wie sollen wir lernen und prüfen? Und welches ist die geeignete Lern- und *Prüfungsmethode*?

Kompetenzen sind allgemeine intellektuelle Fähigkeiten im Sinne von Dispositionen, die eine Person befähigen, in sehr unterschiedlichen Situationen anspruchsvolle Aufgaben zu meistern. Kompetenzen sind dabei „auf bestimmte Klassen von Situationen und Anforderungen bezogene kognitive Leistungsdispositionen, die sich psychologisch als Kenntnisse, Fertigkeiten,

Strategien, Routinen oder auch bereichsspezifische Fähigkeiten beschreiben lassen".[1] Daher stellt sich die Frage, was gelernt und geprüft werden soll, d. h. die Frage nach den Lern- und Prüfungs*zielen*.

Ausgehend von der Aussage Kliemes „Eine Disposition, die Personen befähigt, bestimmte Arten von Problemen erfolgreich zu lösen." (Klieme et al. 2003: 72) kann man diese für die Kompetenz im Fremdsprachenlernen wie folgt abändern: „Eine Disposition, die Personen befähigt unterschiedliche Arten von *kommunikativen* Problemen durch *interkulturelle, fremdsprachige Handlungsfähigkeit* erfolgreich zu lösen."

Schematisch lassen sich die verschiedenen Faktoren, die das Unterrichten, Lernen und Prüfen von Fremdsprachenkenntnissen an der Hochschule bedingen, wie folgt darstellen:

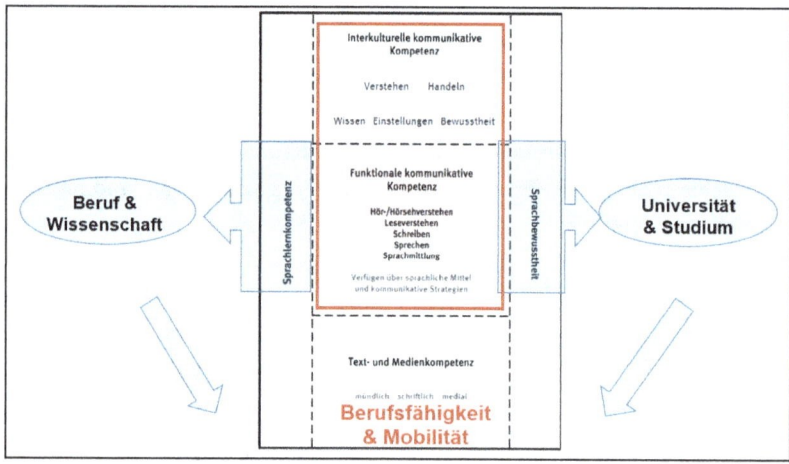

Abb. 1: Umgang mit Fremdsprachenkenntnisse an der Hochschule.
  In Anlehnung an KMK (2014: S. 12)

Ein zentrales Ziel des Fremdsprachenunterrichts an der Hochschule ist es, eine kommunikative Kompetenz zu entwickeln (oder aufbauend auf bereits

---

[1] Vgl. Weinert (1999) zitiert nach Klieme et al. (2001: S. 182). Weinert erstellte 1999 ein Gutachten zur Definition und Auswahl von Kompetenzen für internationale Schulleistungsstudien mit Empfehlungen zur adäquaten Durchführung solcher Studien.

durch Schule und andere Kontexte bereits vorhandene Kompetenzen weiter auszubauen), um in Studium und Beruf/ Wissenschaft einen mündlichen und schriftlichen Diskurs zu ermöglichen. Diese Kompetenz sollte Lernende dazu befähigen, ihre Sprachkenntnisse sowohl im Studium als auch im Beruf situationsadäquat und adressatengerecht sowie pragmatisch und interkulturell angemessen einzusetzen. Hierbei sollen die im Fremdsprachenunterricht an der Hochschule (weiter)entwickelten Kompetenzen die Lernenden zu Mobilität und zur Bewältigung von Aufgaben insbesondere in einem beruflichen internationalen und interkulturellen Kontext innerhalb und außerhalb der Hochschule befähigen.

Die zu entwickelnde Diskursfähigkeit kann in fünf Bereiche untergliedert werden: funktionale kommunikative Kompetenz, interkulturelle Kompetenz, Text- und Medienkompetenz, Sprachbewusstheit und Sprachlernkompetenz"[2]. Die Teilkompetenzen der kommunikativen Kompetenz orientieren sich am GER.

Ein weiteres elementares Ziel des Fremdsprachenunterrichts an der Hochschule ist die Weiterentwicklung interkultureller kommunikativer Kompetenzen, die auf das Verstehen und Handeln insbesondere in universitären und beruflichen Kontexten ausgerichtet ist. Die Lernenden erarbeiten sich die in fremdsprachigen und fremdkulturellen Texten enthaltenen Informationen und Aufforderungen zum Handeln. Der Lernkontext muss hierbei Voraussetzungen für die Reflexion der Texte und Aufgaben vor dem eigenen kulturellen Hintergrund schaffen und das Zusammenspiel funktionaler kommunikativer Kompetenz, Sprachbewusstheit sowie Text- und Medienkompetenz der Lernenden fördern. Dies lässt sich durch den Ansatz der Handlungsorientierung in hohem Maße erreichen.

Das Grundprinzip der Handlungsorientierung besteht darin, dass die Person durch eine Aufgabe zum Handeln angeregt wird. Die Aufgabe ist dabei von ganz zentraler Bedeutung für das Unterrichts- bzw. Prüfungskonzept. Dabei verstehen wir „Aufgabe" gemäß folgender Definition des englischen Begriffs „task" von Skehan:

---

2   Vgl. KMK (2014: S. 12).

> A task is an activity which requires learners to use language, with emphasis on meaning, to attain an objective.[3]

D. h. die Aufgabe muss für die jeweilige Zielperson sinnvoll sein und eine Bedeutung haben. Außerdem muss mit der Aufgabe ein (kommunikativer) Zweck erfüllt werden. Es geht nicht darum, etwas zu sagen um des Sagens willen, sondern darum, Inhalte, Erkenntnisse, Wissen etc. der jeweiligen Gesprächsperson zu kommunizieren. Die Wichtigkeit des Bedeutungsaspektes beschreibt Skehan auch in folgendem Text:

> Tasks [...] are activities which have meaning as their primary focus. Success in tasks is evaluated in terms of achievement of an outcome, and tasks generally bear some resemblance to real-life language use. So task-based instruction takes a fairly strong view of communicative language teaching.[4]

Hier betont Skehan nochmals, dass mit der Aufgabe ein bestimmtes Ziel verfolgt werden soll und am Ende ein Ergebnis bzw. ein Produkt vorliegen sollte. Weiterhin betont er, dass sich die Aufgaben nahe an der Lebenswirklichkeit orientieren sollten.

Für die Umsetzung des handlungsorientierten Konzeptes im Unterricht gilt es, den jeweiligen Kurs bzw. die jeweilige Aufgabensequenz als Einheit zu denken, d. h. die Lehrkraft überlegt sich, was am Ende herauskommen soll (Definition der übergeordneten Aufgabe), und definiert anschließend die einzelnen Schritte (Festlegen der Einzelaufgaben und Schritte).

Dies betont z. B. Puren in seinem Konzept, wenn er schreibt:

> La mise en œuvre de la perspective actionnelle suppose logiquement un passage à une « entrée par l'action », l'unité affichée de l'unité didactique (son titre) étant désormais celle d'une action unique.[5]

bzw.:

> [...] l'« entrée par l'action », c'est-à-dire un modèle d'unité didactique où toutes les activités dans tous les domaines (CO, CE, PO, PE, lexique, culture, grammaire

---

3 Skehan 2003: S. 3.
4 Skehan 2003: S. 20.
5 Puren 2008: S. 4.

et graphie-phonie) sont conçues en fonction d'une action unique à partir de laquelle et à propos de laquelle est construite l'unité didactique.[6]

Was die Begrifflichkeiten betrifft, so stehen u. E. die Begriffe „Aufgabenorientierung" und „Handlungsorientierung" in engem Zusammenhang: Während „Aufgabenorientierung" den Blick auf die Lehrkraft richtet, konzentriert sich der Begriff „Handlungsorientierung" stärker auf die bzw. den Lernenden. Anders formuliert: Die Lehrkraft gibt den Lernenden eine Aufgabe, die dadurch zur Aktion animiert werden und kommunikativ auf den Input reagieren:

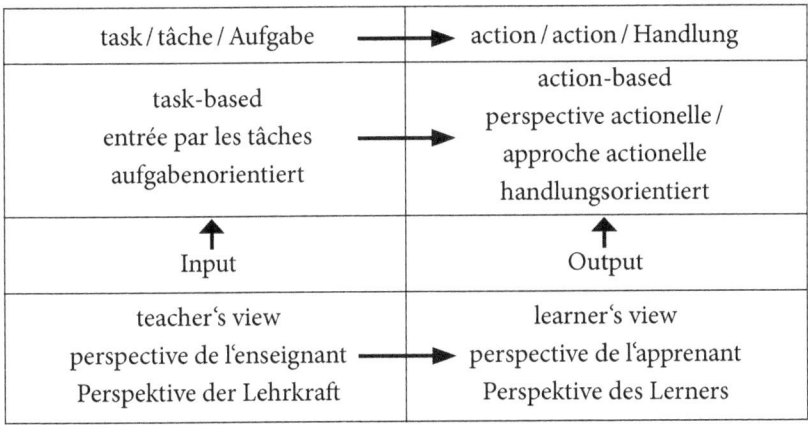

Abb. 2: Interaktion Lehrer/Lerner, vgl. Fischer et al. (2011: S. 17)

Als methodische Schwerpunkte der Handlungsorientierung können festgehalten werden:
- lernerzentrierter Ansatz,
- Individualisierung des Lernprozesses,
- aufgabenbasierter und handlungsorientierter Ansatz für den Unterricht,
- problembasierter Ansatz (PBL),
- Authentizität des Materials und der Situationen.

Der handlungsorientierte Ansatz stellt dabei die bzw. den Lernenden ins Zentrum des Unterrichts bzw. des Lernens, d. h. ihre bzw. seine Interessen,

---
6   Puren 2008: S. 12.

Kenntnisse, Kompetenzen, sprachlichen Fertigkeiten, und fordert sie bzw. ihn auf, eine (authentische) Aufgabe zu bewältigen, wobei sie bzw. er ihre bzw. seine Kompetenzen, sprachlichen Fertigkeiten und auch ihr bzw. sein Wissen einsetzen kann.[7]

Was das Verhältnis zwischen kommunikativem Ansatz und Handlungsorientierung anbelangt, so lässt sich festhalten:

> Task-based language learning and testing can best be seen as a more focused development of the communicative approach to teaching languages. The hallmarks of the communicative approach include a focus on communicating meaning, using authentic materials, integrating skills, and centring instruction on the students and their communicative needs. What the task-based approach adds is an emphasis on embedding holistic communicative acts into a specific context and situation, with a specific aim that mirrors the actual or future communicative aims of the learner.[8]

Im Rahmen des Projektes „Guidelines for task-based university language testing" (GULT) des Europäischen Fremdsprachenzentrums des Europarates in Graz hat das Team dieses Verhältnis wie folgt schematisch dargestellt, um deutlich zu machen, dass sich der handlungsorientierte Ansatz als eine Weiterentwicklung des kommunikativen Ansatzes versteht und so die Tradition der Fremdsprachendidaktik berücksichtigt:

---

7 Vgl. hierzu auch Alonso (2009: 115 f.).
8 Fischer et al. 2011: S. 18.

Abb. 3: Kommunikativer Ansatz und Handlungsorientierung, Fischer et al. (2011: S. 21)

3. Handlungsorientierung beim Unterrichten und Lernen

Handlungsorientierte Konzepte für den Unterricht sind – wie erläutert – aufgabenbasiert. Als geeignete Konzepte haben sich dabei Projektarbeit, globale Simulation und Fallstudie erwiesen, wobei die Fallstudie aufgrund ihres problembasierten Ansatzes besondere Möglichkeiten bietet, sowohl in Bezug auf Authentizität von Aufgabe, Situation und Rolle, als auch auf die Motivation der Lernenden.

3.1 Handlungsorientierte Ansätze

3.1.1 Globale Simulation

Debyser definiert die globale Simulation wie folgt:
> Une simulation globale est un protocole ou un scénario cadre qui permet à un groupe d'apprenants pouvant aller jusqu'à une classe entière d'une trentaine d'élèves, de créer un univers de référence – un immeuble, un village, une île, un cirque, un hôtel – de l'animer de personnages en interaction et d'y simuler

toutes les fonctions du langage que ce cadre, qui est à la fois un lieu-thème et un univers du discours, est susceptible de requérir.[9]

Globale Simulationen[10] weisen folgende Kennzeichen auf:

- Es wird eine fiktive Welt geschaffen, d. h. ein Raum, in dem die Lernenden eine fiktive Lebenswirklichkeit erschaffen. Als Rahmen für diese fiktive Welt kann z. B. ein Wohnblock, eine Insel, ein Dorf, ein Unternehmen oder eine Konferenz von der Lehrkraft (bzw. den Lernergruppen) gewählt werden.[11]
- Dieser Rahmen wird anschließend mit Leben gefüllt, d. h. es werden bestimmte Situationen simuliert und Dokumente – schriftlicher und mündlicher Natur – produziert.

Wenn man, wie bei der Simulation eines fiktiven Unternehmens im Rahmen eines Wirtschaftssprachkurses, den Business Plan für ein fiktives Unternehmen in einer Stadt im Zielsprachenland im Rahmen des Kurses entwickeln und schriftlich abfassen lässt, identifizieren sich die Lernenden in zunehmendem Maße mit dem Projekt. Die Studierenden müssen so reelle bzw. realistische Aufgaben bewältigen. Die Identifikation mit diesem Projekt wird noch weiter gefördert, wenn die Studierenden ihren Business Plan Fachleuten (wie z. B. Mitarbeitenden von IHK, einer Bank oder eines potenziellen Konkurrenten) vorstellen und verteidigen müssen. So werden die Kompetenzen in einer „fiktiven Lebenswirklichkeit" überprüft. Die Fiktion wird zunehmend authentischer und aus Fiktion wird eine neue Realität.[12]

3.1.2 Projektarbeit

Bei der Projektarbeit[13] erarbeiten die Lernenden gemeinsam ein Produkt, wie z. B. eine Broschüre, ein Poster, einen Flyer oder ein Marketingkonzept, das für einen konkreten Zweck eingesetzt wird. Die Projektarbeit zeichnet sich

---

9 Debyser 1996: IV.
10 Vgl. hierzu auch: Caré / Debyser (1995); Debyser (1996); Fischer et al. (2008: S. 12–18); Yaiche (1996).
11 Beispiele von globalen Simulationsprojekten für den Fremdsprachenunterricht an der Hochschule sind im Internet abrufbar unter: http://www.zess.uni-goettingen.de/explics/.
12 Fischer 2005.
13 Vgl. z. B. Ribé / Vidal 1993; Schart 2003.

dabei durch Authentizität, durch ein hohes Maß an Relevanz und einen realen Nutzwert für die Lernenden aus.

3.1.3 Fallstudie

Die Arbeitsgruppe des Projektes „LCaS – Language Case Studies" des Europäischen Fremdsprachenzentrums definierte eine Fallstudie als die Analyse eines Problems in einer bestimmten Situation, zu dem es keine eindeutige bzw. richtige Lösung gibt[14]. Kaiser[15] bot bereits 1983 folgende Definition:
> Darstellung einer konkreten Situation aus der betrieblichen Praxis oder dem Alltagsleben, die anhand bestimmter Tatsachen, Ansichten und Meinungen dargestellt wird, auf deren Grundlagen eine Entscheidung getroffen werden muss.

Bei Fallstudien sollte nach unserem Verständnis mit authentischem Material aus Printmedien und gegebenenfalls mit authentischen Audio- und Videodateien gearbeitet werden. Dabei handelt es sich um eine quantitativ relativ umfangreiche Dokumentation. Bei der Fallstudienarbeit wird ein Problem analysiert, das einen gewissen Grad an Komplexität aufweist (also nicht einfach mit „ja" oder „nein" zu beantworten ist) und zu einer kontroversen Diskussion anregt.[16]

3.1.4 Service Learning

Auch Service Learning-Modelle nutzen den handlungsorientierten Ansatz sehr erfolgreich und bieten durch die praktische Umsetzung in der Realität der sozialen Projekte ein noch höheres Maß an Authentizität.[17]

---

14 Fischer et al. 2008: S. 17.
15 Zitiert nach Kiefer 2004: S. 70.
16 Beispiele von Fallstudien für den Fremdsprachenunterricht an der Hochschule sind im Internet abrufbar unter: http://www.zess.uni-goettingen.de/explics/.
17 Vgl. z. B. Altenschmidt et al. 2009; Backhaus-Maul / Roth 2013; Backhaus-Maul et al. 2015; Boos et al. 2016; Stark et al. 2013.

3.2 Die Handlungsorientierung im Fremdsprachenunterricht

Grundsätzlich gilt für handlungsorientierte Ansätze, dass die Lernenden aufgrund ihrer mannigfaltigen Vorkenntnisse, Kompetenzen und Interessen die Aufgaben unterschiedlich angehen und so sehr verschiedenartige Ergebnisse erarbeitet werden, wie folgendes Schema zeigt:

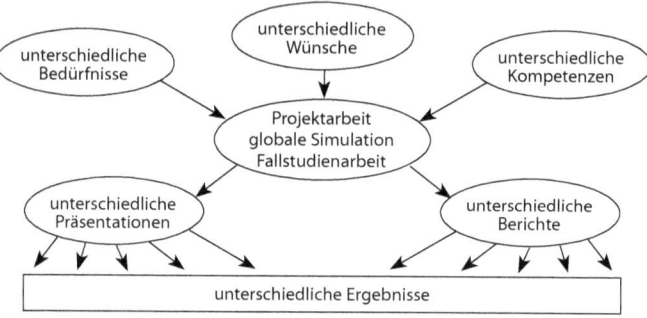

Abb. 4: Handlungsorientierter Ansatz

Die handlungsorientierte Fremdsprachenlehre an der Hochschule sollte dabei folgende Charakteristika aufweisen:
- Es sollten Situationen bearbeitet werden, die für die Berufsausübung bedeutsam sind (Lernen für das Handeln).
- Die Handlungen sollten möglichst selbst ausführbar sein oder eine gedankliche Nachvollziehbarkeit aufweisen (Lernen durch Handeln).
- Die Handlungen sollten von den Lernenden möglichst selbstständig geplant, durchgeführt, überprüft, ggf. korrigiert und schließlich evaluiert werden.
- Die Handlungen sollten ein ganzheitliches Erfassen der (beruflichen) Wirklichkeit fördern (authentische Texte verwenden, Komplexität der Realität abbilden).
- Die Handlungen müssen in die Erfahrungen der Lernenden integriert und in Bezug auf ihre Auswirkungen reflektiert werden.

Die Handlungsorientierung bedeutet nicht eine völlige Umkehr von der bisherigen Lehr-Lernpraxis, sondern eine Ergänzung praktischer Anwendungsmodelle im Unterricht, d. h. handlungsorientierte Aufgaben geben den Rahmen für eine Lehrveranstaltung und die „traditionell" erlernten Kompetenzen und Kenntnissen werden in den handlungsorientierten „Projekten" angewandt, geübt und bewertet. Für die konkrete Unterrichtssituation bedeutet dies einen kontinuierlichen Wechsel zwischen Vermittlung und Anwendung, wie folgendes Schema zeigt:

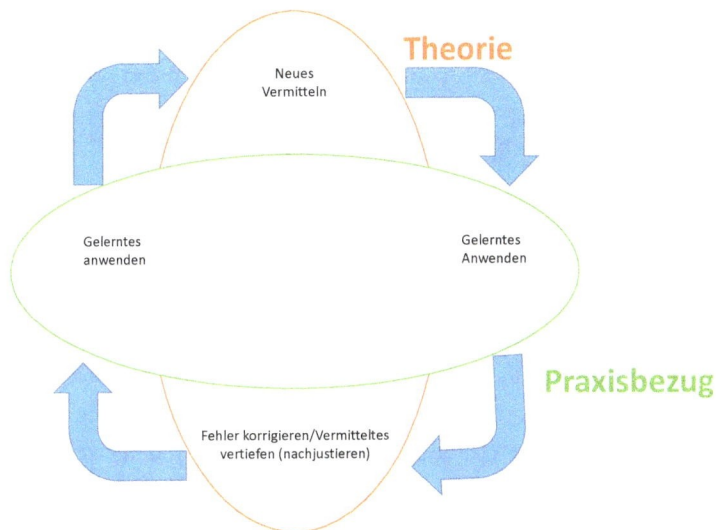

Abb. 5: Kreislauf Theorie und Praxisbezug

Was das Kurskonzept anbelangt, so gibt es verschiedene Nutzungsmöglichkeiten für handlungsorientierte Ansätze. So kann z. B. das Material für eine konkrete Fallstudie in Abhängigkeit von der Schwerpunktsetzung im Kurs zu unterschiedlichen Zwecken auf unterschiedliche Art und Weise eingesetzt werden. So können z. B. Fallstudien auch für das gezielte Training einer der vier Fertigkeiten genutzt werden, u. a. wenn die Lehrkraft mit einer bestimmten Lernergruppe z. B. den mündlichen Ausdruck im Hinblick auf Präsentationen oder den schriftlichen Ausdruck im Hinblick auf das Abfassen eines Berichtes gezielt bearbeiten möchte, weil in dieser konkreten Gruppe ein entsprechender Bedarf besteht. Auch bieten handlungsorientierte Ansätze die Möglichkeit zur Individualisierung innerhalb der Lernergruppe, denn je nach Stärken und Schwächen der einzelnen Lernenden müssen einzelne Personen schwerpunktmäßig die eine oder andere Aufgabe erledigen oder Fertigkeit bearbeiten.

4. Handlungsorientierung beim Sprachtesten

4.1 Konzeption

Während handlungsorientierte Unterrichtskonzepte in den letzten Jahren zunehmend Einzug in den Fremdsprachenunterricht an der Hochschule gehalten haben, sind Sprachprüfungen häufig noch sehr traditionell konzipiert. Dies ist sicherlich bedingt durch die Tatsache, dass Richtlinien und Empfehlungen zum Sprachtesten sehr stark von den ausbildungsunabhängigen standardisierten Testanbietern für die einzelnen Sprachen erarbeitet wurden. Diese arbeiten jedoch unter völlig anderen Bedingungen und werden so den Bedarfen eines ausbildungsbezogenen Sprachtests im Rahmen eines Fremdsprachenmoduls an der Hochschule nicht gerecht.[18]

In ausbildungsunabhängigen Sprachtests lauten die Aufgaben für die einzelnen Fertigkeiten traditionellerweise vereinfacht dargestellt wie folgt:
- Leseverstehen: *„Lesen Sie den Text und beantworten Sie die Fragen!"*
- Hörverstehen: *„Hören Sie zu und beantworten Sie die Fragen!"*
- Schriftlicher Ausdruck: *„Schreiben Sie einen Aufsatz zum Thema ..."*
- Mündlicher Ausdruck: *„Was halten Sie von ..."* / *„Präsentieren Sie ..."* / *„Stellen Sie sich vor, Sie sind ... und ..."*

Aber sind dies authentische Aufgabenstellungen, denen die Kandidatinnen und Kandidaten auch in der Lebenswirklichkeit begegnen? Wie valide sind sie hinsichtlich einer Aussage über die tatsächliche Sprachkompetenz? Inwieweit sind die Aufgaben für die Testnehmenden überhaupt relevant? Gerade der letzte Aspekt hat einen bedeutenden Einfluss auf die Motivation der Kandidatinnen und Kandidaten, sich mit der Thematik zu befassen: Wenn ich mich durch die Aufgabe als Individuum persönlich angesprochen fühle, werde ich

---

18 Vgl. hierzu Fischer 2013.

mich aktiv mit ihr befassen und diese zu lösen versuchen. Wenn ich aber nicht verstehe, warum ich eine bestimmte Aufgabe machen muss, welcher Zweck – abgesehen von der Sprachtestsituation – damit verbunden ist, was meine Rolle ist, wer ein möglicher Adressat für das sprachliche Produkt ist und wofür ich diesen Text schreibe bzw. diese Ausführungen mündlich vortrage, befasse ich mich nur gezwungenermaßen bzw. ungern mit der Aufgabe, kann mich gegebenenfalls nicht mit ihr (oder der Rolle) identifizieren oder kann mich eventuell gar nicht mit der Aufgabenstellung anfreunden. Aufgrund der ggf. geringen intrinsischen Motivation hat dies folglich einen direkten Einfluss auf das Ergebnis und meine Leistungen.

Vielmehr ist es in einer authentischen Kommunikationssituation wichtig, dass ich meine eigene Meinung zu einem bestimmten Thema äußern kann, dass ich meine individuellen Wünsche und Bedürfnisse erläutern und dass ich bestimmte Informationen zum Thema vermitteln kann. Um überzeugen zu können bzw. um als Gewinnerin oder Gewinner aus einer Verhandlungssituation herauszugehen, ist neben dem Verstehen der Kommunikationspartnerin bzw. des Kommunikationspartners wichtig, die produktiven Fertigkeiten situationsadäquat mit dem richtigen sprachlichen Register kompetent zu beherrschen.

Im Rahmen des Projektes „GULT – Guidelines for task-based university language testing"[19] ist das Projektteam daher folgender Frage nachgegangen:
> Wie kann man die Prüfungen gestalten, damit die Sprachkompetenz besser gemessen werden kann, d. h. damit erkennbar wird, inwieweit sich die einzelnen Personen in konkreten Situationen kommunikativ erfolgreich äußern können?

Ziel war es auch, dazu beizutragen, dass an den Hochschulsprachenzentren in noch stärkerem Maße die Kompetenzen der Lernenden in den Fokus genommen werden, wie vom GER angeregt, und man sich noch stärker von der „Fehlerfixiertheit", die durchaus beim Bewerten der Fremdsprachenkompetenzan der Hochschule noch anzutreffen war und ist, verabschiedet. Es ging auch darum, die Objektivität, die Validität, die Reliabilität und die Relevanz,

---
19 Fischer et al. 2011.

aber auch die Transparenz der Prüfungen in der Fremdsprachenausbildung an der Hochschule zu erhöhen.

So wurde im Rahmen dieses Projektes, basierend auf der von der UNIcert®-Kommission erarbeiteten Struktur – „Dötlinger Modell" genannt (vgl. Anhang 1) –, ein Rahmenkonzept für das handlungsorientierte Sprachtesten an der Hochschule entwickelt, bei dem in der Prüfung – ob nun „achievement test" oder „prochievement test"[20] – für alle Fertigkeiten und Aufgaben ein einziges Thema behandelt wird. D. h. es wird nicht eine Vielfalt sprachlicher, fachsprachlicher und / oder inhaltlicher Aspekte abgeprüft, sondern anhand eines konkreten Themas wird die Kandidatin bzw. der Kandidat auf die sprachliche Kompetenz genau abgetestet; man geht also beim Prüfen nicht in die Breite, sondern in die Tiefe.

Was die Struktur einer derartigen Prüfung anbelangt, so kann diese wie folgt aussehen:

- Aufgabenstellung: Einführung in *DAS Thema,*
- Hörverstehen und Leseverstehen,
- *Fallstudienarbeit* (Partner- / Teamarbeit),
- schriftlicher Ausdruck,
- mündlicher Ausdruck.

Im Vergleich zu „traditionellen" Prüfungen unterscheidet sich dieses Format in zwei wichtigen Punkten:

- Zum einen muss zu Beginn der Prüfung eine Einführung in das Thema erfolgen, damit – entsprechend dem Konzept Purens einer „unité didactique"[21] – allen klar ist, worum es in der Prüfung geht.
- Zum zweiten wird den Prüfungskandidatinnen und -kandidaten nach der Bearbeitung der rezeptiven Fertigkeiten die Möglichkeit gegeben, sich in Zweierteams oder Kleingruppen mithilfe eines umfassenden Dossiers und ggf. eigener Recherchen z. B. im Internet tiefer in die Thematik einzulesen, wie dies z. B. auch beim CLES[22] („Certificat de compétences en langues de l'enseignement supérieur") schon mit Erfolg geschieht.

---

20 Fischer 2013: S. 92; Gonzalez Pino 1998.
21 Puren 2008.
22 Vgl.: https://www.certification-cles.fr/ (letzter Zugriff: 27.04.2017).

In der Praxis bedeutet dies, dass
- bei der Prüfungserstellung die Lernziele beachtet werden müssen,
- dass eine Kompetenz- bzw. Handlungsorientierung tatsächlich ermöglicht wird,
- dass „authentische" Kontexte angeboten werden,
- dass die Aufgaben situiert sind und
- dass sich diese an den Bedürfnissen der Lernenden orientieren.

Hierzu müssen übliche Gütekriterien des Sprachtestens eingehalten werden. Hierzu zählen z. B.:
- Die Leistungsanforderungen müssen im Vorfeld der Prüfung transparent gemacht werden.
- Es muss eindeutige Anweisungen geben.
- Die Prüfungsteile müssen klarstrukturiert sein, was auch konkrete Angaben zur Gewichtung beinhaltet.
- Die vier Fertigkeiten Hörverstehen, Leseverstehen, Schriftlicher Ausdruck, Mündlicher Ausdruck müssen gleichgewichtet sein.
- Es sollte eine Mischung der Aufgabenformate geben, d. h. unterschiedliche Leistungsaspekte sollten geprüft werden.
- Es muss sichergestellt sein, dass vorhandenes Welt- und Vorwissen keinen Einfluss auf die Bewertung der sprachlichen Kompetenz hat.

Für das Hör- und Leseverstehen bedeutet dies, dass die Aufgabenstellung in eine Situation eingebettet werden muss, so dass die Kandidatinnen und Kandidaten wissen, wozu sie die Texte lesen bzw. hören und sie sich bemühen, die Inhalte zu erfassen, da sie wissen, dass sie diese in der späteren Phase der produktiven Aufgabenstellung nutzen können. Die Texte sind nun in einen Kontext eingebunden, erfüllen im Kontext der Gesamtfragestellung eine Funktion und sind Teil einer übergeordneten Aufgabe, die ein bestimmtes Ziel verfolgt. Die Inhalte werden nicht mehr punktuell abgefragt. Das Verstehen der Texte ist vielmehr Voraussetzung für die Bearbeitung der produktiven Aufgabe, wobei sichergestellt werden sollte (z. B. durch die Phase der eingeschobenen Fallstudienarbeit zwischen rezeptivem und produktivem Prüfungsteil), dass die Aufgaben zum Testen der produktiven Fertigkeiten auch dann erfolgreich bearbeitet werden können, wenn der rezeptive Prüfungsteil teilweise oder ganz erfolglos war. Durch die Einbettung des rezeptiven Prüfungsteils in eine Gesamtaufgabe wird das Verstehen in gewissem Maße indirekt überprüft. Auf jeden Fall lautet die Lese- bzw. Hörverstehensaufgabe nicht mehr „Lies bzw. höre den Test und beantworte die Fragen!", sondern „Untersuche das Problem und erarbeite eine Lösung dazu!".

Wichtig ist dabei zu prüfen, inwieweit die Texte (und die Aufgaben) authentisch und für die Studierenden relevant sind bzw. ob sie einen sinnvollen Fachbezug ermöglichen. Weiterhin gilt es, bei der Textauswahl und Fragenkonzeption folgende Aspekte zu reflektieren:
- Aufgabenformat,
- Komplexität,
- Hör- bzw. Lesearten, Strategien,
- Informationsentnahme aus einer oder mehreren Quellen,
- Durchführbarkeit,
- Zeitaufwand,
- Abhängigkeit von der Gedächtnisleistung,
- geringe Häufigkeit von Zufallslösungen.

Von zentraler Bedeutung ist jedoch die Zielsetzung: Was will ich hierbei überprüfen?

Wie in der Lebenswirklichkeit können die Testteilnehmenden in gewissem Umfang auf authentische Ressourcen zurückgreifen, können sich inhaltlich mit Kommilitoninnen und Kommilitonen abstimmen und werden so auf authentische Situation ihrer Studien- und späteren Berufs- bzw. Lebenswelt vorbereitet. Hierzu gehört auch die adäquate Nutzung von Hilfsmitteln (wie Wörterbüchern oder Internetressourcen).

Was die produktiven Fertigkeiten – mündlicher und schriftlicher Ausdruck – anbelangt, so müssen die Prüfungskandidatinnen und -kandidaten ein konkretes sprachliches Produkt (z. B. Bericht, Antrag, Präsentation, Verhandlung) erarbeiten und vorstellen, wobei sie ein klar formuliertes Ziel in einem konkreten Kontext verfolgen. D. h. auch hier gibt es für die Erledigung der Aufgabe eine konkrete Funktion.

4.2 Bewertungsraster

Zur Bewertung der produktiven Fertigkeiten ist die Erarbeitung von Bewertungsrastern erforderlich, die die Kompetenzen der Prüfungskandidatinnen und -kandidaten erfassen und sich nicht (mehr) auf die Fehler konzentrieren. Hierzu bieten GER[23], das sogenannte „Manual for Relating Language Examinations tothe CEFR"[24] sowie weitere ergänzende Materialien des Europarates[25] eine hilfreiche Basis. So hat das UNIcert®-Netzwerk[26] auf einem Workshop an der Universität Rostock im November 2009 basierend auf diesen Unterlagen sinnvolle Kriterien zur Bewertung des schriftlichen Ausdrucks gesammelt und sich anschließend auf eine Grobstruktur für ein Bewertungsraster geeinigt. Ziel war es, ein für interessierte Einrichtungen des Netzwerks ein teilweise einheitliches Bewertungssystem zu entwickeln. Als Bewertungskriterien wurden dabei zusammengetragen:

- globale Wertung
- Inhalt – inhaltliche Vollständigkeit – inhaltliche Richtigkeit – Relevanz – Textaufbau / Organisation – Themenentwicklung – Gliederung
- Kohärenz und Kohäsion
- sprachliche Korrektheit – Wortschatzspektrum
- Ausdruck / Stil – Register
- Interpunktion / Orthographie
- Aufgabenbewältigung
- Beschreibung – Argumentation
- Nutzung Quellmaterialien

Weiterhin hat sich die Arbeitsgruppe auf folgende Struktur für das Bewertungsraster geeinigt:

---

23 Europarat (2001).
24 Council of Europe (2009); abrufbar unter: http://www.coe.int/t/dg4/linguistic/Manuel1_EN.asp#Manual (letzter Zugriff: 24.04.2017).
25 Vgl.: http://www.coe.int/t/dg4/linguistic/Manuel1_EN.asp#Manual (letzter Zugriff: 24.04.2017).
26 Vgl.: http://www.unicert-online.org/ (letzter Zugriff: 27.04.2017).

Inhalt: 30 % / 25 %	Sprachliche Kompetenz: 40 % / 50 %
• Vollständigkeit	• Sprachliche Korrektheit
• Korrektheit	– Grammatik
• Relevanz	– Wortschatz
• Ggf. Originalität, Substanz	– Orthographie / Interpunktion
Pragmatische Kompetenz: 30% / 25%	• Variabilität der sprachlichen
• Funktionalität: Wirkung auf	Mittel
Adressaten (inkl.	– Grammatik
Textsortenadäquatheit)	– Wortschatz
• Textorganisation / Kohärenz /	• Stil / Register
Kohäsion	

Auf diesem Workshop blieben folgende Aspekte offen:
- Details zur Gewichtung der Kriterien für die einzelnen UNIcert®-Stufen,
- Bewertungsprinzip: Notenskala oder Punkteskala mit Grenze zu „nicht bestanden" bei x % (50–60–66)?,
- Formulierung der Deskriptoren bzw. Kann-Beschreibungen für die einzelnen Stufen (in Abhängigkeit vom jeweiligen Bewertungsprinzip).

Nicht abschließend diskutiert wurde auch die Frage, ob ein durchgängiges Erreichen der Kompetenzstufen – gerade beim schriftlichen Ausdruck – realistisch ist, was wiederum Auswirkungen auf die Formulierung der Deskriptoren hat. Die Ergebnisse dieses Workshops boten den beteiligten Sprachenzentren die Möglichkeit, durch Ergänzung der Deskriptoren für die eigene Einrichtung Bewertungsraster zu entwickeln bzw. zu überarbeiten. Dabei zeigte sich schnell, dass veränderte Bedürfnisse und Gegebenheiten eine regelmäßige Überarbeitung der Bewertungsraster erforderlich machen.

4.3 Ergebnisse eines handlungsorientierten Prüfungskonzeptes in der Praxis

Die Zentrale Einrichtung für Sprachen und Schlüsselqualifikationen (ZESS) der Georg-August-Universität Göttingen nutzt seit Anfang 2009 erfolgreich ein handlungsorientiertes Prüfungskonzept, das innerhalb kurzer Zeit für alle Sprachen und Stufen umgesetzt wurde.

Nachdem die Studierenden mit einer gewissen Unsicherheit in die ersten UNIcert® III-Prüfungen für Wirtschaftsenglisch gingen, da sie im Vorfeld mit dem Konzept nicht vertraut waren bzw. vertraut gemacht werden konnten, zeigte sich jedoch sehr schnell, dass sie die Neukonzeption ausgesprochen positiv bewerten. Dies lässt sich an folgenden Punkten festmachen:

- Die Prüfungsangst wird (sichtbar) reduziert (soziale Komponente).
- Die Kandidatinnen und Kandidaten sind viel stärker in die jeweilige Aufgabe und Thematik vertieft, was sich u. a. an der Tatsache zeigt, dass sie sich im Nachgang der Prüfung an zahlreiche Details z. B. der Hörverstehenstexte erinnern können.
- Es zeigt sich ein viel stärkerer inhaltlicher Bezug zur Aufgabe (höheres Maß an Authentizität und Relevanz).
- Die Kandidatinnen und Kandidaten beziehen Aspekte und Inhalte des Hörverstehens und des Leseverstehens in die Prüfung zum mündlichen Ausdruck ein.
- Studierende zeigen vielfach bessere Ergebnisse als bisher. Dies betrifft insbesondere Studierende mit guter Sprachkompetenz, die nun gerade im Leseverstehen oder im schriftlichen Ausdruck bessere Ergebnisse zeigen. Dies erklärt sich u. E. aus der Tatsache, dass sie einen Sinn im Lesen der Lesetexte erkennen können und ganz anders, nämlich wie in der Studienrealität, an die Texte herangehen: Sie wollen die Inhalte verstehen, um sie anschließend in den Prüfungsteilen zu den produktiven Fertigkeiten adäquat nutzen zu können, und suchen gezielt nach verwertbaren Inhalten.

Auch die Prüfenden zeigten eine andere Herangehensweise an das Prüfen und Bewerten: Aufgrund der großen Bandbreite unterschiedlicher Berichte und Präsentationen sind auch sie von der Thematik viel stärker angesprochen, was zu einem intensiveren Austausch mit den Studierenden über die Problematik oder Fragestellung führt als bei stark schematisierten Prüfungen z. B. mit standardisierten Rollenspielen.

Zusammenfassend konnte eine stärkere Motivation sowohl der Prüflinge als auch der Prüfenden festgestellt werden. Auch zeigte sich bei beiden eine stärkere inhaltliche Auseinandersetzung mit der Thematik. Die Augenscheinvalidität der Prüfungen konnte deutlich erhöht werden. Die Ergebnisse spiegeln laut Aussage der Lehrkräfte zudem in höherem Maße die im Unterricht gemessen Sprachkompetenzen wieder, so dass nicht nur die Zufriedenheit der Studierenden mit den Prüfungen deutlich gestiegen ist, sondern auch die Zufriedenheit der Lehrkräfte.

Aus Sicht des Autorenteams hat sich der Aufwand daher gelohnt: Der Mehrwert der Handlungsorientierung wird darin gesehen, dass
- lernerzentriert gearbeitet wird,
- Unterricht und Prüfungen deutlich mehr der Lebenswirklichkeit entsprechen und somit
- authentischer sind,
- Schlüsselkompetenzen integrativ mit vermittelt werden,
- die Resonanz von Prüflingen und Prüfenden ausgesprochen positiv ist und
- ggf. in höherem Maße Rückschlüsse auf den zukünftigen Erfolg der Lernenden in kommunikativen Kontaktsituation mit der Sprache möglich sind.

5. Ist-Zustand, Potenziale, Bedarfe

Die Teilnehmenden am Panel haben sich abschließend über die Unterrichts- und Prüfungspraxis an den einzelnen Einrichtungen ausgetauscht und sich dann mit der Frage befasst, welche Chancen die Kompetenz- bzw. Handlungsorientierung bietet und welche Herausforderungen zu meistern sind.
Als Chancen wurden dabei festgehalten:
- Die multimodalen Stimulationen führen zu einer Intensivierung des Lehr-/Lernprozesses.
- Der Unterricht ermöglicht eine gezielte Vorbereitung auf die Berufswelt.

Als Herausforderungen wurden genannt:
- Die Komplexität der Aufgabe, Lehrveranstaltung und Prüfungen in Einklang zu bringen.

- Die Problematik der zur Verfügung stehenden Materialien, da kommerzielle Lehrwerke nur bedingt geeignet sind, andererseits aber Lernplattformen eine gute Unterstützung bieten können.
- Für die Prüfungsentwicklung und -durchführung wurden genannt:
  – die Umsetzung des Ansatzes bei der großen Zahl an Prüfungspersonen,
  – der (gefühlte bzw. vermutete) zeitliche Aufwand bei der Prüfungserstellung, gerade in der Umstellungsphase,
  – die Herausforderung, geeignetes Audiomaterial für das Hörverstehen zu finden, und
  – die mangelnde Ausbildung der Lehrkräfte in diesem Bereich.

Als positive Aspekte des Ansatzes wurden von den Teilnehmenden festgehalten:
- die gleiche Berücksichtigung und Wertung der vier Fertigkeiten,
- die klare Orientierung am GER,
- die Konzeption der Prüfungen,
- die Zielsetzung des Ansatzes, nämlich die Einbettung der Aufgaben in einen kommunikativen Kontext,
- der Bezug zur Lebenswirklichkeit und
- die Zielorientierung bzw. Produktorientierung des Ansatzes.

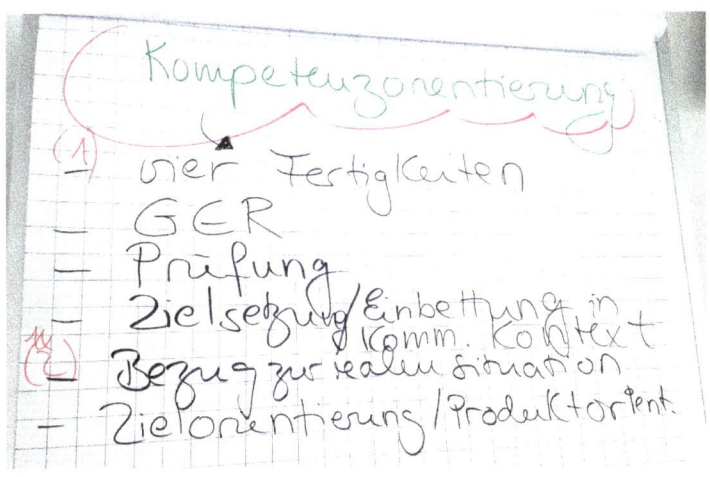

Abb. 6: Kompetenzorientierung

Anhang 1

Structure GULT test / Konzeption eines GULT-Tests / Conception d'un test GULT
(„Dötlinger Modell")

1.	presentation of task / *Aufgabenstellung* / *Présentation des tâches*					
	↓					
2.	receptive skills / *rezeptive Fertigkeiten* / *Compétences réceptives (ca. 90 min.)*					
	2.a	listening / *Hörtext* / *compréhension orale* ↓ reading / *Lesetext* / *compréhension écrite* ↓ task completion / *Aufgabenbearbeitung* / *réalisation de la tâche*	2.b	reading (brief overview) / *einleitender Lesetext (Überblick)* / *compréhension écrite (texte introductif à lire)* ↓ listening / *Hörtext* / *compréhension orale* ↓ reading / *Lesetext* / *compréhension écrite* ↓ task completion / *Aufgabenbearbeitung* / *réalisation de la tâche*		
				↓		
(3.)	research activities / *Themenvertiefung* / *activités de recherche (ca. 60 min. / optional)*					
	3.a	individual research activities / *eigene Recherche* / *activités de recherche individuelle*	3.b	pair research / *Partnerrecherche* / *recherche avec pair*	3.c	team research / *Teamrecherche* / *recherche en équipe*
				and / or – *und* / *oder* – *et/ ou*		and / or – *und* / *oder* – *et/ ou*
				oral interaction / *mündliche Interaktion* / *interaction orale*		oral interaction / team work – *mündliche Interaktion* / *Teamarbeit* – *interaction orale* / *travail en équipe*
				↓		
4.	productive skills / *produktive Fertigkeiten* / *compétences productives*					
	4.1	writing / *schriftlicher Ausdruck* / *expression écrite (ca. 90 min.)*				
		↓				
	4.2	speaking / *mündlicher Ausdruck* / *expression orale (ca. 30 min.)*				
		↓				
5.	evaluation & feedback / *Evaluation und Feedback* / *évaluation et feedback*					

Literaturverzeichnis

ALONSO, G. (2009). *Kompetenzförderung an der Hochschule. Eine hochschuldidaktische Konzeption von Lernszenarien zur integrativen Vermittlung von Schlüsselkompetenzen.* Göttingen: Sierke Verlag.

ALTENSCHMIDT, K. / MILLER, J./STARK, W. (Hrsg.) (2009). *Raus aus dem Elfenbeinturm? Entwicklungen in Service Learning und bürgerschaftlichem Engagement an deutschen Hochschulen.* Weinheim und Basel: Beltz Verlag.

BACKHAUS-MAUL, H. / ROTH, C. (2013). *Service Learning an Hochschulen in Deutschland. Ein erster empirischer Beitrag zur Vermessung eines jungen Phänomens.* Wiesbaden: Springer VS.

BACKHAUS-MAUL, H. / EBERT, O./FREI, N./ROTH, C./SATTLER, C. (2015). *Service Learning mit internationalen Studierenden. Konzeption, Erfahrungen und Umsetzungsmöglichkeiten.* Weinheim und Basel: Beltz Juventa.

CARÉ, J.-M. / DEBYSER, F. (1995). Simulations globales. Sèvres: CIEP.

CERTIFICAT DE COMPÉTENCES EN LANGUES DE L'ENSEIGNEMENT SUPÉRIEUR (CLES): https://www.certification-cles.fr/ (letzter Zugriff: 27.04.2017).

COUNCIL OF EUROPE (2009). *Relating Language Examinations to the Common European Framework of Reference for Languages: Learning, Teaching, Assessment (CEFR). A Manual*; abrufbar unter: http://www.coe.int/t/dg4/linguistic/Manuel1_EN.asp#Manual (letzter Zugriff: 24.04.2017).

DEBYSER, F. (1996). *L'immeuble.* Paris: Hachette.

EUROPARAT (2001). *Gemeinsamer europäischer Referenzrahmen für Sprachen: lernen, lehren, beurteilen.* Straßburg: Europarat / Berlin et al.: Langenscheidt.

FISCHER, J. (2013). Zum Verhältnis von standardisierten und ausbildungsbezogenen Sprachtests im Hochschulkontext. In: Mügge, R. (Hrsg.). *Gekonnt, verkannt, anerkannt? – Sprachen im Bologna-Prozess. Dokumentation der 27. Arbeitstagung 2012.* Bochum: AKS-Verlag, S. 89–99.

FISCHER, J. / CASEY, E. / ABRANTES, A. M. / GIGL, E. / LEŠNIK, M. (Hrsg.) (2008). *LCaS: Language Case Studies. Teacher training modules on the use of case studies in language teaching at secondary and university level. A handbook.* Strasbourg: Council of Europe.

FISCHER, J. / CHOUISSA, C. / DUGOVIČOVÁ, S. / VIRKKUNEN-FULLENWIDER, A. (2011). *Guidelines for task-based university language testing*, Strasbourg / Graz: Council of Europe.

FISCHER, J. / MUSACCHIO, M. T. / STANDRING, A. (Hrsg.) (2009). *EXPLICS – Exploiting Internet Case Studies and Simulation Templates for Language Teaching and Learning. A Handbook.* Göttingen: Cuvillier Verlag.

GONZALEZ PINO, B. (1998). *Prochievement testing of speaking: Matching instructor expectations, learner proficiency level, and task type.* In: Texas Papers in Foreign Language Education, 3.3, S. 119–133.

KAISER, F. J. (Hrsg.) (1983). *Die Fallstudien. Theorie und Praxis der Fallstudiendidaktik.* Bad Heilbrunn: Klinkhardt.

KIEFER, K.-H. (2004). *Fallstudien – zum Umgang mit einer erfolgreichen Lernmethode im Fachsprachenunterricht Wirtschaftsdeutsch.* In: Info DaF 1, S. 68–98.

KLIEME, E. / AVENARIUS, H. / BLUM, W. / DÖBRICH, P. / GRUBER, H. / PRENZEL, M. / REISS, K. / RIQUARTS, K. / ROST, J. / TENORTH, H.-E. / VOLLMER, J. (2003). *Zur Entwicklung nationaler Bildungsstandards. Eine Expertise.* Bonn: Bundesministerium für Bildung und Forschung.

KLIEME, E. / FUNKE, J. / LEUTNER, D. / REIMANN, P. / WIRTH, J. (2001). *Problemlösen als fächerübergreifende Kompetenz: Konzeption und erste Resultate aus einer Schulleistungsstudie.* In: Zeitschrift für Pädagogik, 47(2), S. 179–200.

PUREN, C. (2008). *Formes pratiques de combinaison entre perspective actionnelle et approche communicative: analyse comparative de trois manuels.* In: Langues Modernes 5 Janvier 2008, S. 1–19.

RIBÉ, R. / VIDAL, N. (1993). *Project Work.* Oxford: Heinemann.

SCHART, M. (2003). *Projektunterricht – subjektiv betrachtet. Eine qualitative Studie mit Lehrenden für Deutsch als Fremdsprache.* Hohengehren: Schneider Verlag.

SKEHAN, P. (1996). *Second language acquisition research and task-based instruction.* In: Willis, J./Willis, D. (Hrsg.). Challenge and Change in Language Teaching. Oxford: Heinemann, S. 17–30.

SKEHAN, P. (2001). *Tasks and language performance*. In: Bygate, M./Skehan, P./ Swain, M. (Hrsg.). Researching Pedagogic Tasks: Second Language Learning, Teaching and Testing. Harlow: Longman, S. 167–187.

STÄNDIGE KONFERENZ DER KULTUSMINISTER DER LÄNDER IN DER BUNDESREPUBLIK DEUTSCHLAND (2014). *Bildungsstandards für die fortgeführte Fremdsprache (Englisch/Französisch) für die Allgemeine Hochschulreife (Beschluss der Kultusministerkonferenz vom 18.10.2012)*. Köln: Carl Link.

STARK, W. / MILLER, J. / ALTENSCHMIDT, K. (2013). *Zusammenarbeiten – Zusammen gewinnen. Was Kooperationen zwischen Hochschulen und Gemeinwesen bewirken können und was dafür nötig ist. Potenzialanalyse Campus Community Partnerships*. Essen: Universität Duisburg-Essen.

YAICHE, F. (1996). *Les simulations globales – mode d'emploi*. Paris: Hachette.

Panel B5

Sabine Klüner

Kompetenzbedarf beim Übergang von der Hochschule in den Beruf

Thema: Studium beendet, und wie geht's weiter? Welche Kompetenzen – neben den fachlichen – brauchen Absolventen, um in der Arbeitswelt Fuß zu fassen, und wie können Career Center oder andere Serviceeinrichtungen der Hochschule sie dabei lancieren?

Schwerpunkt: Bewerbungsportale / Formularbewerbungen und deren Anforderungen an Bewerber.

Gliederung

1. Ausgangslage – Status Quo bei Bewerbern und Unternehmen
2. Vorteile von Bewerbungsportalen für Unternehmen
3. Vor- und Nachteile von Bewerbungsportalen für Bewerber
4. Inhaltliche und technische Regeln für die Nutzung von Bewerbungsportalen
    4.1 Grundsätzliches
    4.2 Felder im Drop-Down-Menü
    4.3 Freitextfelder
    4.4 Dateianlagen
    4.5 Technische Fallstricke
    4.6 Umgang der Unternehmen mit den Bewerberdaten
5. Unternehmenseinblicke
    5.1 Typische Bewerberfehler
    5.2 Tipps und Hinweise der Unternehmen
6. Fazit

1. Ausgangslage – Status Quo bei Bewerbern und Unternehmen

Unternehmen nutzen heute unterschiedliche Kanäle für den Bewerbungseingang. Dass der Trend weg von der Papierbewerbung hin zur Bewerbung per E-Mail und über Bewerbungsportale geht, ist offensichtlich und selbstverständlich. Laut einer Studie der Universität Bamberg[1] erhalten Unternehmen derzeit über die Hälfte aller Bewerbungen per Online-Formular, 36 % per E-Mail und 13 % per Post. Die Tendenz zur Online-Bewerbung über ein Bewerbungsportal ist zunehmend: Drei Viertel der befragten Unternehmen favorisieren die Formularbewerbung. Währenddessen ist die Bewerbung über ein Online-Formular bei Karriereinteressierten weniger beliebt: Über 80 % bevorzugen die E-Mail-Bewerbung und nur knapp 8 % die Formularbewerbung – fast gleichauf mit der papierbasierten Bewerbungsmappe. Hier findet sich also eine große Diskrepanz zwischen dem Wunsch der Unternehmen und der Wirklichkeit der Bewerber. Für knapp 7 % der befragten Karriereinteressierten stellt die Formularbewerbung sogar einen Grund dar, sich gar nicht zu bewerben.

2. Vorteile von Bewerbungsportalen für Unternehmen

Gerade für große Unternehmen mit einer stark beanspruchten Personalabteilung liegen die Vorteile eines Bewerbungsportals auf der Hand. Eine softwaregestützte Filterung der Bewerbungen unterstützt durch Suchfunktionalitäten und vereinfacht die Sichtung und den Vergleich; ein Zugang aller involvierten Mitarbeiter zum System sorgt für Transparenz im gesamten Bewerbungsprozess. Auch Zeit und Kosten werden durch eine automatisierte Verarbeitung gespart; und nicht zuletzt ermöglicht ein Bewerbungsportal den professionellen Aufbau eines Bewerberpools mit möglichst wenig Aufwand.

---

1 „Bewerbung der Zukunft. Ausgewählte Ergebnisse der ‚Recruiting Trends 2016', einer empirischen Studie der Top 1.000 Unternehmen aus Deutschland sowie der Top 300 Unternehmen aus den Branchen Automotive, Handel und IT, und der ‚Bewerbungspraxis 2016', einer empirischen Studie mit über 4.800 Stellensuchenden und Karriereinteressierten im Internet."

3. Vor- und Nachteile von Bewerbungsportalen für Bewerber

Bewerbungsportale stellen nicht die bevorzugte Form für Bewerber dar, um ihre Bewerbung an Unternehmen zu übermitteln. Dabei bieten sie durchaus Vorteile; z. B. besteht auch bei erfolgloser Bewerbung auf eine ausgeschriebene Stelle oder bei einer Initiativbewerbung die Chance, in den Bewerberpool des Unternehmens aufgenommen zu werden. Zudem genießen die Bewerber größtmögliche Transparenz im Bewerbungsprozess. Durch sofortige Eingangsbestätigungen, automatische Zwischenbescheide oder das Verfolgen des Bewerbungsstatus über den eigenen User-Account ist man immer auf dem Laufenden. Sobald sich beim Ausfüllen von Bewerbungsformularen eine gewisse Routine eingestellt hat, sind Zeitersparnis und Fehlervermeidung Pluspunkte. Jedoch befürchten die Bewerber, ihre Qualifikationen in der Kürze eines Formulars mit festgelegten Feldern nicht optimal darstellen zu können oder allein wegen objektiver Faktoren wie Noten oder Studiendauer durch das Raster zu fallen. Daher ist es umso wichtiger, die Besonderheiten der Online-Bewerbung zu kennen und für sich zu nutzen.

4. Inhaltliche und technische Regeln für die Nutzung von Bewerbungsportalen

4.1 Grundsätzliches

Firmen, die mit Bewerbungsportalen arbeiten, machen auf ihren Recruiting-Seiten den Bewerbungsvorgang transparent und geben von sich aus viele Tipps und Hinweise zur optimalen Bewerbung und Fehlervermeidung. Diese sollte sich jeder Karriereinteressierte aufmerksam durchlesen, und das bei jedem Unternehmen erneut, da es Abweichungen gibt. Die Formularbewerbung hat per se einen anonymen Charakter, der sich durch die Tipps und Hinweise etwas verliert. Denn auch wenn die Bewerbung durch eine Computersoftware läuft: Am Ende sitzt immer eine Person – das sollte man sich als Bewerber immer vor Augen führen. Viele Unternehmen geben an, keine Pre-Selection durch Filter zu nutzen, sondern sich jede Bewerbung anzusehen. Doch auch, wenn dies zutrifft, belegt die Studie der Universität Bamberg, dass Recruiter sich im Schnitt nur mit 42,2 % der eingegangenen Bewerbungen intensiv beschäftigen. Daher sollten Bewerber einige Regeln beachten, die für die Formularbewerbung gelten. Unabhängig vom Übermittlungsweg ist natürlich das Gleiche zu beachten wie bei jeder Bewerbung, also die Vollständigkeit der Bewerbungsunterlagen, überzeugendes Anschreiben, Aktualität des Lebenslaufes etc.

4.2 Felder im Drop-Down-Menü

In den Bewerbungsformularen sind die Angaben zu Ausbildung und Berufserfahrung weitestgehend standardisiert. So wird sichergestellt, dass der Personalentscheider über verschiedene Suchfunktionen eine Liste der passenden Bewerber erhält. Vom Bewerber sollten daher möglichst alle Felder ausgefüllt werden. Sind beispielsweise der Ausbildungsgang oder die Branche im Drop-Down-Menü nicht aufgeführt, wählt man die beste Alternative, denn jedes nicht ausgefüllte Feld kann den Bewerber aus dem Suchprozess werfen. Oft arbeitet die Software zusätzlich mit einer Ranking-Funktion, d. h. die Ergebnisliste wird bewertet. Zudem sollte im Drop-Down-Menü die Auswahlmöglichkeit „Sonstiges" vermieden werden, da sie in der Regel dafür sorgt, dass der Bewerber in der Auswahlliste ganz unten erscheint. Auch Felder, die keine Pflichtfelder sind, sollten unbedingt ausgefüllt werden.

4.3 Freitextfelder

Wenn ein Freitextfeld für das Anschreiben vorgesehen ist, gelten auch hier die Regeln der Briefkommunikation. Darüber hinaus sind Freitextfelder häufig mit Suchfunktionalitäten hinterlegt, weshalb der Bewerber für die ausgeschriebene Position wichtige Schlüsselworte verwenden sollte. Unnötige Schriftzeichen wie Aufzählungszeichen, Sternchen, Rauten o. ä. sollten hingegen vermieden werden, da diese mit manchen Software-Programmen nicht dargestellt werden können. Bei begrenzter Zeichenzahl gilt es, sich auf die eigenen Stärken zu konzentrieren und keine Dopplungen – wie Stationen aus dem Lebenslauf – aufzuzählen. Wie im Anschreiben üblich, sollte man auf das geforderte Profil eingehen und darauf, welchen Gewinn das Unternehmen durch den Bewerber hätte. Das Freitextfeld mit Floskeln („Wenn mein Profil für Sie interessant ist, dann freue ich mich über eine Kontaktaufnahme") zu füllen, ist weder aussagekräftig noch höflich.

4.4 Dateianlagen

Anlagen sollten vom Bewerber immer in PDF-Form hochgeladen werden, auch wenn andere Dateiformate wie Word, Excel oder JPG erlaubt sind. Der Vorteil von PDFs: Sie sind nicht editierbar, man kann mehrere Seiten in einer Datei zusammenfassen, und es ist ein komprimiertes Format, also von relativ kleiner Dateigröße. Der Anhang sollte für den Personaler aussagekräftig benannt sein, optimalerweise mit dem eigenen Namen und der Job-ID. Kostenlose Programme zur Zusammenführung und Komprimierung verschiedener Dateiformate in eine PDF-Datei finden sich kostenlos im Internet, z. B. unter den Stichworten „Online PDF convert".

4.5 Technische Fallstricke

Viele Unternehmensportale bieten automatische oder interaktive Hilfe (z. B. bei nicht ausgefülltem Pflichtfeld) und FAQs an. Damit gehen Bewerber sicher, dass sie das Online-Formular mit den Informationen gespeist haben, welche das System zur objektiven Auswertung benötigt. Um einen möglichen Session Time Out zu umgehen, kann der Bewerber die Anhänge und Texte für auszufüllende Felder offline vorbereiten und sich erst nach nochmaliger Durchsicht der Unterlagen einloggen und diese hochladen. Hat man einen eigenen Bewerber-Account angelegt, ist es sinnvoll, sich das Passwort zu notieren. Eine automatische Eingangsbestätigung kann aufgrund technischer Einstellungen im Spam-Ordner landen – also sollte zunächst dort nachgesehen werden, bevor man beim Unternehmen nachfragt.

4.6 Umgang der Unternehmen mit den Bewerberdaten

Um zu erfahren, wie mit den versendeten Daten umgegangen wird, sollten Bewerber unbedingt die Nutzungsbedingungen des Unternehmens lesen. Manche Firmen verwenden die Daten zum Aufbau eines Bewerberpools, d. h. die Angaben und Dateien werden über einen längeren Zeitraum gespeichert, wenn der Bewerber sich nicht explizit dagegen ausspricht – wie bei einer E-Mail-Bewerbung auch. Einige Unternehmen geben die Daten auch an Dritte weiter, z. B. eine mit der Selektion beauftragte Personalberatung. Gegebenenfalls sollte man hierfür die Genehmigung nicht erteilen.

5. Unternehmenseinblicke

Fünf Unternehmen[2], die mit einem Bewerbungsportal arbeiten, wurden per Telefoninterview von der Autorin über ihre Erfahrungen mit Formularbewerbungen befragt. Da sich zahlreiche Aussagen glichen, sind diese hier in den folgenden zwei Kapiteln zusammengefasst.

5.1 Typische Bewerberfehler

Fehler technischer Art kommen bei Bewerbungen selten vor, da es sich um eine junge, IT-affine Zielgruppe handelt. Ein Problempunkt sind allerdings die Anhänge; oft werden viele einzelne PDFs übermittelt, statt diese zu einem Dokument zusammenzufügen. Auch das Hochladen von editierbaren Dateien wird bemängelt. Formate wie Word erreichen nur in „zerschossener" Form die Empfänger, also mit falsch dargestellten Sonderzeichen, verschobenen Formatierungen etc. Oft fehlen Dokumente, die dann nachgefordert werden müssen. Diese mangelnde Sorgfalt spiegelt sich auch in inhaltlichen Fehlern wie der laxen Beantwortung von Fragen (z. B. „siehe Lebenslauf"), Rechtschreibfeh-

---

2 Teach First gGmbH, insgesamt rd. 1.000 Bewerbungen pro Jahr | Allied Vision, 300 MA weltweit, rd. 50 Bewerbungen pro Woche und Personalverantwortlichem | Smaato, 220 MA weltweit, rd. 50 Bewerbungen pro Stellenanzeige | Hermes Fulfilment, 14.000 MA weltweit | NXP Semiconductors, weltweit tätig, 2.000 MA in Deutschland, 95 % der Bewerbungen über Online-Formular eingehend.

lern, fehlenden Umgangsformen oder unvollständigen Angaben wider. Auch die mangelnde Qualifikation für eine Stelle kommt vor – ebenso wie bei Bewerbungen in anderer Form auch. Diese Fehler führen jedoch nicht gleich zum Ausschluss der Bewerbung, da sie für die Unternehmen im Pre-Screening noch nicht sichtbar sind. Auch die Vorstellung der Bewerber, dass sie bei „falschen" Antworten gleich durch das Raster fallen, ist lt. der befragten Unternehmen unbegründet.

5.2 Tipps und Hinweise der Unternehmen

Viele der Tipps und Hinweise der befragten Unternehmen gelten für eine Formularbewerbung ebenso wie für Bewerbungen auf jedem anderen Weg: Wichtig ist eine authentische Bewerbung, in der klar wird, warum man sich auf die ausgeschriebene Stelle bewirbt und warum man das Unternehmen interessant findet. Auch sollte man eine Bewerbung nicht zu lax nehmen, bloß, weil sie einfach abzuschicken ist – es empfiehlt sich also nicht das Gießkannenprinzip, nur, weil das Formular schnell ausgefüllt ist. Es wird Wert auf eine intensive Beschäftigung mit dem Unternehmen und dem Programm gelegt, Fragen sollten telefonisch im Vorfeld geklärt werden. Da der erste Blick oft auf den Lebenslauf fällt, sollte hierauf der Fokus für Karriereinteressierte liegen. Erst wenn der Lebenslauf beim Unternehmen auf Zustimmung trifft, werden Anschreiben und Zeugnisse gesichtet. Erfahrungen und Kenntnisse, die für die ausgeschriebene Vakanz zutreffend sind, sind unbedingt dort zu erwähnen. Speziell bei der Bewerbung über ein Online-Formular wird Wert auf kurze konkrete Antworten gelegt. Abgeraten wird von einer Bewerbung per Mobile oder Tablet; diese ist zwar möglich, technisch aber nicht ausgereift. Oft werden die Anhänge nicht übermittelt. Wenn per Mobile App (Dropbox, WeTransfer o. ä.) ein Download-Link für die Anhänge mitgeschickt wird, dürfen diese aus datenrechtlichen Gründen nicht vom Unternehmen heruntergeladen werden. Unbedingte Empfehlung lautet also, Bewerbung immer über den Desktop-PC zu versenden. Der Wandel vom Arbeitgeber- zum Arbeitnehmermarkt macht sich hier bemerkbar: Haben vielversprechende Bewerber vergessen, ihre Dokumente anzuhängen, haken die Unternehmen telefonisch nach. Auch der händische Datenbankeintrag von Bewerberdaten, die per E-Mail eingegangen sind, ist bei den Unternehmen keine Seltenheit.

6. Fazit

Je mehr der Bewerber über die Funktionsweise der Bewerberportale und die Intention der Unternehmen weiß, desto eher kann er sich darauf einlassen. Es gilt also für die Career Services, Aufklärungsarbeit bei den Studierenden und Absolventen zu leisten. Auch über eine Formularbewerbung ist es möglich, seine Motivation, Qualifikation und individuelle Persönlichkeit darzustellen, wenn man einige Hinweise beachtet. Auch wenn Unternehmen die Möglichkeit der Filterung haben, wird diese nicht ausgiebig genutzt – es sind immer Personen, die über eine Einladung zum Bewerbungsgespräch entscheiden.

Panel B6

Natalie Böddicker / Simone Kroschel
Überfachliche Angebote in der Hochschulstruktur

1. Experten-Input

1.1 Hochschulpolitischer Rahmen

Im Panel wurde zunächst die Frage aufgeworfen, welche hochschulpolitischen Rahmenbedingungen den Einzug überfachlicher Angebote in die Hochschulen bedingen. Einfluss hat hier unter anderem die Bildungspolitik der Europäischen Union (EU). So wurde in der Lissabon Erklärung von 2000[1] Bildung als Motor der wirtschaftlichen Entwicklung propagiert. In diesem Zusammenhang durchzieht die Vision, dass Menschen sich durch Kompetenzen unterschiedlicher Art auszeichnen, unabhängig davon, wo und wann diese erworben wurden, verschiedene bildungspolitische Debatten und Prozesse innerhalb der EU. Dabei stellt der Bologna-Prozess jenen Strang dar, der sich auf den europäischen Hochschulraum bezieht. Ein bildungspolitisches Ziel ist es, dass über formale Bildungsgänge hinaus Kenntnisse und Fähigkeiten, die durch nonformales und informelles Lernen erworben wurden, anerkannt und nutzbar gemacht werden. Während eine Gefahr dieser Tendenzen in der Perspektive auf die wirtschaftliche Verwertbarkeit liegen mag, ergeben sich auf der anderen Seite auch Chancen aus der angestrebten Wertschätzung aller Kompetenzen, die einen Menschen über einen formalen Bildungsabschluss hinaus auszeichnen, auch wenn die Realität zum Beispiel von Bewerbungsverfahren davon häufig noch weit entfernt sein dürfte.

---

1 Europäischer Rat, Schlussfolgerungen des Vorsitzes, 2000: www.europarl.europa.eu/summits/lis1_de.htm, zuletzt abgerufen am 14.07.2016.

Die oben skizzierte Vorstellung schlägt sich auch im Europäischen Qualifikationsrahmen für lebenslanges Lernen (EQR)[2] nieder, in dem Kenntnisse, Fähigkeiten und Kompetenzen auf einer abstrakten, überfachlichen Ebene klassifiziert und Niveaustufen zugeordnet werden, damit so in erster Linie eine „Übersetzungshilfe" zwischen den Bildungssystemen der verschiedenen europäischen Länder geschaffen wird. Für das deutsche Bildungssystem wurde der EQR in den Deutschen Qualifikationsrahmen für lebenslanges Lernen (DQR)[3] überführt.

Von den Zielen, die auf EU-Ebene verfolgt werden, ist auch eine Reihe von Entwicklungen im Hochschulbereich gekennzeichnet: So stellt zum Beispiel das Ziel, die Curricula von Studienprogrammen an den zu vermittelnden Kompetenzen auszurichten, eine zentrale Forderung im Rahmen des Bologna-Prozesses dar. Leitend für die Konzeption soll nicht die Frage sein, welchen Input die anbietende Institution leisten möchte, sondern die Orientierung an dem, was die Lernenden nach erfolgreichem Abschluss des Studiengangs können sollen. Weiterhin sind die zahlreichen Programme und Initiativen, die auf lebenslanges Lernen und Aufstieg durch Bildung zielen, in diesem Kontext zu sehen. Eine besondere Rolle spielen die Verknüpfung von hochschulischen und nicht-hochschulischen Bildungsgängen und – in Verbindung damit – die Forderung, dass Kompetenzen unterschiedlicher Art, die von Lernenden einmal erworben wurden, auf weitere Bildungsgänge anerkannt werden.[4]

Für den deutschen Hochschulbereich gibt es zudem einen eigenen Qualifikationsrahmen für Deutsche Hochschulabschlüsse[5], in dem den Abschlüssen auf Bachelor-, Master- und Doktoratsebene jeweils Merkmale in den Bereichen „Wissen und Verstehen", „Können (Wissenserschließung)" und „Formale As-

---

2   Europäische Kommission, Der europäische Qualifikationsrahmen für lebenslanges Lernen, 2008: https://ec.europa.eu/ploteus/content/descriptors-page, zuletzt aufgerufen am 14.07.2016.
3   Bundesministerium für Bildung und Forschung; Kultusministerkonferenz, Der Deutsche Qualifikationsrahmen für lebenslanges Lernen, 2013: www.dqr.de, zuletzt abgerufen am 14.07.2016.
4   Vgl. für den Hochschulbereich „Anrechnung von außerhalb des Hochschulwesens erworbenen Kenntnissen und Fähigkeiten auf ein Hochschulstudium" I und II (Beschlüsse der Kultusministerkonferenz vom 28.06.2002 und vom 18.09.2008).
5   Kultusministerkonferenz, Qualifikationsrahmen für Deutsche Hochschulabschlüsse, 2005: https://www.hrk.de/fileadmin/redaktion/hrk/02-Dokumente/02-03-Studium/02-03-02-Qualifikationsrahmen/2005_Qualifikationsrahmen_HSAbschluesse.pdf, zuletzt abgerufen am 14.07.2016.

pekte" zugeordnet werden. Die nachfolgende Übersicht zeigt einige Beispiele auf der Bachelorebene:

Wissen und Verstehen	Können (Wissenserschließung)	Formale Aspekte
Wissensverbreiterung: z.B. breites und integriertes Wissen und Verstehen der wiss. Grundlagen des Lerngebietes	Instrumentale Kompetenzen: z.B. Wissen und Verstehen auf Tätigkeit oder Beruf anwenden	...
	Systemische Kompetenzen: z.B. relevante Informationen sammeln, bewerten und interpretieren	
Wissensvertiefung: z.B. kritisches Verständnis der wichtigsten Theorien, Prinzipien und Methoden des Studienprogramms	Kommunikative Kompetenzen: z.B. sich mit Fachvertretern und Laien über Informationen, Ideen, Probleme und Lösungen austauschen	

Abb. 1: Qualifikationsrahmen Bachelorebene

Wie insbesondere am Bereich „Können (Wissenserschließung)" deutlich wird, beinhaltet der DQR keineswegs nur fachliche Aspekte, sondern geht davon aus, dass überfachliche Kompetenzen entscheidend dafür sind, dass Fachwissen umgesetzt und an unterschiedliche Zielgruppen kommuniziert werden kann.

1.2 Qualitätssicherung

Eine weitere politische Vorgabe in diesem Zusammenhang ist die Qualitätssicherung von Studium und Lehre, die im deutschen Hochschulsystem intern durch die Hochschulen selbst und extern durch Akkreditierung gewährleistet werden soll. Hierzu gibt es Vorgaben der Kultusministerkonferenz und des Akkreditierungsrates[6], die unabhängig von der jeweiligen Akkreditierungsagentur

---

6 Eine Zusammenstellung der für die Akkreditierung relevanten Vorgaben findet sich unter der Rubrik „Regeln und Beschlüsse" auf den Seiten des Akkreditierungsrates: www.akkreditierungsrat.de, zuletzt abgerufen am 14.07.2016.

oder der Art des Verfahrens – Programm- oder Systemakkreditierung – gelten, sowie ggf. weitere landesspezifische Vorgaben.

In Bezug auf das Konzept eines Bachelor- oder Masterstudiengangs gilt das Kriterium 2.1 des Akkreditierungsrates:

> Das Studiengangskonzept orientiert sich an Qualifikationszielen. Diese umfassen fachliche und überfachliche Aspekte und beziehen sich insbesondere auf die Bereiche wissenschaftliche oder künstlerische Befähigung, Befähigung, eine qualifizierte Erwerbstätigkeit aufzunehmen, Befähigung zum gesellschaftlichen Engagement und Persönlichkeitsentwicklung.[7]

Es macht deutlich, dass mit einem Studiengang, neben fachlichen, auch überfachliche Bildungsziele angestrebt werden müssen. Diese Forderung wurde von politischer Seite nach den Studierendenprotesten vor etwa zehn Jahren unterstrichen, da es ein Kritikpunkt der Studierenden am gestuften System war, dass viele Studiengänge zu sehr auf die Vermittlung von Fachwissen fokussiert seien.

In Kriterium 2.2 wird die Verbindlichkeit des HRQ festgeschrieben: „Der Studiengang entspricht (1) den Anforderungen des Qualifikationsrahmens für deutsche Hochschulabschlüsse vom 21.04.2005 in der jeweils gültigen Fassung ...".[8]

Kriterium 2.3 bezieht sich auf die curriculare Umsetzung und macht deutlich, dass die angestrebten Lernergebnisse fachlicher und überfachlicher Art auch im Curriculum abgebildet sein müssen. Erwähnt wird in diesem Zusammenhang zudem, dass obligatorische Praxisanteile (zum Beispiel im Rahmen der Berufsfeldorientierung) in das Curriculum integriert sein müssen:

> Das Studiengangskonzept umfasst die Vermittlung von Fachwissen und fachübergreifendem Wissen sowie von fachlichen, methodischen und generischen Kompetenzen. Es ist in der Kombination der einzelnen Module stimmig im Hinblick auf formulierte Qualifikationsziele aufgebaut und sieht adäquate Lehr-

---

7 Akkreditierungsrat, Regeln für die Akkreditierung von Studiengängen und für die Systemakkreditierung vom 08.12.2009 i. d. F. vom 20.02.2013, S. 11: www.akkreditierungsrat.de/fileadmin/Seiteninhalte/AR/Beschluesse/AR_Regeln_Studiengaenge_aktuell.pdf, zuletzt abgerufen am 14.07.2016.
8 Ebd.

und Lernformen vor. Gegebenenfalls vorgesehene Praxisanteile werden so ausgestaltet, dass Leistungspunkte (ECTS) vergeben werden können ...[9]

Bei der Akkreditierung darf den Hochschulen kein bestimmter Weg zur Vermittlung überfachlicher Kompetenzen vorgeschrieben werden, so dass insbesondere bei der erstmaligen Akkreditierung vor allem geprüft werden kann, ob diese im Konzept eines Studiengangs in irgendeiner Form angelegt ist. Die Erfahrungen bei der Umsetzung der entsprechenden Vorgaben und Kriterien waren zu Beginn des Bologna-Prozesses je nach Hochschule und Studiengang sehr unterschiedlich. Inzwischen kann man beobachten, dass es zunehmend hochschulweite Konzepte zur Vermittlung überfachlicher Kompetenzen gibt und dass fächerübergreifende Wahlpflichtbereiche, die diesem Ziel ganz oder teilweise dienen, bewusst profiliert wurden, damit die Studierenden sie als zielgerichteten Bestandteil des Studiums und nicht als Sammelbecken für Angebote jeglicher Art wahrnehmen. Mittlerweile gelingt die Integration entsprechender Bestandteile in das Studium in vielen Fällen besser, was auch damit zusammenhängt, dass es ein Bewusstsein dafür gibt, dass entsprechende Angebote in die Kreditierung einbezogen sein müssen. Hieraus resultiert tendenziell eine höhere Akzeptanz bei den Studierenden, die im Rahmen des Studiums erworbene und attestierte Qualifikationen außerfachlicher Art auch zunehmend als wichtig für den Übergang in den Beruf erachten.

Diese Entwicklungen werden außerdem durch die Qualitätssicherung an den Hochschulen im Rahmen von Akkreditierungs- und Evaluationsverfahren unterstützt. An der Heinrich-Heine-Universität Düsseldorf wird zum Beispiel von Beginn an bei der Curriculumentwicklung beraten. Dazu gehört auch die Frage nach der Verortung von überfachlichen Kompetenzen. Durch Leitfragen werden die Qualifikationsziele des Studiengangs gemeinsam mit den Fachvertreter/innen herausgearbeitet und mit dem curricularen Angebot abgeglichen. Wo es sinnvoll erscheint, wird auf die Angebote der Studierendenakademie und eine mögliche Kooperation hingewiesen.

Für die Evaluation von Studium und Lehre sind zunächst die universitätsweiten Ziele, die im Leitbild Lehre der Heinrich-Heine-Universität fixiert

---

9 Ebd.

sind, relevant. Zu diesen Zielen zählen auch die bildungspolitisch geforderten überfachlichen Kompetenzen, wie zum Beispiel die Fähigkeit zu lebenslangem Lernen, soziale Kompetenz sowie die Entwicklung zu einer kritischen und selbstständigen Persönlichkeit. In Zusammenarbeit der Qualitätsbeauftragten und der Hochschuldidaktiker/innen in den Fakultäten werden diese Ziele operationalisiert und die Evaluationsinstrumente werden dahingehend überprüft, ob diese Ziele auch erfasst werden. In einem nächsten Schritt müssen an Hand der Ergebnisse die Methoden bzw. die Art der Vermittlung von überfachlichen Kompetenzen hinterfragt werden.

1.3 Strukturelle Verankerung

Die strukturelle Verankerung an Hochschulen lässt sich grob in zwei Arten einteilen:
- Integrativ: Die Vermittlung überfachlicher Kompetenzen ist in das fachwissenschaftliche Curriculum integriert.
- Additiv: Es gibt separate Angebote zur Vermittlung überfachlicher Kompetenzen, die in spezifischen Modulen, fächerübergreifenden Wahlpflichtbereichen o. ä. belegt werden können.

Weiterhin kann beispielsweise noch unterschieden werden, ob überfachliche Kompetenzen von Lehrenden aus dem jeweiligen Fach oder aus zentralen Einrichtungen oder von externen Lehrbeauftragten vermittelt werden. In diesem Zusammenhang kann das Lehrdeputat für entsprechende Angebote der jeweiligen Lehreinheit oder einer zentralen Einrichtung zugeordnet sein.

Für die integrative und additive Form der Vermittlung gibt es jeweils Vor- und Nachteile:

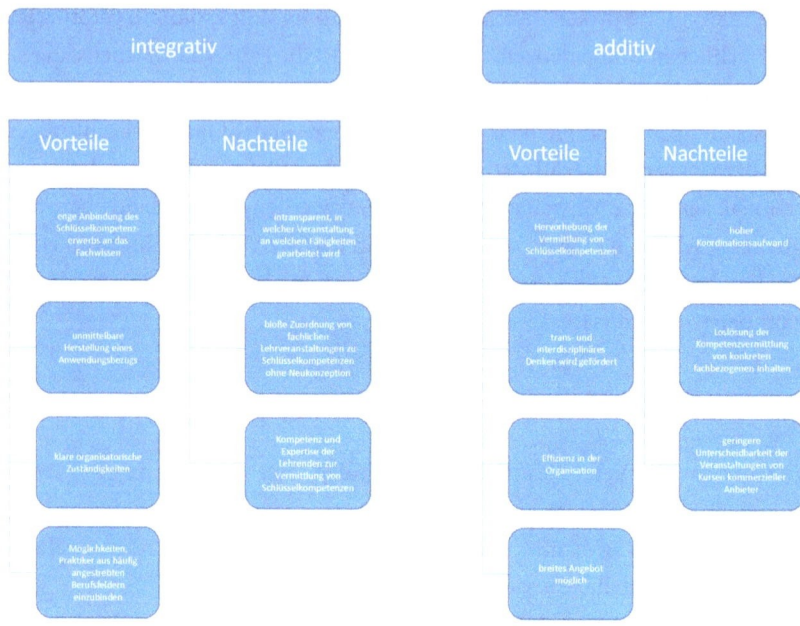

Abb. 2: Integrative und additive Form der Vermittlung

1.4 Beispiele

Abb. 3: Logo des House of Competence

In der Praxis finden sich häufig Mischformen, wie auch in dem Best-Practice-Beispiel des House of Competence (HoC) am Karlsruher Institut für Technologie (KIT).

Das HoC ist eine zentrale, forschungsbasierte Einrichtung, die vor allem additive Angebote macht, aber auch in Zusammenarbeit und Team-Teaching mit Lehrenden integrative Angebote unterstützt.

Das HoC besteht aus einem Zentrum für mediales Lernen, dem Zentrum für Lehrerbildung, dem LernLABOR, dem MedienLABOR und dem SchreibLABOR und ist zuständig für Schlüsselqualifikationen sowie berufsfeldorientierte Zusatzqualifikationen. Die Vermittlung basiert vor allem auf dem Prinzip des forschungsorientierten Lernens. Zusätzlich bietet das HoC Beratung für Studierende zur Entwicklung von Schlüsselqualifikationen an. Dabei kommen auch studentische Lernmentoren zum Einsatz, die durch ihre Qualifizierung und Tätigkeit ihrerseits überfachliche Kompetenz aufbauen können.

2. Diskussionspunkte

Trotz umfangreicher Forderungen und Vorgaben durch Hochschulpolitik und Qualitätssicherung zur Verantwortung für die Vermittlung von überfachlichen Kompetenzen, verschiedenen Entwicklungen in den Hochschulen und vielen guten Beispielen für die Umsetzung überfachlicher Angebote stellt sich für viele Hochschulen immer noch die Frage, ob diese lediglich ein notwendiges Übel oder auch ein Gewinn für die Hochschulen darstellen. Die Erfahrungen zeigen, dass Einrichtungen und Zentren sich immer wieder neu legitimieren müssen. Dies spiegelt sich auch deutlich in der Panel-Diskussion wieder. Die Teilnehmenden sammeln Argumente und Maßnahmen für eine nachhaltige Verankerung von überfachlichen Angeboten:
- Beitrag zur Profilbildung,
- Studieninteressierte überzeugen, Studierende auch in Zukunft gewinnen – und damit Finanzmittel sichern,
- Fördermittel einwerben,
- Beitrag zur Qualitätsentwicklung in Studium und Lehre.

3. Fazit/Ausblick

Die Förderung von überfachlichen Kompetenzen in der Hochschule ist politisch gefordert und wird aktuell bleiben, genauso wie die Frage der Einbindung in die Hochschulstruktur, des Commitments der Leitungsebene und der Akzeptanz einzelner Fächer. Ein weiterer Austausch der Community wird gewünscht, um Synergie-Effekte zur Strategie-Entwicklung nutzen zu können.

Literaturverzeichnis

Susanne In der Smitten/Michael Jaeger (Hrsg.): *Studentischer Kompetenzerwerb im Kontext von Hochschulsteuerung und Profilbildung. Dokumentation zur HIS-Tagung am 03. November 2009 in Hannover,* Hannover 2010. http://www.hoc.kit.edu/lehrangebot.php, zuletzt abgerufen am 12.07.2016.

Kapitel III
Über das Wort hinaus ...

Tagungsimpressionen

Kapitel IV
Über die Lehrendenperspektive hinaus...

Studentische Ansichten

Studentische Ansicht

Fabian Schröer

Gute Lehre für die neue Studierendengeneration kann sich nur im Dialog entwickeln

In den Universitäten und Hochschulen wird allzu oft über Studierende gesprochen: Wie die Studierenden sind, was sie sich wünschen, wie sie sich von den Vorjahren unterscheiden oder was das Bester für sie ist. Eine Sache wird dabei jedoch allzu oft vergessen oder manchmal auch als lästig erachtet: das Gespräch mit den Studierenden. Genau dieser Grund ist Motivation genug, dass Studierende an einer Tagung mit dem Titel „Über das Fach hinaus … Neue Studierendengeneration, neue Herausforderungen" teilnehmen sollten. Das Studierendenparlament der Heinrich-Heine-Universität Düsseldorf empfand dies ebenfalls so und finanzierte daher einigen Studierenden mit Mandaten im Parlament, im Senat oder im AStA die Teilnahme an dieser Tagung.

Die Tagung begann inhaltlich mit dem Impulsvortrag von Herrn Prof. Dr. Christian Scholz zu den Unterschieden der Generationen und den Besonderheiten der aktuellen Studierendengeneration Z. Interessant war zu sehen, dass alle versucht haben, sich zu einer Generation zuzuordnen, jedoch viele in den anschließenden Gesprächen erzählten, dass es schwierig sei, sich mit allen Punkten aus der „eigenen" Generation zu identifizieren. Viele sahen sich als eine Art Hybrid aus den Generationen, die sie durchlebt haben. Ich kann mich, als typisches Mitglied der Generation Y, jedoch auch mit einigen Aspekten der Generation Z identifizieren. Dabei kann natürlich hinterfragt werden, ob die typische Frage der Generation Z „Ist das klausurrelevant?" nicht viel mehr mit dem Modell Bachelor und Master zu tun hat. Zu diesem Zeitpunkt habe ich mir ebenfalls die Frage gestellt, ob es für die neue Studierendengeneration überhaupt Patentrezepte in Sachen Lehre geben kann, wenn man feststellen muss, dass Generationengrenzen schwammig sind und eine Generation nicht als homogene Masse zusammengefasst werden kann. Im Weiteren präsentierte Herr Scholz Ansätze, was Lehrende akzeptieren und nutzen können, welche Dinge nicht zu akzeptieren sind und wo gegengesteuert werden muss. Es war eindeutig zu erkennen, dass hier aus der Sicht der Lehrenden und nicht aus der Sicht der Lernenden gesprochen wurde. Ein Dialog, welche Lehrmethoden am besten sind und zu den verschiedenen Vorlesungstypen, Fachbereichen und Dozierenden passen, sollte zusammen mit den Studierenden stattfinden. Es würde beispielsweise nicht funktionieren, wenn den Studierenden aktive Teilnahme aufgezwungen wird, die Studierenden aber den Mehrwert für sich nicht erkennen. Übungen, bei denen Bonuspunkte für eine Klausur gesammelt werden können, haben zum Beispiel eine viel bessere Beteiligung als Übungen, in denen dies nicht möglich ist. Aber nicht nur Studierende sind durch „Incentives" zu motivieren. Das Zeitkontingent der Dozierenden kann auf Lehre und Forschung aufgeteilt werden. Diese Aufteilung wird jedoch häufig zu Ungunsten der Lehre durch Anreize für Forschung (z. B. Drittmittelerwerb) aus dem natürlichen Gleichgewicht gebracht. Hier müssten die Universitäten gegensteuern und der Lehre die gleiche Wertschätzung durch passende Belohnungsinstrumente für gute Lehre geben. Ebenfalls sollte die Lehre ein größeres Gewicht in Berufungsverfahren erhalten, was zum Beispiel durch verpflichtende Lehrvorträge vor Studierenden und hohe Gewichtung der resultierenden Ergebnisse im Berufungsverfahren ermöglicht werden könnte.

Im nächsten Teil stellte Herr Holger Ehlert das „MenteeModul" der Studierendenakademie vor. Einige Studierende stellen sich während des Studiums die Frage, wie sie dieses erfolgreich beenden können, wie sie ihren Lebenslauf aufpeppen können und was sie mit ihrem Studium überhaupt für Berufsperspektiven haben. Für Außenstehende sehen diese Fragen manchmal sehr merkwürdig aus, da die Studierende sich diese Fragen vorher stellen könnten. Richtig, die Studierenden könnten sich diese Fragen vorher stellen, doch bei der aktuellen Generation von Studierenden ist es häufig auch ein Ausprobieren, was zu einem passt, oder die Wahl fällt auf ein Studium, weil man an den Fächerinhalten interessiert ist. Auch lesen die wenigsten Studierenden die Prüfungsordnungen, die ein guter Wegweiser zur Absolvierung des Studiums sind. Genau an diese Punkte möchte das „MenteeModul" der Studierendenakademie ansetzen. Wichtig ist bei Modulen, die auf die Wünsche und Bedürfnisse der Studierenden angepasst sein sollen, dass diese entsprechend evaluiert werden und sich durch ein ständiges Feedbacksystem immer weiterentwickeln. An diesem Punkt weitergedacht, sollten Universitäten vielleicht ihr Evaluationssystem überdenken und die Dozierenden dieses als interaktive Chance nutzen. Dabei könnten Evaluationen während und am Ende des Semesters, mit der Rückkopplung zu den Studierenden einen höheren Erfolg bringen als aufgezwungene, die in den Schubladen landen. Weiterhin kann das Interesse der Dozierenden und der Studierenden an der Durchführung der Evaluation erhöht werden, wenn es einen Pool an Fragen gibt, aus dem ausgesucht werden kann, sodass diese passgenau für die Veranstaltung sind.

Das erste Panel, welches von mir besucht wurde, trug den Titel „Was bedeutet eine zeitgemäße akademische Bildung als offenes Programm?". Die Expertin Frau Ursula Konnertz führte durch dieses Panel, welches sich mit der Frage beschäftigt hat, was für einen Lehrauftrag die Universitäten eigentlich besitzen. Es standen hierbei die Themen Wissenserwerb und der Erwerb von überfachlichen Schlüsselqualifikationen der Persönlichkeitsentfaltung der Studierenden gegenüber. Auch hier empfand ich es als äußerst interessant, dass auf einer sehr abstrakten Ebene diskutiert wurde, wie Lehre zu sein hat und wie sich Dozierende oder Personen aus der Didaktik zeitgemäße Lehre vorstellen. Es wurde über Humboldt, Bildungsziele von Universitäten und philosophische Theorien gesprochen, bis die Frage aufkam, ob die eigene Universität ein Bildungsziel besitzt. Hier habe ich mich sofort an die Diskussionen der Grundordnungskommission der Heinrich-Heine-Universität Düsseldorf erinnert, die auch einen Passus zum Thema Lehre hervorbrachte: „Die Heinrich-Heine-Universität Düsseldorf dient im Zusammenwirken ihrer Mitglieder der Wissenschaft in Forschung, Lehre und Studium und fördert im Geiste ihres Namenspatrons eine Kultur der Toleranz, Weltoffenheit und Freiheit. Ziel der Forschung ist die Gewinnung wissenschaftlicher Erkenntnisse sowie die wissenschaftliche Grundlegung und Weiterentwicklung von Lehre und Studium. Das Studium soll Methoden, fachliche Kenntnisse und die Fähigkeit zu wissenschaftlicher und beruflicher Arbeit sowie einer kritischen Einordnung wissenschaftlicher Erkenntnisse vermitteln" (Grundordnung der Henrich-Heine-Universität Düsseldorf vom 17.03.2015 § 1 Abs. 2). Diese Zeilen der Grundordnung zeigen, wie ein mögliches Bildungsziel aussehen kann, wenn alle Statusgruppen der Universität zusammen diskutieren, wie sie sich Lehre vorstellen. In diesem Abschnitt sind genau die Punkte vorhanden, über die im Panel diskutiert wurde, wie beispielsweise kritisches Denken oder soziales und ethisches Handeln. Wichtig ist jedoch, dass die Bildungsziele transparent und lebendig sind und den Studierenden nicht als starres, vorgefertigtes und eingefahrenes Konzept präsentiert werden. Studierende müssen die Chance erhalten, diese Ziele mitzubestimmen und diese im Dialog immer wieder an neue äußere Einflüsse und neue Bedürfnisse der Studierenden und Dozierenden anzupassen. Einen Aspekt, den ich bei dem Titel zeitgemäße akademische Bildung vermisst habe, waren allgemeingültige Lehrstandards an Universitäten. Häufig sind diese Themen in den Studiengängen selbst oder in den Fakultäten geregelt, obwohl Universitäten die Möglichkeit haben, transparent für alle Studierende einheitliche Regelungen zu Klausuren oder Vorlesungen zu beschließen. Aus der Sicht der Studierenden fände ich eine Universität attraktiv, bei der ich auf den ersten Blick zum Thema lesen würde, dass man in jedem Studiengang die Möglichkeit zur Klausureinsicht hat und wie diese Einsicht geregelt ist, wie viele Klausuren maximal pro Woche geschrieben werden, dass nur eine Klausur pro Tag geschrieben wird oder dass es keine Überschneidungen von Veranstaltungen gibt.

Im zweiten Panel, welches ich besucht habe, gab Frau Sabine Klüner, die Leiterin des „Stellenwerkes" (einer Art Online-Job-Börse für Studenten) in Hamburg, einen Impulsvortrag über die notwendigen Kompetenzen beim Übergang von der Hochschule in den Beruf und wie Career Center dabei unterstützend wirken können. Anschließend ging der Impulsvortrag in eine Diskussion über, aus der drei Fragestellungen hervorgingen. Zu dieser wurden Lösungsansätze in drei kleineren Gruppen ausgearbeitet. Dieses Panel stand inhaltlich im kompletten Gegensatz zum vorherigen. Die Frage, inwieweit eine Universität überhaupt passgerechte Arbeitnehmerinnen und Arbeitnehmer für die Berufswelt produzieren soll, war eins der Hauptstreitthemen im ersten Panel. Im zweiten wurde die Prämisse gesetzt, dass Universitäten für Studierende attraktiv sind, wenn diese den Studierenden so viel Rüstzeug wie möglich für das spätere Berufsleben mitgeben können. Im Impulsvortrag wurde, bezugnehmend auf Befragungen von Unternehmen, gesagt, dass fast alle Befragten erworbene, nicht-fachliche Schlüsselqualifikationen während des Studiums als eines der Hauptauswahlkriterien ansehen. Dieses Bild passt meiner Erfahrung nach sicherlich nicht auf jede Branche und jede Studienrichtung. Aus gut zwei Dutzend Praktika, Unternehmenspräsentationen und Gesprächen mit Personen aus der Personalabteilung hat sich mir ein anderes Bild gezeigt, sodass ich die Frage in den Raum gestellt habe, warum viele Unternehmen in nicht-offiziellen Gesprächen behaupten, dass die Note das Hauptauswahlkriterium sei. Die Diskussion dazu konnte zwar nicht allumfassend geführt werden, jedoch kam die Gruppe zu dem Ergebnis, dass bei gleicher Note sicherlich die Schlüsselqualifikation den Ausschlag geben wird oder „nur" der passende Notenschnitt als erste Hürde genommen werden muss. Weiterhin sei die Branche, der Grad an Teamarbeit, die Häufigkeit von Kundenkontakt oder die Notwendigkeit von interkulturellem Austauschausschlaggebend für die Wichtigkeit von passenden Schlüsselqualifikationen. In diesem Panel fand ich ebenfalls die Diskussion, ob der Erwerb von Schlüsselqualifikationen überfachlich oder fachspezifisch sein sollte, äußerst interessant. Bei dieser Diskussion habe ich für mich als Ergebnis mitgenommen, dass Studierende selbst gute Ideen einbringen sollen und können, z. B. welche fachlichen Schlüsselqualifikationen sie sich wünschen, damit diese angeboten werden können. Für die Mathematisch-Naturwissenschaftlichen Fächer wäre zum Beispiel ein Kurs zum Thema Labormanagement eine gute Idee.

Zusammenfassend nehme ich von der Tagung für mich viele neue Ideen mit, die ich durch die Hochschulpolitik an unserer Universität einbringen und verwirklichen möchte. Die vielen Gespräche mit Dozierenden und Personen aus der Didaktik oder dem Bereich Career Management haben mir einen ganz anderen Blick auf die Universität ermöglicht. Ein passendes Gesamtfazit der Veranstaltung lautet daher: Gute Lehre für die neue Studierendengeneration kann sich nur im Dialog aller Beteiligten entwickeln.

Studentische Ansicht

Benjamin Bartels
Tagungsbeitrag

Zum ersten Mal wurde ich durch das Studierendenparlament der Heinrich-Heine-Universität auf die Tagung aufmerksam, als dort thematisiert wurde, ob man den Vertretern der Studierendenschaft ermöglichen sollte, an dieser Veranstaltung teilzunehmen oder nicht. Nachdem dies dort bewilligt wurde, habe ich mich für den AStA-Vorstand als Vertreter angemeldet.

Für uns, beziehungsweise mich, war dies eine gute Möglichkeit, sich im direkten Austausch mit Dozierenden und Vertretern verschiedener Institutionen anderer Universitäten zu treffen und auszutauschen. Dabei lag mein Interesse besonders darin herauszufinden, wie mit verschiedenen Problemen oder Situationen an anderen Universitäten umgegangen wird oder welche Lösungswege dort konzipiert wurden. Hier muss ich das erste Lob an die Veranstalter der Tagung aussprechen. Diesen ist es gelungen, sowohl fachlich als auch menschlich hervorragende Gastredner für diese Tagung zu gewinnen.

Besonders möchte ich hier den Vortrag „Wie ‚ticken' die heutigen Studierenden? Ziele, Wünsche, Erwartungen der ‚Generation Z'" von Herrn Prof. Dr. Christian Scholz hervorheben. In diesem wurden die alltäglichen Probleme, die im universitären Alltag auftreten, in Bezug auf die verschiedenen Generationengruppen beleuchtet und herausgestellt. Interessant war zu sehen, inwieweit die einzelnen Generationengruppen voneinander lernen und vor allem besser miteinander zusammenarbeiten und kommunizieren können. Denn das größte Problem in der heutigen Zeit scheint die Kommunikation unter den Generationen zu sein, da sich die Bedeutungen bestimmter Begrifflichkeiten und die Aufnahme dieser drastisch geändert haben.

Im weiteren Verlauf konnte ich feststellen, dass sich so ziemlich jeder anwesende Gast der Tagung bei dem einen oder anderen typischen Merkmal ertappt fühlte. Doch weitaus erstaunlicher war, dass es sehr schwer zu sein schien, sich klar einer Generationengruppe zuzuordnen. Dies hing damit zusammen, dass man Merkmale aus mehreren Gruppen auf sich projizieren konnte.

Nach dem Vortrag ergab sich bereits die Möglichkeit, in die ersten Gespräche einzutauchen und die eben aufgeworfenen Fragen untereinander oder gar mit dem Gastredner persönlich zu besprechen. Was hierbei besonders positiv zu erwähnen ist, war das kollegiale und wertschätzende Verhalten der Tagungsteilnehmer. Unabhängig davon in welcher Position man sich befand, wurden Beiträge und Meinungen hochgeachtet.

Im Anschluss daran ging es in den Panels weiter. In meinem Panel widmete ich mich dem Thema „Man kann nicht nicht kommunizieren – aber falsch. Was Kompetenzen bei Kommunikation bedeutet und wie man sie vermittelt". Recht zügig stellten die Teilnehmer fest, dass alle ähnliche Erfahrungen im Bereich der Kommunikation gemacht haben, unabhängig davon in welcher Position sie sich befanden. Zunächst erfolgte eine kleine Vorstellungsrunde, in der Erwartungen und Themenwünsche geäußert wurden. Bevor man sich dem theoretischen Teil des Panels widmete, erfolgten zunächst in Kleingruppen erste Übungen zur spontanen Kommunikation, um die Situation der sich noch recht unbekannten Teilnehmer etwas aufzulockern. Hierbei wurden die verschiedenen Erwartungen von Sender und Empfänger beleuchtet. Aufschlussreich war, wie schnell Kleinigkeiten, etwa Gestik oder Mimik, die Kommunikation zwischen Personen stören und diese massiv ins Negative beeinflussen können, aber auch wie man dieses Phänomen umgehen und „smart" lösen kann.

Nachdem der theoretische Teil beendet wurde, galt es nun die gewonnenen Erfahrungen in der Praxis anzuwenden, was sehr unterhaltsam und lehrreich war. Eine der wichtigsten Erkenntnisse aus dem Panel war wohl, dass man Kommunikation immer weiter lernen, ausbauen und üben muss, um diese zu beherrschen und sachgerecht für seine Ziele nutzen zu können.

Zum Abend hin wurde ein *Get-together* im Foyer des Hauses der Universität veranstaltet. Die Teilnehmer konnten in einer gemütlichen Runde das Bisherige reflektieren und bekamen nochmals die Möglichkeit, sich austauschen. Geschichts- und kulturinteressierteren Gäste konnten sich auf eine Stadtführung durch Düsseldorf aus dem Blickwinkel von Heinrich Heine begeben. Der Rest gab sich den fußballerischen Künsten von Wales und Belgien hin und genoss ein erstklassiges Fußballspiel im Rahmen der Europameisterschaft in Frankreich bei einigen Kaltgetränken und in entspannter Atmosphäre. Die

Organisatoren haben den Übergang von fachlicher Tagung und guter Abendgestaltung bravourös gemeistert, sodass wohl für jeden ein passender Programmpunkt dabei war.

Am folgenden Tag ging es nach der kurzen Vorstellung der Ergebnisse des Vortages und einem Impuls zum Thema „Schlüsselkompetenzen" weiter mit den Panels des zweiten Tages.

Hier habe ich mich für das Panel „Kompetenzbedarf beim Übergang von der Hochschule in den Beruf" entschieden, da wir als AStA leider feststellen mussten, dass sich dieser für Studierende oft schwieriger gestaltet, als man vielleicht vermuten würde. Herausforderungen seien beispielsweise die fehlende Berufserfahrung, ein Mangel an gewissen Soft Skills und das Phänomen, nicht zu wissen, was man nach dem Studium mit seinem Abschluss machen möchte.

Besonders lehrreich war zu erfahren, dass die Probleme, unabhängig vom Universitätsstandort, vielerorts gleicher Natur, die Lösungswege jedoch andere sind. Hier gilt es, sich aus den vorhandenen Methoden das Beste anzueignen und für unsere Universität umzusetzen. Ein gutes Beispiel hierfür ist das Studierenden-Service-Center, welches unter anderem Studienabbrecher dabei unterstützt, einen Beruf oder eine Ausbildung zu finden. Doch ist dies ja nur einer der vielen Bereiche, der angegangen werden muss.

Ein weiterer Fokus lag auf der Vermittlung von Soft Skills, da es Studierenden oft an diesen mangelt und dies zu vielen Problemen, nicht nur im Berufsleben führt. Jedoch war hier auch die Schwierigkeit zu erkennen, wie den Studierendendie Wichtigkeit dieser Skills nahe zu bringen ist, aber auch wie man den Dozierenden aufzeigt, welche notwendige Bedeutung diesen zuzumessen ist.

Insgesamt besteht hier noch viel Handlungsbedarf und das Panel hat ermöglicht, sich intensiv und differenziert zu diesem Thema auszutauschen. Ein erster Schritt ist nun getan. Jetzt müssen die hier besprochenen Dinge idealerweise aktiv umgesetzt, die Erfahrungen evaluiert und der Austausch in regelmäßigen Abständen wiederholt werden.

Abschließend kann man festhalten, dass diese Tagung der Universität aus meiner Sicht sehr gut getan hat, da dadurch ermöglicht wurde zu zeigen, dass man bereit ist, sich aktuellen Thematiken und Problemen proaktiv zu stellen und diese zum einen für die Universität zu verbessern und zum anderen den Standort zu stärken. Weiterhin soll die Qualität der Lehre verbessert werden, womit man sich auch in diesem Bereich für die Zukunft aufstellt.

Für mich als Vertreter der Studierendenschaft bot die Tagung eine gute Möglichkeit, direkt mit den Leuten in Austausch zu treten, die die Probleme und Thematiken an die entsprechenden Institutionen weiterleiten oder gar direkt und selbst angehen können. Des Weiteren bekam ich einen Einblick in die reflektierte Welt der Dozierenden, die selbst feststellten, dass sich einiges verändern muss, wenn man das Studieren langfristig aufstellen möchte und zukunftsfest machen will. Besonders erfreulich war, dass sich sehr über das Feedback und die Sichtweise aus der studentischen Mitte gefreut wurde, da so die verschiedensten Blickwinkel zum Tragen kamen, wodurch man einige Sachverhalte ganz anders wahrgenommen hat und für die Zukunft anders machen möchte.

Deshalb ist es von größter Wichtigkeit, dass Studierende den Diskurs mit Dozierenden und der Universität suchen, um dies, im Sinne beider Seiten, langfristig und nachhaltig zu verbessern.

Zum Abschluss möchte ich mich herzlich bei der Studierendenakademie der Heinrich-Heine-Universität für die Einladung zu der Tagung bedanken. Diese war hervorragend organisiert und eine durch und durch gelungene Veranstaltung.

Studentische Ansicht

Jessica Schäfers

Beitrag zu Panel: Praxis- und Berufsorientierung an Hochschulen II

Hinter Berufsberatung an Hochschulen steckt unheimlich viel Leidenschaft. Das wurde im Panel „Praxis- und Berufsorientierung an Hochschulen II" mehr als deutlich. Schon im kurzen Impuls, den Holger Ehlert zu Beginn der Diskussion gegeben hat, zeigt sich das. Viel passiert hier durch Eigeninitiative und durch Interesse an den Studierenden.

Sind Career-Service & Co. „Kümmerer"? Diejenigen, die aufarbeiten, was Professoren nicht mehr leisten können? Das war die erste Frage, die sich stellte. Trotz Uneinigkeiten fand man eine gemeinsame Antwort: Auf jeden Fall sind sie Kümmerer im positiven Sinne. Berater legen viel Wert auf den individuellen Blick, den sie auf studentische Probleme haben. Das ist, was sie auszeichnet, sagt einer der Teilnehmer.

In der Diskussion zeigt sich schnell, dass sich die Probleme der Teilnehmer, obwohl ihre Ausgangssituationen sehr unterschiedlich sind, doch oft ähneln. Die nicht gesicherte Finanzierung der Projekte und die vielen befristeten Stellen, durch die beispielsweise ein Career-Service besetzt wird, wirken sich verheerend auf Arbeitsmotivation und laufende Projekte aus. Der curriculare Rückhalt lässt auch zu wünschen übrig. Oft kommt aus den Fachbereichen die Aussage, dass Praxisorientierung außerhalb des Fachs gar nicht mehr nötig wäre. Kontrovers diskutiert wurde die Rolle der Bundesagentur für Arbeit an den Hochschulen.

Teilweise wurde diese als Gegenspieler wahrgenommen, insbesondere wenn es um die Streichung von Geldern für die hochschulinterne Berufsberatung geht. Einige Teilnehmer sahen aber auch eher einen Kooperationspartner, der nur bedingt eine Rolle spielt. Einigkeit herrschte beim Thema Wertschätzung der Hochschulen. Diese scheint oft zu fehlen, was insbesondere an der Raumsituation deutlich wird. „‚Ja ja, packt die [Kollegin] zu dem von der Berufsberatung ins Büro.' Auf Datenschutz bei Beratungen und Ähnliches wird da null Rücksicht genommen."

Auch bei den Studierenden wurde man sich einig. Das Studium stehe heute nicht mehr an erster Stelle, gerade dann, wenn SHK-Stellen nicht unter 20 Stunden Arbeitszeit pro Woche angeboten würden. „Da bleibe dann halt keine Zeit mehr", so eine der Teilnehmerinnen.

Am Ende der Diskussion stand eine Frage klar im Vordergrund, die wohl einer Problemlösung am nächsten kommt: Wenn man gute Angebote bereitstellt und eine angenehme Beratungssituation geschaffen hat – Wie vermittelt man den Studierenden dann, was man anzubieten hat?

Studentische Ansicht

Christian Lentz

„Über das Fach hinaus ... Neue Studierendengeneration, neue Herausforderungen"

Als Wissenschaftliche Hilfskraft der Geschäftsführung der Studierendenakademie wurde mir die Möglichkeit gegeben, beim gesamten Prozess der Planung und Durchführung der Tagung dabei zu sein. Aus einer dualen Perspektive, einerseits als Mitarbeiter der Studierendenakademie und andererseits als Student, erlebe ich die Angebote der überfachlichen Schlüsselkompetenzvermittlung an der Heinrich-Heine-Universität und war auch deswegen gespannt auf die Sichtweisen der Vertreterinnen und Vertreter anderer Universitäten und wie sich diese vor dem Hintergrund der Leitfrage der Tagung auf die neue Studierendengeneration einstellen.

Im Zuge der Tagungsvorbereitung übernahm ich unter anderem diverse Recherchetätigkeiten wie das Erstellen von E-Mail-Verteilern, Adress- und Kontaktlisten, die (Mit-)Gestaltung von Flyern und diversen anderen Infomaterialien zur Bewerbung der Veranstaltung, aber auch die Registrierung der Anmeldungen sowie den Rechnungseingang. Auch durch diese Tätigkeiten konnte ich mir bereits recht früh in der rund einjährigen Planungs- und Organisationsphase ein Bild davon machen, wie die Tagung final aussehen wird.

Während der Tagung umfassten die Aufgaben von meinen Kolleginnen und mir an beiden Tagen unter anderem die Besetzung des Tagungsbüros, die Unterstützung der Referentinnen und Referenten bei technischen Fragen sowie die Bestückung der Räumlichkeiten mit entsprechenden Präsentationsmaterialien. Im Tagungsbüro, das absichtlich etwas aus dem „Ankommenstrubel" des Foyers an den Treppenbereich, der zum großen Saal des Hauses führte, verlagert wurde und während der beiden Veranstaltungstage als zusätzlicher

Informationspunkt im Haus diente, bekamen die Teilnehmer auch die für sie wichtigen Unterlagen überreicht. Darunter befanden sich neben Informationsmaterialien auch für die Tagung unbedingt notwendige Dokumente wie der Ablaufplan der beiden Veranstaltungstage, die personalisierten Namensschilder der jeweiligen Person sowie eine Übersicht über die entsprechenden Raumbelegungen, der auch zu entnehmen war, wann welches Panel an welchem Ort stattfand. Als gute Idee, so bestätigten es viele Teilnehmer im Gespräch, erwies sich zudem die Beilage eines Stadtplans von Düsseldorf, mit dem die Orientierung abseits der Tagung doch erheblich erleichtert wurde.

Nachdem die erste Orientierung am noch unbekannten Veranstaltungsort abgeschlossen war und sich die meisten Teilnehmer im großen Saal des Hauses der Universität eingefunden hatten, konnte die Tagung offiziell mit der Begrüßung durch den Leiter der Studierendenakademie, Herrn Prof. Dr. Pretzler und der thematischen Einführung durch Herrn Prof. Dr. Scholz beginnen.

Die Frage danach, wie eine Hochschule, deren Hochschulsystem für den Umgang mit Studierenden nach dem Muster der „Generation Y" ausgerichtet ist, damit umgehen soll, dass sich der durchschnittliche Studierende heutzutage eher nach dem Typus der „Generation Z" verhält, erscheint mir hier als besonders spannend. Denn wie schwierig diese Frage in der Praxis wirklich zu beantworten ist, wird deutlich, wenn man die verschiedenen Generationen von Studierenden im Universitätsalltag betrachtet. Hier wird deutlich, dass „die Studierenden" keine gänzlich homogene Masse darstellen und bei vielen von ihnen oftmals eher eine Mischung aus typischen Merkmalen verschiedener Generationen zu beobachten ist. So lassen sich durchaus auch Vertreter „älterer" Generationen in Vorlesungen und Seminaren finden, die typische Fragen eines „Generation Z"-Vertreters stellen. Etwa danach, ob entsprechende Lehrinhalte klausurrelevant sind. Klar ist aber auch, dass man entsprechend typische Merkmale und Kriterien definieren muss, wenn man die entsprechenden Generationen als Masse greifbar machen möchte.

Interessant finde ich hinsichtlich des so oft im öffentlichen Dialog geforderten Auftrags der Universitäten die Frage, inwieweit es sich eine Hochschule überhaupt leisten kann, ideale, in Schablonen passende Arbeiter für die entsprechenden Berufsfelder zu produzieren. So scheint es, mit Blick auf die akademische Laufbahn, neben den Geisteswissenschaftlern beispielsweise auch bei den Wirtschaftswissenschaftlern und den Juristen der Fall zu sein, dass sie mit ihrem reinen Fachstudium auf dem Arbeitsmarkt mit immer mehr vermeintlich fachfremden Bewerbern um dieselben Arbeitsplätze konkurrieren. Hieran zeigt sich deutlich, welche (positiven) Auswirkungen das Aneignen von überfachlichen Schlüsselkompetenzen haben kann. Denn eben jenes Fachstudium, so mein Eindruck, gibt in vielen Studierendenbiografien bloß die ungefähre Richtung vor. Der Schlüsselkompetenzerwerb, kombiniert mit Praktika und dem Erfahrungsgewinn durch verschiedene Tätigkeiten während des Studiums, stellt aber, neben der Abschlussnote, gewissermaßen das „Salz in der Suppe" dar, das einen für diverse, teils auch fachfremde, Tätigkeitsbereiche qualifiziert, ein breites Spektrum an möglichen Arbeitsfeldern auffächert und oftmals die Türe zumindest für das erste Vorstellungsgespräch öffnet.

Neben Themenfeldern wie der Selbstpräsentation bei der Jobsuche im Internet oder der Frage über die Wichtigkeit und Notwendigkeit von Schlüsselkompetenzen und deren Vermittlung war auch die Digitalisierung und deren Auswirkung auf das Lern- und Lehrverhalten an den Hochschulen ein Aspekt, der während der Tagung behandelt wurde.

Dieser Punkt ist aus meiner Sicht auch ein beinahe durchweg positives Beispiel für die Modernisierung der Hochschulen und für das gelungene Einstellen auf die neuen Studierendengenerationen. Während meines Studiums konnte ich beobachten, wie die Dozenten den Spagat zwischen analogen und digitalen Medien gemeistert haben, ohne dabei das eigentliche Ziel der Veranstaltung (Wissensvermittlung und Motivation zum Selbststudium) aus den Augen zu verlieren. Dabei habe ich diesen Spagat zumeist als absolut gelungen und sinnvoll umgesetzt erlebt, da niemand versuchte, künstlich ein anderes Lehrverhalten an den Tag zu legen, sondern die digitalen Medien und Plattformen (etwa die Lernplattformen „Moodle" und „Ilias" oder die Möglichkeit, anstelle mit Folien und einem Overheadprojektor eine Power Point Präsentation und den Beamer zu nutzen) eher als sinnvolle Ergänzung zur Vermittlung von Vorträgen und Materialien verstanden wurde.

Auch der Eindruck, dass die während des Studiums gesammelten Schlüsselkompetenzen von den allermeisten Arbeitgebern gern gesehen werden, wurde im Rahmen der Vorträge, die ich während der Tagung mithören konnte, bestätigt. Bei all den im Rahmen der Tagung behandelten Themen wurde, so mein Eindruck, auch nie das notwendige Zusammenspiel von Hochschule und Arbeitsmarkt und den damit aufkommenden Fragen, aus den Augen verloren. Hierbei geht es aus Hochschulsicht wohl vor allem um die Angebote und Entwicklungsmöglichkeiten von Serviceeinrichtungen wie am Beispiel der Heinrich-Heine-Universität, dem Career Service, der die Studierenden für ihren Übergang von der Hochschule in die Berufswelt berät, oder der Abteilung KUBUS (Karriere Und Berufsorientierung Und Studium), die den Praxisbezug in die Berufswelt herstellen. Hier kommt es vor allem auf die realistische Einschätzung des Kompetenzbedarfs an, den die Berufswelt an die Absolventen stellt und den diese idealerweise mitbringen und in der Bewerbungsphase unter Beweis stellen können.

Aus den Vorträgen heraus ließ sich dabei ein sich gegenseitiges Bedingen erkennen: Die Wirtschaft ist davon abhängig, gut ausgebildete, geeignete Absolventen aus den Hochschulen zu bekommen, die sie in ihre breiten Anforderungsprofile integrieren kann. Dass dabei in vielen Branchen, bei den über die Jahre gestiegenen Anforderungen, mehr gefragt ist, als die bloße fachspezifische, universitäre Ausbildung, liegt auf der Hand. Gefragt sind gut ausgebildete Akademiker, die aber auch über ein gewisses Maß an Lebenserfahrung verfügen und dabei gerne auch breit aufgestellt sein dürfen.

Es scheint nie von Nachteil zu sein, bereits Einblicke in die fachbezogenen Berufsfelder und darüber hinaus gehabt zu haben. Ein soziales und gesellschaftliches Engagement wird ebenso gerne gesehen wie Kenntnisse in einer oder mehreren Fremdsprachen. Zudem wird von einem Hochschulabsolventen erwartet, dass er sich im Rahmen seiner universitären Ausbildung und darüber hinaus, neben dem fachlichen Wissen, auch ein breites Spektrum an Präsentationsfähigkeiten, die Fähigkeit zur Selbstreflektion sowie Methoden- und Sozialkompetenz angeeignet hat.

Somit ist wohl die Angleichung der Kompetenzanforderungen von Studierenden, Hochschulen und Unternehmen aneinander einer der wichtigen Schritte und gleichzeitig die große Herausforderung, die in Zukunft noch stärker angegangen werden wird. Diesbezüglich wird es auch interessant sein zu beobachten, ob es umsetzbar sein wird, ein konkretes Verständnis von Schlüsselkompetenzen über die Universität hinaus zu etablieren, um ein noch zielorientierteres Vermitteln entsprechender Kompetenzen sowohl für den Studierenden selbst als auch für den potentiellen Arbeitgeber zu ermöglichen.

Hinsichtlich dessen war auch der Impulsvortrag von Frau Prof. Dr. Alonso äußerst informativ, in dem unter anderem die kontroversen Diskussionen in den verschiedenen Bildungskontexten zu den Themen „Qualifikation" und „Kompetenzen" skizziert wurden und der Hinweis darauf erfolgte, dass das Hochschulrahmengesetz die Hochschulen verpflichtet, neben der wissenschaftlichen Ausbildung auch einen Beitrag hinsichtlich der Vorbereitung auf die Berufswelt zu leisten. Für diesen Aspekt dienlich waren Frau Prof. Dr. Alonsos Ausführungen zum so genannten Projekt „SQ 21", bei dem Studierende, Hochschulvertreter sowie Unternehmensvertreter ihren Standpunkt bezüglich ihrer Methoden, Erfahrungen, Vorstellungen und Erwartungen rund um das Thema Schlüsselkompetenzen deutlich machten und, in einem zweiten Schritt, in einen Dialog miteinander fielen. Das Ziel dieses Austauschs war es, mit den Ergebnissen die Bachelor- und Masterstudiengänge hinsichtlich der Vermittlung von fachübergreifenden Schlüsselkompetenzen zielgerichtet zu optimieren.

Um all diese Dinge gewährleisten zu können, haben viele Hochschulen bereits seit längerem Maßnahmen ergriffen und Einrichtungen installiert und etabliert, die dafür sorgen sollen, dass es den Studierenden ermöglicht wird, ihr persönliches Profil zu schärfen und überfachliche Kenntnisse zu erwerben. Dabei soll den Studierenden durch ein breites, facettenreiches Angebot die Wahl gegeben werden, in welchen über ihr Fach hinaus vorhandenen Gebieten sie sich weiterbilden und Schlüsselkompetenzen erwerben möchten.

Vor dem Hintergrund all dieser Erfahrungen und Kompetenzen, die vom heutigen Hochschulabsolventen erwartet werden, ist es äußerst fraglich, wie sinnvoll ein G8-Abitur, der Wegfall von Wehrpflicht und Zivildienst sowie das Durchpeitschen durch ein eng bemessenes, oftmals stark verschulischtes Regelstudium in Bachelor und Master für diesen Prozess ist. Schließlich muss die Frage gestellt werden, wie viel Lebenserfahrung sowie Sozial-, Methoden- und Selbstkompetenzen von einem Anfang 20-jährigen Menschen erwartet werden kann, der, oftmals in Rekordzeit, die Schule und Universität absolviert hat und anschließend auf den Arbeitsmarkt drängt.

Mit der Beschreibung „Über das Fach hinaus ... " lässt sich auch eine weitere, die Tagung betreffende Idee benennen, die erst nach der Veranstaltung so richtig zum Tragen kommen und gewürdigt werden konnte. So wurde eigens ein Blog erstellt, der mit crossmedialen Elementen gefüllt wurde. Hierfür verantwortlich waren zwei Workshops aus der Abteilung KUBUS der Studierendenakademie, die die Tagung begleitet haben. Der Geschäftsführer des Düsseldorfer Hochschulradios, Herr Andreas Meske, war mit seinem Radioworkshop vor Ort und nahm mit den Studierenden O-Töne auf, führte Interviews durch und bearbeitete und schnitt gleich in einem entsprechend ausgestatteten Raum im Haus der Universität die Beiträge. Der Schwerpunkt in dem Workshop des Filmemachers und Autors Herrn Dr. Klaus Bergner lag im Bereich Foto und Video. Beide Gruppen nahmen verschiedene Veranstaltungsschwerpunkte wie die gehaltenen Vorträge crossmedial auf. Dabei waren beide Workshops durchaus sportlich unterwegs und wechselten im Laufe des Tages immer wieder die Etagen, um verschiedene Geschehnisse mit der Kamera und dem Aufnahmegerät zu dokumentieren und festzuhalten. Das am 2. Juli stattfindende Viertelfinale der Fußballeuropameisterschaft zwischen Deutschland und Frankreich nahm der Video-Workshop zudem zum Anlass, um die Tagungsteilnehmer das mögliche Endergebnis dieser Partie tippen zu lassen und dies per Aufnahme festzuhalten. Auch diese launige Abwechslung vom eigentlichen Tagungsthema kam gut an und wurde ebenfalls auf dem Internet-Blog verewigt.

Durch die Bewertungen und Einschätzungen der Teilnehmer, die aus den insgesamt 26 zurückgegebenen Evaluationsbögen hervorgingen, wurde zudem ein umfassendes Bild ermöglicht und den Organisatoren die Möglichkeit gegeben, von den wichtigen Anregungen und Kritikpunkten, aber auch von den vielen lobenden Worten für die Zukunft zu profitieren.

Mein persönliches Fazit zur Tagung fällt absolut positiv aus. Es war eine interessante Erfahrung, die Perspektiven und Sichtweisen der verschiedenen Experten zu hören und dabei mitzuhelfen, dass am Ende ein reibungsloser Tagungsablauf zu Buche stand. Dazu gehört auch die Gewissheit, dass sich –

spätestens nach der Auswertung der Evaluationsbögen – Teilnehmer wie Referenten zum allergrößten Teil wohl gefühlt, die Möglichkeit des Netzwerkens auch außerhalb der Panels und Vorträge genutzt und zwei für sie interessante Tage im Haus der Universität verbracht haben.

Kapitel V
Über fünf Jahre hinaus ...

Die Studierendenakademie
der Heinrich-Heine-Universität Düsseldorf

Nina Leibinnes
Die Studierendenakademie der Heinrich-Heine-Universität Düsseldorf

Die Studierendenakademie der Heinrich-Heine-Universität Düsseldorf (HHU) ist im Jahr 2012 gegründet worden, um überfachliche Angebote an der HHU zu bündeln und damit ihre Sichtbarkeit zu erhöhen. Verschiedene Aktivitäten in diesem Bereich hatten an der HHU bereits eine Tradition. Sie waren aber in unterschiedlichen Organisationsstrukturen verankert und es bestand kaum Vernetzung untereinander. Für Studierende waren die einzelnen Angebote zudem schwer zu überblicken.

Unter dem Dach der Studierendenakademie sollten die Programme stärker aufeinander abgestimmt und gemeinsame Angebote entwickelt werden. Ziel war eine neue Einheit, die maßgeblich zur Erreichung der Ziele des Bologna-Prozesses und der Ziele der HHU in Lehre und Studium beiträgt, indem sie die Employability der Studierenden verbessert, ihre Mobilität fördert, den Praxisbezug erhöht und die Internationalisierung der HHU ebenso unterstützt wie Optimierung von Service und Beratung. Durch die Studierendenakademie sollte somit die Qualität und die Attraktivität des Studiums an der HHU weiter erhöht werden. Für die Studentinnen und Studenten wurde mit der Studierendenakademie eine zentrale wissenschaftliche Einrichtung an der HHU geschaffen, die sich als die Anlaufstelle für Aktivitäten außerhalb des eigentlichen Fachstudiums etabliert hat.

Jedes Semester nutzen aktuell ca. 500 Studierende die Möglichkeit, ihr akademisches Wissens- und Kompetenzspektrum sinnvoll zu ergänzen, um sich persönlich weiterzuentwickeln. Gleichzeitig verbessern sie damit ihre Berufsaussichten, weil Qualifikationen, die über die rein fachliche Kompetenz hinausgehen, auf dem Arbeitsmarkt ein immer größeres Gewicht bekommen.

Mit dem facettenreichen Programm der fünf Abteilungen der Studierendenakademie – Zentrum Studium Universale, Studiengebiet Deutsch als Fremdsprache, Sprachenzentrum, KUBUS (Praxis- und Berufsorientierung) und Career Service – können Studentinnen und Studenten ihr Profil schärfen und einen Blick über den Tellerrand wagen. Zusätzlich wird Ihnen ermöglicht, individuell zu lernen und bei der Qualifizierung ihren persönlichen Interessen zu folgen. Sie können Schwerpunkte setzen, Stärken ausbauen – und auch eventuellen Schwächen entgegenwirken. Denn nicht zuletzt sieht es die Studierendenakademie als ihre Aufgabe an, mit ihren Veranstaltungen im Sinne des Diversity-Gedankens alle Studentinnen und Studenten in jeder Phase des Studiums unmittelbar zu fördern und sie auf ihrem Weg zu einem guten Studienabschluss und einem erfolgreichen Start in das Berufsleben optimal zu unterstützen. Sie möchte außerdem auf spätere berufliche Herausforderungen und auf die Rolle in der Gesellschaft vorbereiten sowie die intellektuelle Persönlichkeitsbildung fördern. Um dabei auf möglichst viele individuelle Bedürfnisse eingehen zu können, steht den Studierenden jedes Semester ein Programm mit fast 300 Workshops, Kursen und Seminaren sowie diversen Beratungsformaten zur Verfügung. In interdisziplinären und allgemeinbildenden Veranstaltungen, in Sprachkursen oder mit Angeboten zu Zusatz- und Schlüsselqualifikationen sowie zu Berufsorientierung und Karriereberatung trägt die Studierendenakademie bei zur Entwicklung sehr unterschiedlicher Kompetenzen bei den Studentinnen und Studenten. Diese Vielfalt und der Facettenreichtum des Programms finden auch im Logo der Studierendenakademie Ausdruck und werden dort durch den stilisierten Fächer symbolisiert.

Die Zusammenführung der verschiedenen Angebote unter dem Dach der Studierendenakademie vereint das Know-how und die unterschiedlichen Perspektiven der fünf Abteilungen und schafft so den Nährboden für interessante gemeinsame Projekte – wie die Tagung „Über das Fach hinaus ... Neue Studierendengeneration, neue Herausforderungen" im Juli 2016. Zusätzlich können organisatorische Abläufe und Verwaltungsstrukturen gestrafft und optimiert sowie mit einem zentralen Qualitätsmanagement gemeinsame Standards etabliert werden. Der ständige Austausch untereinander sorgt für ein abgestimmtes Programm und erzeugt zahlreiche weitere Synergieeffekte. Darüber hinaus wird die Vernetzung mit ähnlichen Einrichtungen an anderen Hochschulen erleichtert.

Vor dem Hintergrund der gegebenen Herausforderung der Modularisierung des Wahl(pflicht)bereichs sind indes vor allem die gemeinsamen und abteilungsübergreifenden Angebote von Bedeutung. Verschiedene Zertifikate und Module, z. B. „fit4career", das Karriere-Modul für internationale Studierende, oder das „MenteeModul" existieren bereits. Bei der Entwicklung weiterer Angebote setzt die Studierendenakademie auf den Dialog mit Fächern, Fakultäten und dem Rektorat, um maßgeschneiderte Programme zu etablieren. Denn nur so kann das Programm der Studierendenakademie das Fachstudium auch in Zukunft optimal und bedarfsgerecht ergänzen. Unterstützt wird sie bei diesen Bestrebungen durch den Beirat, in dem alle fünf Fakultäten vertreten sind. Die Beiratsmitglieder stehen der Studierendenakademie beratend zur Seite und fördern als „Botschafter/innen" die Kommunikation mit den Fakultäten. Zusätzlich werden Studierendenvertreterinnen und -vertreter regelmäßig zu Wünschen und Bedarfen befragt. Denn die Studierendenakademie versteht sich als Dienstleisterin – für die Hochschulleitung, die Fakultäten und für die Studierenden.

Die Abteilungen der Studierendenakademie

Ilke Kaymak
Career Service

Der Career Service ist Teil der Studierendenakademie der Heinrich-Heine-Universität Düsseldorf und zentrale Anlaufstelle für alle Studierenden, Absolventinnen und Absolventen bei Fragen zum Übergang von der Hochschule in den Beruf. Das Angebot umfasst eine psychologisch fundierte Individualberatung für Studierende und Absolventinnen und Absolventen sowie die Organisation von Veranstaltungen und Exkursionen mit renommierten Unternehmen und Arbeitgebern.

Karriereplanung ist für Studierende sowie Absolventinnen und Absolventen immer eine individuelle Angelegenheit, denn: Beruflicher Erfolg ist bestimmt durch die Faktoren „Persönliche Fähigkeiten" und „Eigene Leistungsbereitschaft". Biografien werden immer flexibler, klassische, vorgezeichnete Karrierewege können immer seltener gegangen werden.

Der erste Schritt der Karriereplanung ist: Herausfinden, was man eigentlich kann und will. Die eigenen Ziele und Fähigkeiten müssen definiert werden. Die umfangreichen Beratungsangebote des Career Service sollen helfen, individuelle Berufseinstiegspläne zu entwerfen und umzusetzen.

Für Unternehmen und weitere Arbeitgeber (NPO, NGO etc.) ist der Career Service zentraler Ansprechpartner und „Tor zur Universität" bei allen Fragen rund um die Nachwuchsgewinnung. Als konstruktiver Kooperationspartner berät und unterstützt der Career Service, um passende Nachwuchskräfte für die eigene Organisation zu gewinnen. Dabei kann auf eine mehrjährige Erfahrung mit universitären Formaten zurückgegriffen werden.

Mit dem Jobportal www.stellenwerk-duesseldorf.de schafft der Career Service eine Infrastruktur für die kurz- und mittelfristige Vermittlung von studentischen Hilfskräften und Aushilfen, Praktikantinnen und Praktikanten und von Hochschulabsolventinnen und Hochschulabsolventen.

Für die eigene Qualitätssicherung ist der Career Service seit 2009 institutionelles Mitglied im Career Service Netzwerk Deutschland e. V. (csnd), dem Dachverband der Career Services im deutschsprachigen Raum.

Die Abteilungen der Studierendenakademie

Peter Hachenberg
Studiengebiet Deutsch als Fremdsprache (DaF)

Erfolgreich studieren heißt Deutsch lernen

Von kaum einem anderen Faktor hängt der Studienerfolg internationaler Studierender so sehr ab wie von guten Deutschkenntnissen. Das Studiengebiet Deutsch als Fremdsprache hilft internationalen Studentinnen und Studenten mit einem auf sie zugeschnittenen Programm und hochkompetenten Lehrkräften, diese Kenntnisse zu erwerben.

Deutschkurse während des Fachstudiums

Während ihres Fachstudiums an der Heinrich-Heine-Universität können internationale Studierende kostenfrei am umfangreichen studienbegleitenden Deutschprogramm teilnehmen, das Kurse von der Grund- bis zur Oberstufe sowie zur Grammatik, Phonetik und zu den Fertigkeiten Hören, Sprechen und Schreiben umfasst. Kurse zur Landeskunde, insbesondere auch zu Geschichte und Kultur der Stadt Düsseldorf mit Exkursionen in der Stadt runden unser Deutschkursangebot ab. Auch Gastwissenschaftlerinnen und -wissenschaftlern der Heinrich-Heine-Universität steht dieses Programm offen.

Angeboten werden Kurse für Anfänger bis Fortgeschrittene (Niveau A1.1 bis C1 gemäß dem Europäischen Referenzrahmen für Sprachen (GER)). Nach Absprache mit den Fachbereichen organisieren wir zudem eigene Kurse für spezielle Zielgruppen (z. B. für das MA-Programm „European Studies").

Peter Hachenberg

Deutschkurse vor dem Fachstudium

Für Studierende aus dem Erasmus-Programm und andere Programmstudierende veranstalten wir schon vor Semesterbeginn zweiwöchige Intensivkurse (20 Stunden pro Woche).

Internationale Sommerkurse

Seit vielen Jahren finden in den Sommerferien an der Heinrich-Heine-Universität gegen moderate Gebühren Deutschkurse für Studierende aus aller Welt statt. Bestandteil der Kurse ist ein abwechslungsreiches Nachmittagsprogramm, mit dem die Teilnehmenden die Stadt Düsseldorf und ihre Umgebung kennen lernen können.

Kursinhalte: Erlernen, Auffrischung und Vertiefung allgemeinsprachlicher Fertigkeiten, Hör- und Leseverstehen mit aktuellen Texten, Übungen zur Grammatik, zum Wortschatz und zur Idiomatik, Verbesserung der Sprechfertigkeit sowie der schriftlichen Ausdrucksfähigkeit, interkulturelle Landeskunde, deutsche Filme und Alltagskultur. Die Sommerkurse richten sich an Anfänger bis Fortgeschrittene (Niveau A1.2 bis C1 gemäß GER, keine Kurse für Null-Anfänger (Niveau A1.1)).

Modul: Zusatzqualifikation Deutsch als Fremdsprache

Mit der „Zusatzqualifikation Deutsch als Fremdsprache" bieten wir Studierenden der Heinrich-Heine-Universität als fächerübergreifendes Wahlmodul (3 Seminare zu je 2 Semesterwochenstunden) eine methodisch-didaktische Grundausbildung für Lehrkräfte im Bereich DaF an. Zielgruppe sind deutsche und ausländische Studierende, die im Rahmen einer Auslandstätigkeit (z. B. als Lektor/in des DAAD, Sprachassistent/in, Dozent/in des Goethe-Instituts, als einheimische Lehrkraft im Ausland) oder im Unterricht mit Jugendlichen oder Erwachsenen an nicht-schulischen Trägern im Inland (z. B. Goethe-Institute, VHS und andere öffentliche Träger, private Sprachschulen usw.) Deutsch als eine fremde Sprache unterrichten wollen.

Zertifikat: Zusatzqualifikation Deutsch als Fremd- und Zweitsprache

Das Studiengebiet Deutsch als Fremdsprache bietet zudem in einer einzigartigen Kooperation mit dem Goethe-Institut Düsseldorf eine einjährige Zusatzqualifikation Deutsch als Fremd- und Zweitsprache inkl. eines umfangreichen Praktikums an. Adressaten dieses gebührenpflichtigen Programms sind Lehrende in der Erwachsenenbildung und Studierende mit muttersprachlichen Deutschkenntnissen (mit Studienabschluss oder kurz vor Studienabschluss). Die Absolvent/innen erhalten ein benotetes Zertifikat der Heinrich-Heine-Universität und des Goethe-Instituts als Nachweis über die Fähigkeit zur Planung und Durchführung eines allgemeinsprachlichen DaF-und DaZ-Unterrichts in der Erwachsenenbildung sowie zur Erteilung von Unterricht in Integrationskursen. Das Zertifikat ist vom Bundesamt für Migration und Flüchtlinge (BAMF) anerkannt.

Die Abteilungen der Studierendenakademie

Dominique Brasseur
Das KUBUS-Programm der Studierendenakademie an der Heinrich-Heine-Universität Düsseldorf

KUBUS ist ein fachübergreifendes Programm zur Berufsorientierung und Praxisqualifizierung im Studium an der Heinrich-Heine-Universität Düsseldorf. Das Kürzel KUBUS steht für die programmatische Verbindung von **K**ARRIERE UND **B**ERUFSORIENTIERUNG UND **S**TUDIUM.

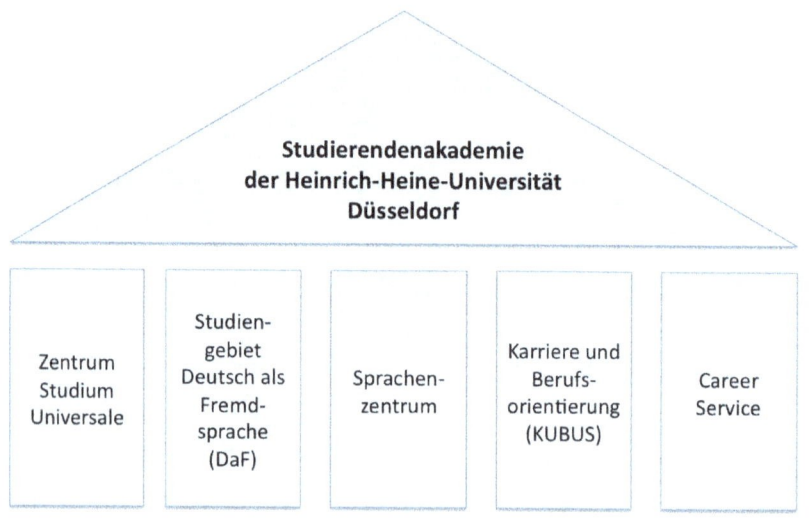

Abb. 1: Die Studierendenakademie der HHUD

KUBUS ist institutionell seit dem Wintersemester 2012 / 2013 gemeinsam mit weiteren Studien- und Serviceangeboten wie dem Beratungsangebot des Career Service, den Sprachen und dem Studium Universale in der zentralen wissenschaftlichen Einrichtung „Studierendenakademie" angesiedelt.

Die Heinrich-Heine-Universität Düsseldorf ist eine mittelgroße Hochschule mit aktuell circa 30.000 Studierenden an fünf Fakultäten. Bedingt durch die Lage in der Landeshauptstadt Düsseldorf mit ihren guten wirtschaftlichen und kulturellen Rahmenbedingungen bietet die Heinrich-Heine-Universität einen sehr attraktiven Studienstandort mit vielfältigen Möglichkeiten, bereits studienbegleitend wichtige Praxiserfahrungen zu sammeln, um so nach der Graduierung, sei es als Bachelor oder Master, erfolgreich und nahtlos in den Beruf einzusteigen. Diese optimalen Rahmenbedingungen prägen auch, bzw. ermöglichen erst, das KUBUS-Programm. So kooperiert KUBUS seit über zwei Jahrzehnten mit aktuell über 100 Partnern aus der Wirtschaft, Kultur und Politik – von den Großunternehmen der Region (z. B. Henkel), über die Medien (z. B. WDR), Institutionen der Presse und Öffentlichkeitsarbeit, der Werbung, dem Verlagswesen, den Kultureinrichtungen, politische Institutionen, der Anwaltskanzlei bis hin zu einzelnen Freiberuflern.

Durchschnittlich fragen rund 5.000 Studierende aller Fakultäten das KUBUS-Programm pro Semester nach. Die Studierenden nutzen dieses seit über 20 Jahren bewährte Angebot, wenn sie sich schon während des Studiums auf den späteren Übergang von der Universität in den Beruf optimal vorbereiten möchten.

KUBUS-Module

Alle KUBUS-Veranstaltungen sind als Module konzipiert, die gemäß der fakultätsspezifischen Anforderungsprofile ausgestaltet sind. Das erprobteste und umfassendste Modul wird für die Philosophische Fakultät angeboten und daher hier exemplarisch vorgestellt:

Das KUBUS-Modul für Studierende der Geistes-, Kultur- und Sozialwissenschaften besteht aus vier Modulteilen, die mit insgesamt acht Credit

Points im fachübergreifenden Wahlpflichtbereich kreditiert werden. Im ersten Schritt wird semesterbegleitend das sogenannte Praxisfelderseminar besucht, wo erfolgreiche Berufspraktikerinnen und -praktiker, welche selbst ein Geistes-, Kultur- oder Sozialwissenschaftliches Studium absolviert haben und sich der Alumni-Idee verpflichtet fühlen, ihren beruflichen Werdegang und den aktuellen Beruf vorstellen. Hier erhalten die Teilnehmenden nicht nur frühzeitig direkte, persönliche Kontakte in die Berufswelt, sondern lernen exemplarisch mögliche Berufsläufe und Berufsfelder im Detail kennen. Im zweiten und dritten Modulteil sind ein Praktikum sowie mindestens ein dreitägiges KUBUS-Blockseminar zu absolvieren. Pro Semester umfasst das Angebot etwa 60 Blockseminare zu verschiedensten berufsvorbereitenden Themen und Schlüsselkompetenzen. Diese Seminare finden an Wochenenden bzw. in der vorlesungsfreien Zeit statt, um inneruniversitäre Terminüberschneidungen möglichst zu vermeiden.

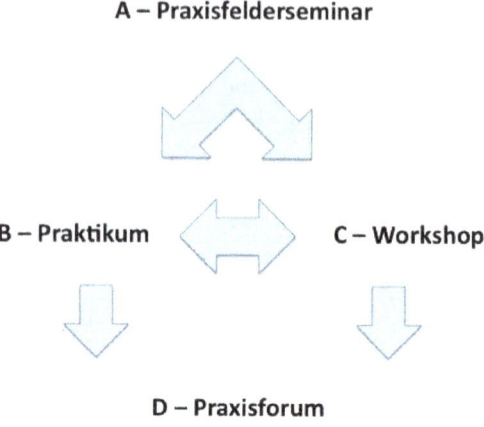

Abb. 2: Das KUBUS-Modul für Studierende der Geistes-, Kultur- und Sozialwissenschaften

In der Modulabschlussveranstaltung – dem Praxisforum – wird die bisherige Qualifizierungsbiographie sowie die individuelle Karriereperspektive im Kontext der jeweiligen Fachkultur reflektiert. Das Praxisforum wird von geschulten Praxismoderatorinnen und -moderatoren aus den jeweiligen Instituten der Universität unterrichtet.

Für Bachelorstudierende der Mathematisch-Naturwissenschaftlichen Fakultät wurde ein reines Blockseminarmodul konzipiert. Die Studierenden der übrigen Fächer wählen individuell einzelne Seminare als Modulteile aus dem KUBUS-Programm und bestimmen so, Inhalt und Umfang selbstständig. Das

KUBUS-Master-Modul ist aufgrund der geringeren Studiendauer komprimierter. Es umfasst nur zwei Modulteile, von denen eines frei wählbar ist, während das zweite der Reflexion und Standortbestimmung am Ende der Studienzeit dient.

Nach erfolgreichem Abschluss der jeweiligen KUBUS-Module erhalten die Studierenden für die Kreditierung und für spätere Bewerbungsunterlagen ein entsprechendes KUBUS-Zertifikat, das alle erbrachten Leistungen dezidiert ausweist.

Interdisziplinarität

Mit Ausnahme einiger fachspezifischer Angebote stehen die KUBUS-Seminare Studierenden aller Fächer gleichermaßen offen. Das langjährige positive Feedback – sowohl seitens der Dozierenden als auch der Studierenden – zeigt, dass die Teilnehmerinnen und Teilnehmer von dieser fachübergreifenden Seminarform nachhaltig profitieren und diese auch einfordern. Durch das Aufeinandertreffen der unterschiedlichen Herangehens- und Denkweisen verschiedener Fachkulturen entstehen kreativere und vor allem auch umfassendere Ergebnisse. So werden nicht nur Seminarinhalte, sondern by the way direkt auch wichtige Erkenntnisse zur Teamarbeit vermittelt.

KUBUS-Dozierende

KUBUS arbeitet nahezu ausschließlich mit externen Referentinnen und Referenten, die entweder in den jeweiligen Berufsfeldern selbst erfolgreich tätig oder aber professionelle Trainerinnen und Trainer sind. Dieser direkte Kontakt in die Berufswelt ermöglicht nicht nur eine wertvolle Erfahrungsweitergabe, sondern auch oftmals die Übernahme teilnehmender Studierender als PraktikantInnen oder MitarbeiterInnen. Im Rahmen des KUBUS-Programms können so regelmäßig auch Seminare angeboten werden in denen reale Aufträge im Mittelpunkt stehen.[1]

---

1 Vergleiche dazu Kapitel VI.1 „Projektintegrierte studentische Praxis- und Berufsorientierung".

Qualitätssicherung und Weiterentwicklung des Programms

Die KUBUS-Veranstaltungen werden von den teilnehmenden Studierenden im Anschluss seit über einem Jahrzehnt konsequent im Online-Verfahren evaluiert. Die einzelnen Evaluationsbögen werden automatisch anonymisiert ausgewertet und als Gesamtergebnisse ausnahmslos online veröffentlicht. Seitens der Abteilungsleitung werden die Ergebnisse zeitnah mit den Mitarbeiterinnen und Mitarbeitern besprochen, so dass ggf. sofort auf Reaktionen der Studierenden reagiert werden kann. Auch die KUBUS-Dozierenden erhalten so ein direktes Feedback über Ihre Veranstaltungen. Die Studierenden gestalten durch dieses Procedere mit ihren Angaben, ihren Vorschlägen und ihrer Kritik die Ausrichtung bzw. Veränderung der KUBUS-Veranstaltungsangebote aktiv mit und unterstützen die Abteilungsleitung dabei, das gesamte Programm kontinuierlich hinsichtlich der sich verändernden Bedarfe der Studierenden zu optimieren. Durch die konsequente Veröffentlichungspraxis der Evaluationsergebnisse wird zudem Transparenz gegenüber den Lehrenden und Lernenden sowie der Öffentlichkeit sicher gestellt.

Kontakt und weitere Informationen:

Heinrich-Heine-Universität Düsseldorf
Studierendenakademie
Abteilung Karriere und Berufsorientierung (KUBUS)
Gebäude 25.13, Ebene 00, Raum 38
Universitätsstraße 1
40225 Düsseldorf
Email: kubus@hhu.de

Weitere Informationen zu KUBUS finden Sie unter:
www.kubus-programm.de oder auf der KUBUS-Facebook-Seite.

Die Abteilungen der Studierendenakademie

Claudia Boes
Fremdsprachen – mehr als ein Tor zur Welt

Globalisierung und Internationalisierung, Mobilität, zunehmende Migration und die dynamische Entwicklung der Medien haben die Begegnung mit Mehrsprachigkeit im Europa des 21. Jahrhunderts alltäglich werden lassen. Für den beruflichen Erfolg und die gesellschaftliche Teilhabe, aber auch für die Entwicklung des Menschen zu einer „sogenannten mündigen" Persönlichkeit ist das Erlernen einer oder mehrerer Fremdsprachen daher unabdingbar notwendig geworden.

Das Sprachenzentrum der Studierendenakademie bietet den Studierenden der Heinrich-Heine-Universität Düsseldorf die Möglichkeit, sich kostenfrei in über 120 Kursen aus rund 23 Fremdsprachen zu qualifizieren und zugleich weiterzuentwickeln. Das Angebot reicht dabei von Arabisch, Deutscher Gebärdensprache und Englisch über Latein und Altgriechisch bis hin zu Polnisch, Spanisch und Türkisch – je nach Bedarf vom Anfänger- bis zum Fortgeschrittenen-Niveau (A1 bis C1). Das Programm umfasst einerseits allgemeinsprachlich orientierte Kurse gemäß des Gemeinsamen Europäischen Referenzrahmens für Sprachen (GER); andererseits beinhaltet es auch Fachsprachenkurse für die verschiedenen Fakultäten: Englisch für Medizinerinnen und Mediziner, Italienisch für Kunsthistorikerinnen und Kunsthistoriker oder Japanisch für Linguistinnen und Linguisten. Durch eine einzigartige Kooperation mit dem Konfuzius-Institut an der Heinrich-Heine-Universität Düsseldorf organisiert das Sprachenzentrum zudem ein vielfältiges Programm für Chinesisch auf dem Campus.

Neben dem Erlernen oder Auffrischen einer oder mehrerer Fremdsprachen bietet das Sprachenzentrum der Studierendenakademie an der Heinrich-Heine-Universität Düsseldorf den Studierenden aber auch den Erwerb von

Sprachnachweisen für die Bewerbung um ein Auslandsstipendium oder einen Masterplatz an.

In seiner Tradition als Ort der Kommunikation, aber auch als Ort, an dem Schlüsselkompetenzen vermittelt werden und das Testen und Prüfen von fremdsprachlichen Kompetenzen zu den täglichen Aufgaben zählt, hat es sich das Sprachenzentrum der Studierendenakademie im Rahmen der Tagung „Über das Fach hinaus … Neue Studierendengeneration, neue Herausforderungen" zum Ziel gesetzt, über die Anforderungen, denen die heutigen Studierenden, aber auch die Universitätsangestellten in Bezug auf genau diese Themenbereiche ausgesetzt sind, zu informieren und zu diskutieren.

Die vom Sprachenzentrum initiierten und begleiteten Panels auf der Tagung der Studierendenakademie befassen sich daher mit den folgenden Frage- bzw. Aufgabenstellungen:

- Man kann nicht nicht kommunizieren – aber falsch. Was Kompetenz bei Kommunikation bedeutet und wie man sie vermittelt.
- ‚Mehr als nur Sprachunterricht!' – Welche (weiteren) Schlüsselkompetenzen vermitteln wir im Fremdsprachenunterricht?
- Handlungs- und Kompetenzorientierung im Bereich des Lehrens, Lernens und Überprüfens von Fremdsprachenkompetenzen

Die Abteilungen der Studierendenakademie

Christoph auf der Horst
Die „Bildung" des Studium Universale (der Studierendenakademie) an der Heinrich-Heine-Universität Düsseldorf

Das abendländische Europa verfügt bis in die Gegenwart hinein über reiche Praxisformen und Theoriebestände zu Bildung (und Kultur), die häufig und nur unzulässig auf den deutschen Begriff „Bildung" oder im Rahmen einer strategisch und inhaltlich unterkomplexen Herangehensweise ausschließlich auf das tradierte Humboldt-Konzept verkürzt werden.

So wenig „Bildung" angemessen in das Englische (education, formation, culture, learning) oder in das Französische (civilisation, culture, formation, instruction) übersetzt werden kann, so vieldeutig kann „Bildung" heute ausgelegt werden. Stammt der Herkunft nach der Bildungsbegriff aus der christlichen Imago-dei-Lehre, derzufolge die menschliche Seele zum Bilde Gottes „überbildet" werden sollte, wird unter „Bildung" seit der zweiten Hälfte des 18. Jahrhunderts v. a. die menschliche Selbstentfaltung, die „Bildung der Persönlichkeit" verstanden. Heute sind diese und weitere Bedeutungen des Bildungsbegriffs – Allgemeinbildung im Bildungsbürgertum etwa – und die Kritik am Bildungsbegriff als „individualistisch", „elitär" oder „bürgerlich" verloren gegangen und unsichtbar, wenn Bildung oft nur noch als (universitäre) qualifikatorische Maßnahme gilt, die das Individuum für den Arbeitsmarkt ausbildet.[1]

---

[1] Martha Nussbaum, Nicht für den Profit. Warum Bildung Demokratie braucht. Tibia Press 2012. OECD 2003.

Ausgehend davon, dass jede Gesellschaft entsprechend ihrer Zeit den ihr eigenen Bildungsbegriff und abhängig davon die ihr eigene Bildungspraxis ausprägt, und vor dem Hintergrund, dass Wissen und Information die zentralen Kennzeichen der modernen und globalisierten Gesellschaft sind, verlangt der Bildungsbegriff heute nach einer Aktualisierung. Eine Anknüpfung an die Paradigmen des humboldtschen Bildungsideals im Sinne einer der Aufklärung und der Selbstwerdung (Selbstbildung der Persönlichkeit) verpflichteten Bildung muss dabei ebenso Bestand haben, wie die Aspekte der Bildung als Allgemeinbildung und der Bildung als Qualifikation Berücksichtigung finden müssen. Auch dem Begriff des „Life Long Learning" sollte durch eine entsprechende Ausgestaltung der akademischen Praxis und einer Ausweitung der Angebote der Hochschulen für verschiedene Zielgruppen (z. B. Public Understanding of Sience and Humanities) Rechnung getragen werden. So kann der Bildungsbegriff um Aspekte des aus dem anglophonen Bereich stammenden Begriffs der Literacy ergänzt werden:

> Literacy is the ability to identify, understand, interpret, create, communicate, compute and use printed and written materials associated with varying contexts. Literacy involves a continuum of learning in enabling individuals to achieve their goals, to develop their knowledge and potential, and to participate fully in their community and wider society.[2]

In Rücksicht auf die zentralen Aufgaben einer Universität – Wissenschaft in Forschung und Lehre – muss Bildung oder Literacy im Hinblick auf ihr Subjekt (1), auf ihren Ort (2), auf ihre Inhalte (3) und ihren Zweck (4) wie folgt konkretisiert werden:

Das Subjekt ist zweifellos der Studierende, wobei zugleich deutlich zu machen ist, dass lernbiografisch sowohl Schüler, die bereits vor der Hochschulzulassung die Universität besuchen, als auch Absolventen, die zur Fortbildung die Hochschule wieder besuchen, ebenfalls Subjekte des Erwerbs von Bildung/Literacy sind. Der Begriff „Subjekt" ist mehrdimensional unter Einschluss der geistigen und im weiteren Sinne der musischen und leiblichen Persönlichkeitsmerkmale zu denken.

---

2 OECD 2003.

"Sich bilden" wird hierbei semantisch ernst genommen, insofern den Studierenden neben/vor den Dozierenden die Hauptrolle im eigenen Bildungsprozess zuerkannt wird. "Sich bilden" als intransitives Verb meint zuallererst, dass Studierende sich selbst bilden; "man" oder ein Lehrverantwortlicher bildet nicht etwa jemanden.[3]

Dieses "sich bilden" wird dabei verstanden als eine kritische Reflexion des Menschen in der

1.1 Selbstbeziehung (Beziehung eines Menschen zu sich selbst),

1.2 Fremdbeziehung (Beziehung eines Menschen zu seinen Mitmenschen),

1.3 Außenbeziehung (Beziehung eines Menschen zu anderen Welten und Kulturen).

Diese "kritische Reflexion" des "sich bildens" ist insofern reflexiv, als dass sie gedanklich-sprachlich vollzogen wird, und in der distanzierenden, in Frage stellenden Ausübung wird die Reflexion kritisch gewendet.[4]

Vor dem Hintergrund des solcherweise profilierten Bildungsbegriffs des Studium Universale organisiert das Zentrum Studium Universale ein Lehrveranstaltungsangebot, das fakultätsübergreifend ausgerichtet ist, auch die Vermittlung von Schlüsselkompetenzen beinhaltet und allen Studierenden aller Fakultäten offen steht. Das Lehrveranstaltungsangebot des Zentrum Studium Universale integriert hierbei Lehrveranstaltungen aller Fakultäten, entwickelt eigene Lehrveranstaltungen, kooperiert hochschulintern mit weiteren Wissenschaftlichen Einrichtungen und beauftragt externe Referenten.

Diese aus den fünf Fakultäten der Heinrich-Heine-Universität ausgewählten Lehrveranstaltungen einführenden und überblicksartigen Charakters werden Studierenden des Studium Universale geöffnet und angeboten. Studierende sollen in diesen Lehrveranstaltungen einen Einblick in die zugrunde liegende Fachdisziplin, ihre speziellen Methoden und ihr besonderes Ethos erhalten und so an die Forschungs- und Denkstile anderer Fakultäten herangeführt werden.

---

3   Jacques Rancière, Der unwissende Lehrmeister. Fünf Lektionen über die intellektuelle Emanzipation. Passagen Verlag 2007.
4   Andreas Dörpinghaus, Bildung. Plädoyer wider die Verdummung. In: Forschung & Lehre Supplement 2009: S. 3–14.

1.1 Das Studium Universale und die Selbstbeziehung

Neben diesem Kernbereich organisiert das Zentrum Studium Universale eigene Lehrveranstaltungen, in denen die aktive Rolle eingeübt werden soll, die den Studierenden nach dem o. a. selbstverantwortlichen und selbst zu gestaltenden Bildungsprozess zukommt.

Zu diesem Bildungsbereich der Selbstbeziehung, in dem Studierende die Beziehung zu sich selbst kritisch reflektieren, zählen auch die Lehrveranstaltungen des Studium Universale, die die Studierenden in die Lage versetzen sollen, ihre musischen und körperlichen Fähigkeiten (selbst) auszubilden.

Im Hinblick auf die individuelle Disposition der Studierenden muss ein angemessen dimensioniertes Bildungsangebot auch die berufsqualifizierenden und die „Employability" erhöhenden Kompetenzen vermitteln. Diese werden vom Zentrum Studium Universale vor allem im Rahmen der Akademie Schlüsselkompetenzen organisiert und angeboten. Ein erster Bereich umfasst dabei die Kompetenzen, über die Studierenden verfügen sollten, wenn sie erfolgreich studieren wollen – mithin die Vermittlung von Study Skills. Neben diesen Workshops, die lernbiografisch in den frühen Semestern liegen, bietet das Zentrum Studium Universale in einem zweiten Bereich Transferable Skills an, die sich auf das Studium verteilen.

1.2 Das Studium Universale und die Fremdbeziehung

Für den aus dem Bildungsbegriff abgeleiteten Bereich des „sich bildens" in einer kritisch reflexiven Beziehung zu seinen Mitmenschen organisiert das Zentrum Studium Universale selbst entwickelte Lehrveranstaltungen zu dem Leitthema Integration von Refugees. Gleicherweise, ebenfalls zur Fremdbeziehung gehörend, muss auch die Kompetenzvermittlung stehen, die Studierende in die Lage versetzt, in einer globalen Welt und an internationalen Arbeitsplätzen in Teams mit Berufstätigen anderer kultureller Hintergründe gemeinsam zu arbeiten und zu kommunizieren, ein Arbeitsbereich, der mit den Modulen und Zertifikaten „Interkulturelle Kompetenzen erwerben", „Diversity-Competence", „Gender-Training" usw. abgedeckt ist.

1.3 Das Studium Universale und die Außenbeziehung

Während in der Fremdbeziehung die Beziehung eines Menschen zu seinen Mitmenschen angesprochen und also personal gedacht ist, wird mit der Beziehung eines Menschen zu anderen Welten und Kulturen die Bildung bezeichnet, die in der Auseinandersetzung mit Fremdem, Unbekanntem, mit unbekannten Werten, Haltungen und kulturellen Überlieferungen entsteht. Der Bildungsbegriff des Studium Universale bezieht deshalb auch die Wechselwirkungen zwischen Ich und Welt mit ein. Beispiele solcher Lehrangebote sind Lehrveranstaltungen, die in Zusammenarbeit mit der „Evangelischen Stadtakademie", dem „Konfuzius-Insitut Düsseldorf", dem „EKO-Haus der japanischen Kultur" etc. entstehen.

2. Der Ort, an dem Bildung erworben werden können muss, ist die Universität, und in der Wissensgesellschaft überhaupt jeder öffentliche Raum, in dem Denken praktiziert wird.[5] Denn die Universität hat heute vielfältige Einflussmöglichkeiten in das Gesellschaftsleben hinein und findet insofern auch extra muros statt. Das Zentrum Studium Universale hält von daher ein Angebot vor, das sich an die Bürgerinnen und Bürger der Stadt Düsseldorf richtet: Das ist einmal in Bezug auf das jüngere Klientel die Kinderuniversität; in Bezug auf Seniorinnen und Senioren ist das einmal die Ringvorlesung Studium Universale und die gemeinsame mit Partnern aus der Stadt Düsseldorf (Heine-Institut, Evangelische Stadtakademie, Volkshochschule) veranstaltete Vortragsreihe „Forschung im Fokus". Mit diesen Veranstaltungsformen richtet sich die Heinrich-Heine-Universität an die Zivilgesellschaft der Stadt und der Umgebung und nimmt somit gesellschaftliche Funktionen wahr.

3. Die Inhalte der zu erwerbenden Bildung sind einmal orientiert an einer Verbesserung kognitiver Leistungsfähigkeiten bereits bei Aufnahme eines Studiums (study skills), dann am künftigen Arbeitsmarkt (transferable skills), selbstverständlich an dem, was gemeinhin Allgemeinbildung bzw. im englisch-

---

5 Jacques Derrida, Die unbedingte Universität. Edition Suhrkamp 2001.

sprachlichen Äquivalent „General Education" genannt wird und schließlich an dem, was die Entfaltung der Persönlichkeit und ihrer Potenziale ermöglicht.

4. Der Zweck der Vermittlung von Bildung/Literacy an einer Hochschule ist somit, dass das Studium die Studierenden zunehmend in die Lage versetzt, pluralistisches Domänenwissen (Wissen um Entitäten von Anwendungsgebieten sowie das Wissen um die strukturellen Beziehungen zwischen ihnen) zu erlangen. Neben dem Domänenwissen sollte auch Methoden- und Handlungswissen in Form von übergreifenden Kompetenzen (Transferable Skills) generiert werden. Die intellektuelle, persönliche und berufliche Entwicklung erfordert in Zukunft ein die eigene Fachdisziplin umfassend ergänzendes Wissensprofil und eine Erweiterung der Grenzen der allein monofachlichen Spezialisierung. Im Ergebnis kann somit davon ausgegangen werden, dass die Absolventen des Studium Universale in die Lage versetzt sind, eine reflexive Haltung zur heutigen, komplexer gewordenen Welt einnehmen und sich in dieser selbst autonom „regieren" (Michel Foucault) können. Ferner wird durch eine gelungene Erzeugung von Sinnbildungskompetenz und Orientierungswissen auch die gesellschaftliche Einbettung der akademischen Ausbildung in einen sozialen Kontext möglich und erfahrbar („Responsible Scientist").

Kapitel VI
Über die Theorie hinaus ...

Zwei tagungsbegleitende Beispiele praxis- und
berufsorientierender Seminare der Studierendenakademie

Tagungsbegleitende Beispiele

Dominique Brasseur
Projektintegrierte studentische Praxis- und Berufsorientierung

KUBUS ist ein fachübergreifendes Programm zur Berufsorientierung und Praxisqualifizierung im Studium und organisatorisch als Abteilung in der zentralen wissenschaftlichen Einrichtung „Studierendenakademie" der Heinrich-Heine-Universität Düsseldorf angesiedelt.[1] Im Rahmen des KUBUS-Programms, das cirka 5.000 Studierende jedes Semester nachfragen, werden regelmäßig und in Zusammenarbeit mit Partnern aus der regionalen Wirtschaft, mit Künstlern, Kulturinstitutionen oder Instituten und Institutionen der Universität, Sonderveranstaltungen konzipiert und durchgeführt.

Diese „Spezial-Seminare" verfolgen das Ziel, eine nachhaltige Verbindung der Elemente des forschenden Lehrens und Lernens[2] mit konkreten Anwendungsbezügen im Kontext von Berufsbezogenheit bzw. Praxisnähe projektbezogen mit Studierenden zu realisieren.[3] Dies bedeutet konkret, dass die Studierenden am Ende dieser KUBUS-Projektseminare gemeinsam unter der fachkundigen Anleitung der jeweiligen Profis Kurzfilme, Radiobeiträge, Werbeslogans, Theaterstücke, Blogs, Drehbücher, Open-Air-Veranstaltungen wie „Heine sucht den Superstar" oder klassische Dokumentationen etc. erarbeitet haben, die in der Regel im Nachgang medial auch veröffentlicht, aufgeführt oder auch von Unternehmen real genutzt werden.[4] Grundsätzlich sind die

---

1 Das Kürzel KUBUS steht für die programmatische Verbindung von KARRIERE UND BERUFSORIENTIERUNG UND STUDIUM. Vgl. die entsprechenden Beiträge unter anderem bezüglich des KUBUS-Programmes in Kapitel V dieser Publikation.
2 Vgl. Huber, Ludwig: Forschungsbasiertes, Forschungsorientiertes, Forschendes Lernen: Alles dasselbe? In: Das Hochschulwesen, 1&2. 2014. S. 32–39.
3 Vgl. Brinker, Tobina: Schlüsselkompetenzen als Brücke zwischen Forschungsorientierung und Berufsbezug? In: Tremp, Peter: Forschungsorientierung und Berufsbezug im Studium. Hochschulen als Orte der Wissensgenerierung und der Vorstrukturierung von Berufstätigkeit. Blickpunkt Hochschuldidaktik, 126. Wbv. Bielefeld, 2015. S. 93.
4 So ist zum Beispiel der bis heute verwendete Slogan des Düsseldorfer Grupello Verlages „Das Auge liest mit" in einem gemeinsam veranstalteten Workshop des Verlages mit KUBUS-Studierenden entstanden.

KUBUS-Projektseminare so konzipiert, dass dem didaktischen Dreischrittkonzept (Initialphase, Aneignungsphase, Nachbereitungsphase) in der Konkretisierung:
1. theoretische Fundierung,
2. inhaltliche / praktische Vertiefung / produktionsorientierte Anwendung / Umsetzung des Gelernten / der Forschungsergebnisse,
3. Reflexion / Nachbereitung

entsprochen wird.

Gekoppelt mit Zielen und Konzepten des Ansatzes „From Teaching to Learning"[5] sowie handlungs- und produktionsorientierten Verfahren steht das methodische Spektrum in Einklang mit der inhaltlichen und praxisorientierten Ausrichtung der Seminare und Module. Dieses in Düsseldorf von KUBUS mit den externen regionalen Partnern über viele Jahre entwickelte, modularisierte und interdisziplinär ausgerichtete Lehr- und Lernkonzept der projektintegrierten studentischen Praxis- und Berufsorientierung kann wahrscheinlich – vor allem unter Nachhaltigkeitsaspekten – als die bislang erfolgreichste KUBUS-Programmlinie angesehen werden.

Insofern lag es nahe, zuletzt auch die „eigene" Düsseldorfer Konferenz der Studierendenakademie „Über das Fach hinaus ..." im Haus der Universität durch KUBUS-Seminare zur projektintegrierten studentischen Praxis- und Berufsorientierung begleiten zu lassen. Erfreulicher Weise konnten der Autor und Filmemacher Dr. Klaus Bergner und der Vorsitzende des Düsseldorfer Hochschulradios, Herr Andreas Meske, hier als erfahrene und professionelle Seminarleiter für die beiden Seminare Fernsehjournalismus und Crossmedia-Journalismus gewonnen werden. Die Ergebnisse der überaus engagierten Studierenden können sich im wahrsten Sinne des Wortes sehen lassen.[6] Diesbezüglich entsteht ein sehr guter und umfassender Einblick anhand des nach

---

5 Vgl.: Wildt, Johannes: „The Shift from Teaching to Learning": Thesen zum Wandel der Lernkultur in modularisierten Studienstrukturen. In: Ehlert, Holger / Welbers, Ulrich (Hrsg.): Qualitätssicherung und Studienreform – Strategie- und Programmentwicklung für Fachbereiche und Hochschulen im Rahmen von Zielvereinbarungen am Beispiel der Heinrich-Heine-Universität Düsseldorf. Grupello. Düsseldorf, 2004. S. 168–178.
6 Siehe hierzu auch den nachfolgenden Beitrag von Dr. Klaus Bergner in diesem Kapitel.

der Konferenz von den Studierenden erarbeiteten und online gestellten Blogs zur Tagung.[7]

Aber bereits während der Fachtagung haben die Studierenden aus den beiden KUBUS-Seminaren die Veranstaltung vor Ort durch ihre Arbeit bereichert. Kein Vortrag, kein Panel, selbst kein Pausengespräch, in dem nicht O-Töne und Interviews für Radiobeiträge oder Fotos und Filmsequenzen aufgenommen wurden. Als besonders beeindruckend nahmen die TagungsteilnehmerInnen einhellig hier die große Professionalität der Studierenden wahr – nicht nur im Umgang mit der Technik, sondern gerade auch hinsichtlich der journalistischen Qualität. So wurden in einem eigens zu diesem Zwecke technisch vollständig ausgestatteten Raum im Haus der Universität, die Beiträge des Crossmedia-Seminars direkt von den Studierenden noch am jeweils gleichen Tag geschnitten und bearbeitet.

Die Studierenden, die an diesen beiden KUBUS-Seminaren mitgewirkt haben, konnten neben der unmittelbaren Erfahrung vielleicht erstmals einer Fachtagung beizuwohnen, vor allem in äußerst komprimierter Form vielfältige Praxiserfahrungen sammeln und so nicht zuletzt auch individuell besser reflektieren, inwiefern die jeweiligen Berufsfelder für die aktuelle persönliche Berufs- und Karriereplanung weiter von Interesse sind.

---

7 Aufrufbar unter: https://ueber-das-fach-hinaus.de.

Tagungsbegleitende Beispiele

Klaus Bergner
Tagungsbegleitende studentische Filmproduktion – Generation Z is making a video

„Warum ist das sinnvoll und vielleicht auch hilfreich, diese Generationen so zu unterteilen und für wen ist das hilfreich?" Lina Lux zusammen mit Sinem Hanbaba stellen diese Frage Prof. Dr. Christian Scholz von der Universität Saarbrücken. Die Studentinnen der HHU befragen den Wirtschaftswissenschaftler für einen Filmbeitrag über die „Generation Z" kurz nach seinem gleichnamigen Vortrag im Rahmen der Tagung „Über das Fach hinaus ... Neue Studierendengeneration, neue Herausforderungen" im Hörsaal des Hauses der Universität. Der Professor hatte in seinem Vortrag die Unterschiede zwischen den Generationen der Babyboomer, Generation Y und auch Z bezüglich ihrer Lebensentwürfe, Werteauffassungen sowie Einstellungen zu Beruf und Karriere erörtert.

Zwei Kommilitonen von Sinem und Lina filmen mit Videokameras die Szene, eine dritte Studentin hält ein Funkmikrofon in der Hand, um das Interview in optimaler Tonqualität aufzuzeichnen. Zusammen mit einer Traube Umstehender sind sie Teilnehmer des KUBUS-Workshops „Fernsehjournalismus", das zeitgleich mit der Tagung abgehalten wird. Und diese kurzerhand zum Thema ihres Films macht.

Das Kompaktseminar „Fernsehjournalismus"

Am Freitag, dem 01. Juli, treffen sich Lehrbeauftragter und Studierende des Kurses zunächst im Medienlabor der Heinrich-Heine-Universität zur Planung und Vorbereitung der Dreharbeiten. Die Aufgabe: einen Filmbeitrag über einen Aspekt der Tagung zu produzieren, das heißt ihn zu planen, drehen, montieren und vertonen.

Die Studierenden werden in diesem Seminar gewissermaßen ins kalte Wasser geworfen. Denn vormals reine Rezipienten von Medienprodukten schlüpfen unter Anleitung plötzlich in die Rolle von Medienproduzenten. Zwar sind Videos und multimediale Inhalte über Smartphone und Notebook für sie omnipräsent, auch hat der eine oder die andere bereits etwa mit dem Handy gefilmt – doch verfügen die meisten von ihnen nur über marginale technische und gestalterische Kenntnisse. Ganz zu schweigen vom Gebiet der Erstellung journalistischer Filmbeiträge. Nun aber müssen sie genau das machen und dafür im Team „funktionieren". Der Dozent bringt seinen beruflichen Hintergrund von mehr als zwei Jahrzehnten TV-Berichterstattung für ARD und ZDF mit ein. Dazu gibt er an wichtigen Positionen der Produktion die Richtungen vor, lässt den Studierenden aber genug Freiraum für eigene Ideen. Denn es soll ja ein Film „von Studies für Studies" werden. Und dabei Spaß machen.

Praxisseminar mit komplexen Inhalten

Die Studentinnen und Studenten des KUBUS-Seminars rekrutieren sich überwiegend aus den Bereichen Medien- und Kulturwissenschaften, Germanistik, Romanistik und Sozialwissenschaften, also sehr theorielastigen geisteswissenschaftlichen Fächern der HHU. In den Seminaren wird diskutiert, hinterfragt, kritisiert, zitiert. Nun müssen sie sehr praxisorientiert handeln, indem sie vier Schritte einer Medienproduktion innerhalb von drei Seminartagen durchexerzieren.

Preproduktion – Themensichtung, Recherche und Drehkonzept: Auf der Grundlage der im Internet verfügbaren Informationen über die Tagung erfolgen diese Arbeiten gemeinsam im Seminar. Im Plenum bestimmen die Teilnehmer die zentralen Inhalte sowie die Form, mit der man diese Inhalte der Zielgruppe vermitteln möchte. Das Seminar entscheidet sich für eine so genannte On-Reportage, bei der zwei Reporterinnen vor der Kamera, sozusagen als Stellvertreter des Zuschauers, die Veranstaltung besuchen.

Produktion – Dreharbeiten: Nach einem Vortrag über Kameraeinstellungen sowie einer kurzen Einführung in die Technik der Videokameras und des begleitenden Equipments fahren die Teilnehmer von der HHU in die Innenstadt zum Tagungsort, dem Haus der Universität. Vor Ort verteilen sie untereinander die Aufgaben: Regie, Co-Regie, Aufnahmeleitung, Kamera 1, Kamera 2, Ton, Redaktion. Nun arbeitet das Team seine Liste ab, welche Experten wann und in welchem Seminar zu befragen sind. An diesem Nachmittag wie auch am folgenden Vormittag konfrontiert das Seminar mit Kamera und Mikrofon zahlreiche Teilnehmer der Veranstaltung mit zwei Kernfragen: „Auf welche Weise und mit welchen Mitteln wollen Lehrende die Generation Z erreichen?" und „Wo ist die Generation Z auf dieser Tagung?"

Postproduktion – Schnitt, Vertonung, Texten: Nach Abschluss der Dreharbeiten befindet sich das gesamte Drehmaterial auf zwei Speicherkarten. Der Dozent lädt es am Sonntagmorgen, 3. Juli, dem dritten Tag des Kompaktseminars, auf einen Datenserver des Medienlabors. Der ist direkt verbunden mit dem Seminar-Rechner. Dann betrachtet er die Aufnahmen zusammen mit seinen Studierenden über einen Beamer und montiert sie auf Anleitung des Plenums in einer sinnvollen Abfolge. Weil bis zum Abend ein rund fünfminütiger Filmbeitrag fertiggestellt werden muss, übernimmt der Dozent hier die Aufgabe des Cutters, da er mit dem Schnittprogramm vertraut ist. Gemeinsam mit den Studierenden bespricht und begründet er, an welcher Position des Films welche Information gestellt wird. Darüber hinaus schlagen die Kursteilnehmer auch vor, wo im Schnitt Musik eingesetzt werden könnte – und natürlich auch welche.

Distribution – Sendung: Nach Fertigstellung des Films und gemeinsamem Betrachten in Kinoformat wird mit den Studierenden diskutiert, auf welcher Informationsplattform dieser Film eingestellt wird, auf welche Internetseite er passt, wie er ins Soziale Netzwerk einzufügen ist. Hier werden neben technischen Fragen zur Datengröße und Komprimierungstechniken auch – sofern sie nicht schon in den Produktionsschritten zuvor angeklungen sind – Fragen zu den Bild- und Musikrechten, zur journalistischen Verantwortung und zur Ethik diskutiert.

Klaus Bergner

Praxisausflug mit Erlebniswert

Die Studierenden merken in der Zusammenarbeit innerhalb dieser Seminarform rasch ihre Selbstwirksamkeit, was sehr motivierend wirkt. Das erfolgt immer dann, wenn der begleitende Dozent Zwischenergebnisse abruft, bei denen gemeinsam vor Ort die Dreharbeiten bewertet werden. Die Tagungsteilnehmer sehen dann eine Gruppe Studierender, die sich um den Kontrollmonitor einer Videokamera schart. Dazu hören sie Äußerungen wie „Das hast du unscharf aufgenommen." oder „Den O-Ton brauchen wir genau so, der passt gut ins Konzept!".

Zum motivierenden Teamspirit gehören in diesem Fall auch die beiden Frontfrauen. Die On-Reporterinnen Lina und Sinem haben sichtlich Spaß an ihrer Rolle und wirken erstaunlich souverän. Dadurch beflügeln sie die gesamten Abläufe innerhalb der studentischen Produktion, was auch die lenkende Arbeit des Dozenten erleichtert. Er kanalisiert einen ständigen Fluss an Einfällen und Ereignissen, an denen jeder im Seminar gleichermaßen beteiligt ist – und dies fast ausnahmslos auch macht. Da sich die Teilnehmer alle zum ersten Mal in dieser Rolle befinden, muss er genau darauf achten, dass journalistische Form und die genaue Verfolgung des Themas eingehalten werden.

Backstage-Einblicke vom Berufspraktiker

Das Seminar über Fernsehjournalismus orientiert sich überwiegend an den aktuellen Abläufen und Inhalten in Redaktionen und Produktionsabteilungen des TV-Sendebetriebs des WDR. Es stützt sich auf die Erfahrungen des Dozenten, die er hier über die Jahre als Autor, Reporter, Regisseur, Redakteur und Produzent gemacht hat. Dabei überblickt er einerseits die journalistischen Standards, die allen Redaktionen zugrunde liegen, kennt andererseits die Unterschiede in den Abläufen. Denn allein schon durch Sendeformat, Sendezeiten und Zielgruppenvorgabe arbeiten die redaktionellen Teams des ARD-Morgenmagazins anders als die einer SWR-Wissenschaftsredaktion, des ZDF-Landesstudios, des WDR-Reportagemagazins „Menschen hautnah" oder von der „Sendung mit der Maus". Während im aktuellen Betrieb des Morgenmagazins Geschwindigkeit zählt und zweiminütige Einspielfilme zusammen mit einem Aufsager des Reporters vor der Kamera innerhalb kürzester Zeit produziert werden müssen, erfordern investigative Recherchen viel mehr personellen und zeitlichen Aufwand oder auch die Beobachtung menschlicher Schicksale über einen Zeitraum von vielen Monaten für einen 45-Minüter eine andere Logistik, Planung und Bildsprache sowie ein anderes Konzept und Drehbuch.

Das didaktische Konzept des Seminars beinhaltet sowohl zahlreiche multimediale Präsentationen aus dem Bereich des Fernsehjournalismus als auch ein rasches Einbinden der Kursteilnehmer in praktische Übungen. Dadurch lernen die Studierenden einerseits die Abläufe innerhalb eines Fernsehsenders und seiner Redaktionen kennen, andererseits auch die Möglichkeiten und Grenzen des Genres. Allein schon die Aufgabe, 30 Sekunden einer Videomontage betexten zu müssen, zeigt ihnen, wie schwer und langwierig es sein kann, das richtige Wort zum bewegten Bild zu finden.

Vor dem Hintergrund eines wachsenden Angebots von frei verfügbaren Informationen, Videos und Tutorials im Internet sowie bereits bestehenden Blended Learning-Angeboten von Hochschulen liegt verständlicherweise der Eindruck nicht fern, dass diese Materie rein virtuell vermittelt werden könnte. Für die bewährte Seminarform eines Workshops spricht allerdings der direkte Austausch, das Erleben zusammen mit anderen, die Gruppendynamik. Und das weiß auch die Generation Z, also die der Digital Natives durchaus zu schätzen.

Generation Z needs videos

Denn im realen Erleben, insbesondere in Verbindung mit dem Teamcharakter, liegt die Chance, rascher zu einem die neu erlangten Fähigkeiten verinnerlichenden Ergebnis zu gelangen. So gab es für die Teilnehmer des beschriebenen KUBUS-Seminars auf der Suche danach, wie Generation Z „tickt" gewissermaßen einen doppelten Aha-Effekt. Für den sorgte die Professorin Gardenia Alonso nach ihrem Vortrag über die Vermittlung von Schlüsselkompetenzen. Denn auf die Frage von Lina und Sinem, warum auf dieser Tagung so wenig Vertreter der Generation Z anzutreffen seien, antwortet sie: „Ich glaube, man muss die Studenten da kriegen, wo sie einen Nutzen sehen. Sie sind ja heute auch nur hier, weil sie einen Nutzen für sich sehen! So funktioniert auch Kompetenzerwerb nur dann, wenn Sie Sinn sehen in dem, was Sie machen."

Den Sinn sahen und sehen Teilnehmer praxisnaher Angebote wie dieses Kurses zum Fernsehjournalismus. Entsprechend zeigt auch das Feedback der Studierenden am Ende der drei Tage, dass sie bzgl. der persönlichen beruflichen Orientierung in dem ihnen präsentierten Bereich der Medien klarer sehen. Nicht wenige lassen sich von der Begeisterung weiter tragen und können sich vorstellen, hier weiter zu engagieren. Anderen geben an, dass ihnen diese Form des Journalismus zu aufwändig sei, so etwa liegen ihnen Hörfunk oder Print/Online mehr. Wieder andere stellen fest, dass ihnen Journalismus als Berufsfeld gar nicht liegt. Der Sinn dieses Seminars ist damit voll erfüllt: Orientierungshilfe.

Persönliches Fazit und Ausblick

Der Dozent dieses Kurses und Autor der vorliegenden Zeilen erhält durch die Rückmeldungen der Studierenden bereits über viele Semester immer wieder erneut die Bestätigung, dass ein großer Markt für Seminare mit Praxisnähe innerhalb der sehr theoretisch aufgestellten Universität besteht. Warum der Terminus „Markt"? Er betont recht treffend die Notwendigkeit und den tatsächlichen Wert dieser Lehrveranstaltungen. Betriebswirtschaftlich betrachtet – und nach solchen ökonomischen Maßstäben stellen sich die Hochschulen nicht erst seit der jüngsten Reform verstärkt auf – rangieren sie unter Ausgaben. Verständlicherweise müssen moderne Hochschulen immer alles im Blick behalten, um den Kostensteigerungen zu begegnen. Allerdings sollten geplante Einsparungen dabei weniger solche Einrichtungen wie die Studierendenakademie der HHU bzw. KUBUS, welche den Studierenden „das Leben da draußen" zeigen, betreffen. Denn von der Gesamtheit aller Bachelorabsolventen schlagen geschätzt weit unter zehn Prozent eine akademische Laufbahn ein. (Mehr kann eine Universität ohnehin nicht aufnehmen, dann i. d. R. ohnehin meist nur im befristeten Angestelltenverhältnis.) Also ist es nur recht (und billig), den neunzig Prozent, also dem größeren Teil der Studierenden eine praxisbezogene Orientierung anzubieten. Hier den Rotstift anzusetzen, wäre Sparen am falschen Ende. Und eine Universität mit einem gut strukturierten, praxisnahen Kursangebot wirkt sehr modern, fair, weltoffen, kurz: attraktiv.

Kapitel VII
Über den Namen hinaus ...

Autorenverzeichnis

Prof. Dr. Gardenia Alonso

Leitung der Zentralen Einrichtung für Sprachen und Schlüsselkompetenzen an der Universität Göttingen und Professorin für International Business Communication an der AKAD University Stuttgart. Studium an der Université Paris-Sorbonne in den Fächern Literatur und Sprachen, an der Universität des Saarlandes in den Angewandten Sprachwissenschaften für die Sprachen Deutsch, Spanisch, Englisch und Französisch sowie am Monterey Institute of International Studies im Fachbereich Translation Studies mit den mit den Schwerpunkten Softwarelokalisierung, Fachübersetzen und Interkulturelle Kommunikation. Promotion zum Thema „Kompetenzförderung an der Hochschule" an der Universität Göttingen.

Benjamin Bartels B. A.

Studium der Geschichte und Philosophie an der Heinrich-Heine-Universität in Düsseldorf. Hochschulpolitische Erfahrung als stellvertretender AStA-Vorsitzender, als Mitglied des Studierendenparlaments und als Vorsitzender des RCDS der HHU.

Dr. Klaus Bergner

Freiberuflicher Fernsehjournalist und Videoproduzent für TV-Sender und das Internet. Tätigkeiten als Autor, Redakteur, Regisseur und Kameramann für verschiedene Redaktion (bspw. ARD-Morgenmagazin, Sendung mit der Maus, Menschen hautnah). Lehrbeauftragter an Hochschulen in den Bereichen Medienwissenschaft, -management, -produktion und -psychologie. Studium der Biologie und Germanistik, Promotion in den Literaturwissenschaften.

Natalie Böddicker

Leiterin der Abteilung Hochschul- und Qualitätsentwicklung sowie Koordinatorin des Projekts „Integrierte Qualitätsoffensive in Lehre und Studium" der Heinrich-Heine-Universität Düsseldorf.

Prof. Dr. Ulf Boes

Professor an der Mediadesign Hochschule Düsseldorf. Hauptlehrgebiet ist das Unternehmerische Medien- und Kommunikationsmanagement mit den Schwerpunkten „Werbliche und vertrauensfördernde Kommunikation". Studium der Publizistik, Kommunikationswissenschaft und Wirtschaftspolitik an der Ruhr-Universität Bochum. Promotion zum Thema Wissenschaftspublizistik.

Claudia Boes M. A.

Wissenschaftliche Mitarbeiterin und Leiterin der Abteilung „Sprachenzentrum" der Studierendenakademie an der Heinrich-Heine-Universität Düsseldorf. Studium der Romanistik und Wirtschaftswissenschaften.

Dominique Brasseur M. A.

Studium der Geschichte, Politikwissenschaft und Allgemeinen Sprachwissenschaft an der Heinrich-Heine-Universität Düsseldorf. Seit 2007 Berufserfahrung in der Organisation und Durchführung von Lehrveranstaltungen im Bereich Berufsorientierung und politische Bildung. Persönliche Referentin des Prorektors für Lehre und Studienqualität 2009. KUBUS-Abteilungsleiterin seit Mai 2009. Geschäftsführerin der Studierendenakademie seit 2016.

Holger Ehlert M. A.

Studium der Germanistik und Philosophie an der Heinrich-Heine-Universität Düsseldorf. Ehemals Beauftragter für die Qualität der Lehre der Philosophischen Fakultät der Heinrich-Heine-Universität und Geschäftsführer der Heinrich-Heine-Gesellschaft Düsseldorf e. V. Wissenschaftlich Beschäftigter am Institut für Germanistik der HHUD und Leiter der Abteilung KUBUS in der Studierendenakademie.

Autorenverzeichnis

Dr. Johann Fischer

Leitung der Zentralen Einrichtung für Sprachen und Schlüsselqualifikation (ZESS) der Universität Göttingen. Studium Englisch, Französisch, Italienisch. Promotion in der Romanistik zum Thema Soziolinguistik. Zuvor Leitung der Sprachenzentren Universität Hohenheim, Tübingen und Würzburg.

Dr. Peter Hachenberg

Leiter der Abteilung „Studiengebiet Deutsch als Fremdsprache" der Studierendenakademie der HHU. Studium Germanistik und Geschichte. 1988 bis 1993 Lektor des DAAD an der Beijing Foreign Studies University, VR China. 1995 bis 1998 Lecturer in German Studies an der University of New South Wales, Sydney, Australien. 2006 bis 2009 Direktor des Konfuzius-Instituts an der Heinrich-Heine-Universität Düsseldorf (HHU).

PD Dr. Christoph auf der Horst

Leiter des Zentrum Studium Universale und stellvertretender Leiter des Hauses der Universität sowie freier Mitarbeiter am Institut für Geschichte, Theorie und Ethik der Medizin. Studium der Germanistik, Philosophie und Theater-, Film- und Fernsehwissenschaften sowie Geschichte und Deutsch in Köln und Clermont-Ferrand. Promotion in den Literaturwissenschaften.

Dr. Ilke Kaymak, Dipl.-Psych.

Leiterin der Abteilung Career Service in der Studierendenakademie. Studium der Psychologie an der Heinrich-Heine-Universität Düsseldorf; Zusatzqualifikation als Psychodynamischer Coach. Nach dem Studium langjährige Mitarbeit in renommierten Personalberatungen, zuletzt als Leiterin einer Recruiting- und Research-Abteilung einer spezialisierten Personalberatung. Promotion und Lehrtätigkeit im Lehrgebiet Arbeits- und Organisationspsychologie der FernUniversität in Hagen.

Sabine Klüner M. A.

Mitarbeiterin im Bereich Conference and Event Management der Universität Hamburg Marketing GmbH.

Dr. Simone Kroschel

Mitarbeiterin bei AQUAS e. V. Studium der Klassischen Philologie und Informationswissenschaft an der Heinrich-Heine-Universität Düsseldorf. Gründungsmitglied des Hochschulradio Düsseldorf e. V. und Vorsitzende des Medientraining Düsseldorf e. V.

Dr. Nina Leibinnes

Wissenschaftliche Mitarbeiterin im Studiendekanat der Medizinischen Fakultät der HHU. Studium der Germanistik und Romanistik in Düsseldorf und Besançon. Promotion im Fach Germanistische Mediävistik. 2012 bis 2014 Persönliche Referentin der Prorektorin für Studienqualität und Gleichstellung der HHU. 2014 bis 2016 Geschäftsführerin der Studierendenakademie.

Christian Lentz M. A.

Promotionsstudent im Fachbereich Germanistik an der Heinrich-Heine-Universität in Düsseldorf. Wissenschaftliche Hilfskraft bei der Studierendenakademie. Studium der Germanistik und Politikwissenschaften. Tätigkeiten u. a. als freier Mitarbeiter bei der Westdeutschen Zeitung und beim Grupello-Verlag.

Elke Muddemann-Pulla, Dipl.-Päd., Dipl. Soz.-Päd.

Mastercoach (DGfC), Supervisorin i. A. und Weiterbildnerin für Menschen in Bildungsinstitutionen, im Gesundheitswesen und im sozialen Bereich bei „fokus-mensch-coaching". Studium der Bildungswissenschaften an der Universität Duisburg-Essen. Zuvor Studienberaterin, psychologische Beraterin und Coach an der Heinrich-Heine-Universität Düsseldorf und der Universität Duisburg-Essen gearbeitet.

Autorenverzeichnis

Prof. Dr. Georg Pretzler

Lehrstuhlinhaber für Laser-Materie-Wechselwirkung an der HHU Düsseldorf. Leiter der Studierendenakademie und des Hauses der Universität. Promotion in Physik (TU Graz), Habilitation in Experimentalphysik (LMU München).

Jessica Schäfers B. A.

Studium der Germanistik und Philosophie an der Heinrich-Heine-Universität in Düsseldorf. Ehemalige Chefredakteurin des Hochschulradios der HHU.

Univ.-Prof. Dr. Christian Scholz

Professor an der Universität Saarbrücken. Lehrgebiet: Personalmanagement. Zentraler Tätigkeitsbereich: Erforschung der Arbeitswelt. Studium an der Universität Regensburg. Bücher: u. a. „Bologna-Schwarzbuch" und „Generation Z". Blog: „Per-Anhalter-Durch-die-Arbeitswelt". Gründungsdirektor des MBA-Programms im Europa-Institut an der Universität des Saarlandes.

Autorenverzeichnis

Fabian Schröer M. A.

Promotionsstudent der Chemie an der Heinrich-Heine-Universität in Düsseldorf. Masterabsolvent der Wirtschaftschemie. Hochschulpolitische Erfahrung u. a. als Präsident des Studierendenparlaments, Senatsmitglied und Fachschaftsrat.

Prof. Dr. Bernd F. W. Springer

Professor für Germanistik an der Universität Autònoma de Barcelona. Forschungsschwerpunkte: Deutsche Literatur zwischen 1750 und 1850; Geschichte des 20. Jahrhunderts in der deutschen Literatur; Deutsche Kultur- und Mentalitätsgeschichte; Interkulturelle (deutsch-spanische) Kommunikation.

Abbildungsverzeichnis

Vortrag: Wie „ticken" Studierende der Generation Z?
Abb. 1: © Scholz, Christian (2014): *Generation Z – Wie sie tickt, was sie verändert und warum sie uns alle ansteckt*. Wiley.
Abb. 2 © Scholz, Christian (2016): *Erwartungen der Generation Z an den Beruf*. GenZ-Panel@orga.uni-sb.de.

Vortrag: Aktuelle Herausforderungen und Zukunft der Vermittlung von Schlüsselkompetenzen
Abb. 1: © Boos, M.; Fischer, J. (2016): *Integrationstandems und Supervised Networking*. Unveröffentlichtes internes Arbeitspapier. Universität Göttingen, S. 2.
Abb. 2: © Schäfer, M. (2004): *Lernstile und e-Learning: Entwicklung und Erprobung eines Kategoriensystems zur Analyse von Lernstilen in problemorientierten virtuellen Seminaren*. Unveröffentlichte Diplomarbeit. Bergische Universität Wuppertal, S. 55.

Vortrag: Das „MenteeModul" der Studierendenakademie
Abb. 1: © Heinrich-Heine-Universität Düsseldorf
Abb. 2: © Holger Ehlert

Panel A3: Man kann nicht nicht kommunizieren – aber falsch. Was Kompetenz bei Kommunikation bedeutet und wie man sie vermittelt
Abb. 1: © Ulf Boes

Panel A4: Mehr als nur Sprachunterricht! – Welche (weiteren) Schlüsselkompetenzen vermitteln wir im Fremdsprachenunterricht?
Abb. 1: © Gardenia Alonso / Johann Fischer
Abb. 2: © Gardenia Alonso / Johann Fischer

Panel B2: Ohne Kulturwissenschaften kein Europa. Vom Nutzen sprachlich-kulturellen Wissens für die Verständigung mit unseren Nachbarn
Abb. 1: © Bernd F. W. Springer

Abbildungsverzeichnis

Panel B3: Handlungs- und Kompetenzorientierung im Bereich des Lehrens, Lernens und Überprüfens von Fremdsprachenkompetenzen?
Abb. 1: © Gardenia Alonso / Johann Fischer: *In Anlehnung an Ständige Konferenz der Kultusminister der Länder in der Bundesrepublik Deutschland (2014). Bildungsstandards für die fortgeführte Fremdsprache (Englisch / Französisch) für die Allgemeine Hochschulreife.* Köln: Carl Link, S. 12.
Abb. 2: © Fischer, J. / Chouissa, C. / Dugovičová, S. / Virkkunen-Fullenwider, A. (2011). *Guidelines for task-based university language testing*, Strasbourg / Graz: Council of Europe, S. 17.
Abb. 3: © Fischer, J. / Chouissa, C. / Dugovičová, S. / Virkkunen-Fullenwider, A. (2011). *Guidelines for task-based university language testing*, Strasbourg / Graz: Council of Europe, S. 21.
Abb. 4: © Gardenia Alonso / Johann Fischer
Abb. 5: © Gardenia Alonso / Johann Fischer
Abb. 6: © Gardenia Alonso / Johann Fischer

Panel B6: Überfachliche Angebote in der Hochschulstruktur
Abb. 1: © Kultusministerkonferenz, Qualifikationsrahmen für Deutsche Hochschulabschlüsse, 2005: https://www.hrk.de/fileadmin/redaktion/hrk/02-Dokumente/02-03-Studium/02-03-02-Qualifikationsrahmen/2005_Qualifikationsrahmen_HSAbschluesse.pdf, zuletzt abgerufen am 14.07.2016.
Abb. 2: © Natalie Böddicker / Simone Kroschel
Abb. 3: © Karlsruher Institut für Technologie (KIT)

Abteilung: KUBUS
Abb. 1: © Heinrich-Heine-Universität Düsseldorf
Abb. 2: © Heinrich-Heine-Universität Düsseldorf

Fotocollage Seite 158 von links oben nach rechts unten:
© Studierendenakademie / Foto: Eleonore Michel
© Studierendenakademie / Foto: Andreas Meske
© Studierendenakademie / Foto: Andreas Meske
© Studierendenakademie / Foto: Vanessa Mittmann

Abbildungsverzeichnis

© Studierendenakademie / Foto: Andreas Meske
© Studierendenakademie / Foto: Vanessa Mittmann

Fotocollage Seite 159 von links oben nach rechts unten:
© Studierendenakademie / Foto: Andreas Meske
© Studierendenakademie / Foto: Vanessa Mittmann
© Studierendenakademie / Foto: Andreas Meske
© Studierendenakademie / Foto: Vanessa Mittmann
© Studierendenakademie / Foto: Vanessa Mittmann
© Studierendenakademie / Foto: Vanessa Mittmann
© Studierendenakademie / Foto: Vanessa Mittmann
© Studierendenakademie / Foto: Vanessa Mittmann
© Studierendenakademie / Foto: Vanessa Mittmann

Autorenfotos
Foto Alonso: © Gardenia Alonso
Foto Bartels: © Benjamin Bartels
Foto Bergner: © Klaus Bergner
Foto Böddicker: © Natalie Böddicker
Foto Ulf Boes: © Ulf Boes
Foto Claudia Boes: © Studierendenakademie
Foto Brasseur: © Dominique Brasseur
Foto Ehlert: © Holger Ehlert
Foto Fischer: © Johann Fischer
Foto Hachenberg: © Studierendenakademie
Foto auf der Horst: © Studierendenakademie
Foto Kaymak: © Ilke Kaymak
Foto Klüner: © Sabine Klüner
Foto Kroschel: © Simone Kroschel
Foto Leibinnes: © Studierendenakademie
Foto Lentz: © Christian Lentz
Foto Muddemann-Pulla: © Elke Muddemann-Pulla
Foto Pretzler: © Studierendenakademie

Foto Schäfers: © Jessica Schäfers
Foto Scholz: © Christian Scholz
Foto Schröer: © Hanne Horn
Foto Springer: © Bernd F. W. Springer

www.ingramcontent.com/pod-product-compliance
Lightning Source LLC
Chambersburg PA
CBHW070400240426
43661CB00056B/2481

CCCC STUDIES IN WRITING & RHETORIC
Edited by Steve Parks, University of Virginia

The aim of the CCCC Studies in Writing & Rhetoric (SWR) Series is to influence how we think about language in action and especially how writing gets taught at the college level. The methods of studies vary from the critical to historical to linguistic to ethnographic, and their authors draw on work in various fields that inform composition—including rhetoric, communication, education, discourse analysis, psychology, cultural studies, and literature. Their focuses are similarly diverse—ranging from individual writers and teachers, to work on classrooms and communities and curricula, to analyses of the social, political, and material contexts of writing and its teaching.

SWR was one of the first scholarly book series to focus on the teaching of writing. It was established in 1980 by the Conference on College Composition and Communication (CCCC) in order to promote research in the emerging field of writing studies. As our field has grown, the research sponsored by SWR has continued to articulate the commitment of CCCC to supporting the work of writing teachers as reflective practitioners and intellectuals.

We are eager to identify influential work in writing and rhetoric as it emerges. We thus ask authors to send us project proposals that clearly situate their work in the field and show how they aim to redirect our ongoing conversations about writing and its teaching. Proposals should include an overview of the project, a brief annotated table of contents, and a sample chapter. They should not exceed 10,000 words.

To submit a proposal, please register as an author at www.editorialmanager.com/nctebp. Once registered, follow the steps to submit a proposal (be sure to choose SWR Book Proposal from the drop-down list of article submission types).

SWR Editorial Advisory Board

Steve Parks, SWR Editor, University of Virginia
Kevin Browne, University of the West Indies
Ellen Cushman, Northeastern University
Laura Gonzales, University of Texas-El Paso
Haivan Hoang, University of Massachusetts-Amherst
Carmen Kynard, John Jay College of Criminal Justice
Paula Mathieu, Boston College
Staci M. Perryman-Clark, Western Michigan University
Eric Pritchard, University at Buffalo
Jacqueline Rhodes, Michigan State University
Tiffany Rousculp, Salt Lake Community College
Khirsten Scott, University of Pittsburgh
Jody Shipka, University of Maryland, Baltimore County
Bo Wang, California State University

WRITING ACCOMPLICES WITH STUDENT IMMIGRANT RIGHTS ORGANIZERS

Glenn Hutchinson
Florida International University

Conference on College Composition and Communication

National Council of Teachers of English

National Council of Teachers of English
340 N. Neil St., Suite #104, Champaign, Illinois 61820
www.ncte.org

Staff Editor: Bonny Graham
Series Editor: Steve Parks
Manuscript Editor: Leigh Scarcliff
Interior Design: Mary Rohrer
Cover Design: Pat Mayer
Cover Image: Glenn Hutchinson

NCTE Stock Number: 58500; eStock Number: 58524
ISBN 978-0-8141-5850-0; eISBN 978-0-8141-5852-4

Copyright © 2021 by the Conference on College Composition and Communication of the National Council of Teachers of English.

All rights reserved. No part of this publication may be reproduced or transmitted in any form or by any means, electronic or mechanical, including photocopy, or any information storage and retrieval system, without permission from the copyright holder. Printed in the United States of America.

It is the policy of NCTE in its journals and other publications to provide a forum for the open discussion of ideas concerning the content and the teaching of English and the language arts. Publicity accorded to any particular point of view does not imply endorsement by the Executive Committee, the Board of Directors, or the membership at large, except in announcements of policy, where such endorsement is clearly specified.

NCTE provides equal employment opportunity (EEO) to all staff members and applicants for employment without regard to race, color, religion, sex, national origin, age, physical, mental or perceived handicap/disability, sexual orientation including gender identity or expression, ancestry, genetic information, marital status, military status, unfavorable discharge from military service, pregnancy, citizenship status, personal appearance, matriculation or political affiliation, or any other protected status under applicable federal, state, and local laws.

Every effort has been made to provide current URLs and email addresses, but because of the rapidly changing nature of the web, some sites and addresses may no longer be accessible.

Library of Congress Control Number: 2020952438

CONTENTS

Acknowledgments vii

Foreword ix
 Angelica Velazquillo

Prologue: Organizer-Writers' Insights and Lessons 1

Community Partner Syllabus Fall 1997 7

1. The Limits of Partnership 13
2. Petitions to Stop Deportations 42
3. A Collective Lens for the Public-Writing Classroom and Op-Eds 68
4. Detention/Writing Center Campaigns for Freedom 96
5. A Shift toward Being an Accomplice 121

Community Accomplice Syllabus Spring 2020 143

Epilogue: Reflections from Student Organizer-Writers 151

Works Cited 157

Index 173

Author 185

ACKNOWLEDGMENTS

SPECIAL THANKS TO Angelica, Julio, Mohammad, Claudio, Viridiana, Nicolas, Francis, Thomas, and all the organizers who inspired this book.

Paula Gillespie and Sara P. Alvarez, thank you for your valuable feedback.

Steve Parks, thank you for your patience, time, and guidance.

And Maria, for your love, strength, and support.

FOREWORD

IT IS STRANGE TO REFLECT ON the various names I have been called. Some people refer to me as illegal, others as undocumented, and then there are the newer categories—Dreamer, DACA recipient— terms used to describe and reduce my identity to a single trait: my *irregular* immigration status. Like millions of others, I came to the United States as a child. I was four years old and my brother was two. We came with my mother with the aim to reunite with my dad, who was working in the US. The plan was for my dad to work for a couple of years, save money, and then we would all return to Mexico. But as time passed, the US became our home. My family moved from New York City to Charlotte, North Carolina, where there were more work opportunities. Thankfully, with community support and multiple scholarships, I attended college. Yet despite my bachelor's degree, there was no change to immigration policy, which meant I could not adjust my immigration status. Unlike my peers, I could not work in my field. Graduate school was too expensive, especially given that I did not qualify for federal aid. Then in 2010, legislation that would have provided a pathway toward legalization for millions of undocumented youth, known as the DREAM Act, fell short of the necessary congressional votes. The glimmer of hope vanished.

As I grappled with the decision—whether to stay in the US with my family or return to Mexico and continue my studies, my brother was detained for driving without a license. In actuality, he was driving with an expired driving permit that he was unable to update because the law in North Carolina changed a few months before he could apply for his full license. It broke my mother's heart to learn that my brother was detained. Nothing prepares you to come home to an empty house knowing your loved one is spending the night in a jail cell. I will never forget the pain of walking into my brother's bedroom and wondering if I would ever see him again. As we consulted immigration attorneys, the answer was the same: there was nothing to do. They suggested my brother ask for "voluntary departure," meaning that he would willingly leave the United States, a fate that is hard to accept when the only home you know is here. . . . I had to decide whether to stay in the US with my family, waiting for my own license to expire and risk being arrested, or leave with my brother. As I debated over what to do, I crossed paths with immigrant rights activists who presented an alternative option: my brother could make his immigration case public. We would denounce the discrepancy between what President Obama was saying, that his administration was not deporting Dreamers, and what local immigration authorities were doing on the ground. Taking a risk, we made his case public, and I came out with him as undocumented. This identity, which we had kept hidden for so long, was finally shared publicly. Thanks to the community support we received, my brother's immigration case was administratively closed. In other words, the federal government decided to close his case, but they maintain the right to reopen it at any time. Overall, it means he does not have to worry about deportation.

After living most of my life in fear and then witnessing the power of community organizing, I felt free from this fear of apprehension; it motivated me to participate in civil disobedience. On September 6, 2011, a group I participated in peacefully protested the unjust treatment that undocumented immigrants were receiving, and we were arrested. We spent three days and two nights in jail. Even though it was a short time, the experience was dehumanizing. Every moment was controlled and dictated by others who told us when to shower, when to eat, and when to go to bed. I remember thinking how hard it must be for those in detention centers or jails who are unexpectedly detained and are not fluent in English. Due to an unexpected and difficult situation that occurred while I was in jail, I became eligible to apply for a U visa. This is a special kind of visa that is available for victims of certain crimes who collaborate with the police.

As I began to work with an attorney to file my U visa application, I also started to explore graduate school options. My civic activism made me realize that I wanted to engage in research that would benefit the undocumented community, particularly in the area of mental health. This interest led me to apply to graduate programs, and eventually I was accepted into a master's program, and subsequently to a doctoral program. These phases offered new opportunities and challenges. Unlike most of my peers who had work experience and were used to living away from their families, this was a first for me. It was encouraging to be in the classroom and realize that my community organizing background had given me the practical experience to understand concepts such as "policy implementation," meaning distinguishing between the written intent of policies when they are drafted and how they are applied by street-level bureaucrats.

It was humbling to be in this academic setting where there was so much to learn. It opened up my eyes to the history of the oppression Mexican Americans have suffered since the acquisition of Mexican territory. I have also had the good fortune to learn more about the civil rights movement and to meet some of its leaders. There have been challenges along the way, such as self-doubt and then seeing a political shift that has led to more restrictive immigration policies. It has been hard to conduct immigration research when I still worry about the safety of my family. Presently, I find myself writing my dissertation, exploring the career paths before me and wondering where I belong. And in these moments of uncertainty, I turn to those mentors who have guided me along the way.

Glenn Hutchinson is a mentor and a friend. He stood alongside my family from the beginning when we fought my brother's deportation. In addition to being a friend and ally, Glenn is a professor who constantly seeks to integrate his academic work with the social issues that impact US society, especially those affecting local communities and his students. In this new book, Glenn provides a tangible resource for students and fellow professors, offering a nuanced approach to community writing in which students can incorporate their lived experiences with their academic assignments. This approach makes teaching more relevant and applicable as students write op-eds or work on petitions that will have a genuine impact, reaching a wider audience. It also acknowledges that all students and instructors enter the classroom with their own unique set of identities and blind spots. Some of these identities may be competing priorities for students. For instance, students may be juggling food insecurity, homelessness, and immigration concerns among other aspects that define who they are. These concerns are supposed to be compartmentalized, as they do not have a place in traditional classrooms. However, considering the health emergency caused by the COVID-19 pandemic in conjunction with shifting political landscapes, it is essential now more than ever to meet students where they are. This is what Glenn accomplishes.

Drawing on his lived experience, Glenn invites the reader to explore his own journey from student to educator, and how his perspective evolved along the way. He examines a course that he codesigned and how the syllabus transformed as he began to question his own assumptions about citizenship and service. This honest and reflective journey brings into conversation academics and the underrepresented perspectives of students as they navigate the educational system with their own intersecting identities.

This book is a resource for students who may share similar struggles as they themselves navigate higher education. It is also a resource for educators who are committed to creating a classroom environment that promotes equity, diversity, and inclusion.

Angelica Velazquillo
December 2020

Prologue: Organizer-Writers' Insights and Lessons

> Yes, I went to high school but I never believed I would go to college. I knew I was undocumented. . . . I still remember when I crossed the border. So I went to high school, Miami Senior High. . . . Right after I graduated, I started working with my dad in construction. And we used to work every day, especially in the summer, even before I graduated. . . . So I started saving money, but never really looking to higher education because I just believed it wasn't for undocumented students. . . .
>
> —Julio

> So I remember I went to transfer. . . . I took my grades and everything. And so the counselor, you know, they looked at my application and everything. And they came out and they said, "You know, Mohammad, you're the perfect student that we're looking for on this campus." And they gave me my acceptance letter and I was sitting there reading my acceptance letter, you know, my student ID number, when I could start and everything, and then, it was maybe ten seconds later, the guy came back and "Oh, shit, we made a mistake. We did not read your application where you mentioned you were born in Iran." So they took my acceptance letter away from me.
>
> —Mohammad

> I know kids who are DACA-applicable and meet all the requirements, but schools are still denying them in-state tuition. So we had some problems trying to explain to the schools that

this is state law and they have to abide by it. And teaching the colleges and schools how to go about it.

—Claudio

[W]hen DACA was under question . . . I remember FIU sent out an email that I have saved that FIU will always be a welcoming place for undocumented immigrants as long as FIU is in compliance with federal law. You might as well just not send anything. Just keep quiet. Because that's insulting at that point. You have like 800,000 students at risk of losing their status . . . and the university releases that level of noncommitment, a school that's 70 or 80 percent Latino—it's embarrassing.

—Tomas

I think working with the student and understanding that when you are someone who has multiple identities—you're not just a student, but you're also someone who doesn't have documentation, or you might be part of a mixed-status family—then you have additional worries. You're not just thinking about your grades and school, but you're sometimes worried about coming home and not seeing your parents or your siblings because they might be detained or you yourself could be detained. . . .

—Angelica

I think the first campaign that I actually did was we just sort of went and spammed, found like twelve thousand email addresses from professors and stuff around the United States who were teachers, thinking that you know this is the population that we can reach out to, that would be the most receptive to young people that have grown up here all their lives who can't move forward in the same way that they see students every single day are being able to move forward . . . No response. Very minimal. Like just one or two people responded. . . . We probably got more people saying take me off the list than we got the same amount, you know, saying, oh, I didn't know this was happening. . . . And so if we had, like even one teacher who reached out, like oh, this was amazing, this really affected me, I didn't know this was happening, that would have really, I think, been helpful to us in maybe our future work when trying harder to build alliances with teachers. . . . I think we might have lost some—not respect—but trust. It's just in the scope of several years of working and maybe not having as much of a receptive space in sort of what people consider the safe space, which is schools.

—Mohammad

We need to raise the level of consciousness of the college campus so that people can make their own decisions and can design activities or organizing, whichever way they want to. As of right now, there's a lot of lobbying going on. I don't advocate for lobbying as much as I advocate for organizing the people and having them lobby themselves. . . .

—Claudio

But I guess the one other thing I would say is in terms of my organizing, I really learned how to organize once I understood how to tell my story. And so, I can sort of see in that same context that learning, like, the real-world application of being able to tell your story, write your story, get your thoughts across—I know that's been, like, an extremely, like, energizing, powerful, therapeutic thing for a lot of undocumented folks I work with. . . .

—Mohammad

[I]t was a coming-out rally, and I had not fully considered what that meant. . . . I think it was the first time in my life as a young adult that I had met people like me. Even though I had shared some about my identity, there was no one close to me at that point that I could relate to. . . . I was fortunate to be a college graduate, but I was stuck. I couldn't work . . . I had been accepted in one [graduate] program but couldn't afford it. . . . When I decided to go to that event, I met other people like me. . . . It was wonderful just to meet people who had a similar trajectory, similar challenges. . . . We were supportive of one another. . . . It was so humbling to see high school students come out and share their stories and just seeing that level of empowerment at that age. . . . I was absolutely devastated with the whole situation with my brother. Did not feel empowered. Did not want to share my story. It did not seem truthful to say that I was undocumented and unafraid, because I was very much afraid. I felt betrayed growing up in a country with certain ideals and then seeing how my brother was being criminalized, and my family was being criminalized, so that was a turning point in finding that support system and finding people like me.

—Angelica

This was about families this whole time. This wasn't about what political party. This wasn't about any of that. It was always about the families—our community, the kids, the parents—that's what it's always about. For me, honestly, as much as I would like to see immigration reform, comprehensive immigration reform, that's not the most important thing for me. The most important thing is organizing . . . creating new strategies. And the fact that years ago, when an attorney told somebody there's nothing we can do on your case . . . we went from people being heartbroken to . . . we're going to organize and pressure ICE and stop your deportation. We're going to keep you united with your family. The fact we can do that . . . is the most important thing. . . . For me the most important thing is organize, organize, organize. Because the community needs to know the power is within us. As corny or cliché or whatever as that sounds, at the end of the day, we are going to be the people that are going to be holding our elected officials accountable. . . .

—Viridiana

The same party that said that they support us was the one who was deporting us. . . .

—Julio

[W]e worked with this Reverend Tim McDonald. He's really cool, and the one thing he told us, because he said he used to preach at Ebenezer Church, Martin Luther King's church. But the one thing he said . . . the thing that Martin Luther King would do and the thing I think you guys should do is, you should always ask for what is already promised to you on paper. Because it's easier to hold people accountable to, but you just ask for what the Obama administration is already promising you that they'd do . . . so my interpretation of that was just sort of like [the Obama administration's] low priority memos [for deportation]. It's the same thing. You know, yes, they say low priority [for deportation] is people XYZ, but they also say if it's in the public benefit [that someone is not deported]. So in our eyes, everyone is a low priority. It's just the matter of the community actually holding them accountable to what they promised you on paper. . . .

—Mohammad

I deal with cases. I'm also part of the Education, Not Deportation Team. . . . You get a case and then we have to help the families try and get out from the detention center. . . . He was a parent, a dad from Arizona. We heard about the case because . . . the daughter was an activist in Arizona, but for some reason they sent [him] to Miami. When we heard about the case, we did everything we could. We did vigils. We went to Krome detention center. I believe he was in Krome and then in Broward as well, in the BTC. And even though I did not know the guy, I had only seen him through fliers and pictures, and people had just talked to me about him, we were able to win his case. He came out of the detention center. When I finally saw him, I had never even met the guy, he just gave me a hug, a handshake, and telling me how proud he was of us, he felt like we were his kids and we were his family, when he saw us and then I noticed that he was skinnier; I guess he wasn't eating as well, they don't really eat much or like rice and beans, I think that's it. So the first thing we did was we went to go eat, and so he was telling us about it. Like that got to me. It could be my dad or my mom too that could be detained. Somebody hopefully helps them out like I did. . . . So that's something that I learned from that. . . .

—Francis

I really enjoyed the Broward campaign because that's the first time we put Immigration on the defensive. They had to react to our allegations. They had to tell people that they're doing their job instead of us having to say you know it was a whole different spin and I think it's very rare that you're going to find any press release from ICE that mentions an organization and responds to their allegations and that's something we were able to do that was very—I mean it comes I think back to the thing of writing to an extent of, you know, we did our own internal investigation and put out the facts as to what they're doing. In their response, I think that gave a lot of credibility to our allegations and that would not have happened if it wasn't for us sort of manipulating the power of the press and our stories and using it for a greater goal beyond. . . .

—Mohammad

That's when I decided to step back and I started doing activism more with the criminalization of people of color. And that really opened my mind to realize that the whole system was created that way just to criminalize people. . . .

—Julio

Community Partner Syllabus Fall 1997

ARSC3480: Citizenship and Service Practicum (V-Values Goal)   FALL 1997

Section 1
Smith Building 203 MW 12:00–12:50PM
Instructor: C. D. ("Dr. Denny") Fernald
Office: Colvard 4024   Office Hours: MW F 8:30–9:45 or by appointment
Phone: 547-4741
E-mail: cdfernal@email.uncc.edu

Section 2
Smith Building 204 MW 12:00–12:50PM
Instructor: Glenn Hutchinson
Office: 290M Fretwell   Office Hours: MW 2–3 PM, F 12–1 PM, or by appointment
Phone: 547-4447/2803 (Voicemail: English office) 547-0776/544-2272 (home)
E-mail: gchutchi@unccvms.uncc.edu

Objectives:
- During this semester, we will wrestle with questions of citizenship and service:
    - What does it mean to be a citizen?
    - What responsibilities does a citizen have for service to others?
    - What are the needs of our community?
    - How are we similar and how are we different from other communities?
    - What are some of the philosophical, social, political, religious, and ethical foundations for community service?
    - What role does community service play in responding to social needs?
    - What role should it play?
    - How can we reconcile self-reliance with volunteerism?
- On campus, we will meet for lectures and seminars to discuss issues such as homelessness, poverty, and social justice.

- Beyond the classroom, we will hit the road and complete forty hours of volunteer work in the community.

Expectations:
- *Regular attendance is essential.* Excessive absences will negatively affect your grade. If a student misses more than three classes, each additional absence will deduct ten points from their final grade.
- Please arrive promptly to class.
- Completion of all assignments is necessary in order to pass the course.
- For our discussions and activities to be successful, we all need to be active participants in class. When discussing these issues of citizenship and service, we hope you will follow Emerson's advice: "Trust thyself: every heart vibrates to that iron string."
- Also, we need to be respectful of our classmates, instructors, speakers, and their ideas, so we can create an atmosphere in which we all feel comfortable expressing our viewpoints.
- Assignments and their due dates are listed on the next page; late work will receive a penalty.
- Please be familiar with the *Code of Student Academic Integrity.* All work submitted must be your own and not used for other courses.
- Volunteer at least once with the UNC-Charlotte Food Recycling Project.
- And finally . . . think, learn, and have fun.

Required Materials:
1. Albert, Gail, ed. *Service-Learning Reader: Reflections and Perspectives on Service.* Raleigh, National Society for Experiential Education, 1994.
2. Three-ring binder (for journal)

Grading:
20% Midterm take-home exam
20% Final exam
25% Volunteer journal
   a. As you complete your forty required hours of community service, please keep a timesheet at the beginning of your notebook.
   b. Each time you volunteer, please make an entry reflecting upon the following questions:
      1. Describe the day's activities. What did you do? What was your purpose? Did anything unusual happen?
      2. What insights have you had about your work and its connections to issues discussed in class?

10% In-class compositions: include responses to quotations and questions from class discussions and guest speakers. These writings will be collected periodically throughout the semester.
15% Concluding essay and portfolio: At the end of the semester, turn in a collection of your writings and a reflection upon what you have experienced this term.
10% Class Participation

Syllabus (subject to change)

Week 1: Orientation
M 8-25 Introduction
W 8-27 *SLR* pp. 140–48, "Experience and Thinking," John Dewey; pp. 172–75, "Three Wondrous Answers," Thich Nhat Hanh

Week 2: Volunteer Fair
M 9-1 LABOR DAY–NO CLASS
W 9-3 Volunteer Fair: ABLE, Hands On Charlotte, United Way, Mallard Creek Tutoring Project, Communities in Schools, Habitat for Humanity, Metrolina AIDS

Week 3: Individualism and Philanthropy
M 9-8 *SLR* pp. 66–89, "Finding Oneself," Robert Bellah; "Self-Reliance," Ralph Waldo Emerson; guest speaker: Becky Davenport
W 9-10 Guest speaker: Dana Bradley
SLR pp. 261–62, "Democracy in America," Alexis de Tocqueville
VOLUNTEER PROJECT CHOICE DUE

Week 4: Values, Community, and the Individual
M 9-15 *SLR* pp. 5–12, "Value Differences in Intercultural Communication," Myron W. Lustig; values clarification exercise
W 9-17 *SLR* pp. 249–61, "The Covenanted Community," Page Smith; pp. 255–61, "Regenerating Community," John L. McKnight; "The Lottery," Shirley Jackson

Week 5: Politics of Service
M 9-22 *SLR* pp. 265–74, "I Only Work Here," John Lachs; project discussion
W 9-24 Guest speakers: Pat McCrory, Mayor of Charlotte; Jim Richardson, Former North Carolina Senator

Week 6: Moral Development
M 9-29   *SLR* pp. 186–87, "The Transformation," Eknath Easwaran; pp. 293–310, "The Evolution of Moral Meaning-Making," Robert Kegan
W 10-1   JOURNAL DUE (#1)

Week 7: Government and Nonprofits
M 10-6   Guest Speaker: Bill Brandon
W 10-8   Follow-up discussion

Week 8: Midterm
M 10-13 FALL BREAK—NO CLASS
W 10-15 Midterm assigned, review of projects

Week 9: Women and Service
M 10-20 Guest speaker: Donna Gabaccia
W 10-22 Midterm due
          Guest speakers: Sharon King, Junior League of Charlotte; Jeri Fischer Krentz, *Charlotte Observer*

Week 10: Role of the Church
M 10-27 *SLR* pp. 184–86, "Righteousness, Not Charity," Jacob Neusner; pp. 198–202, "On Being a Good Neighbor," Martin Luther King Jr.; pp. 323–30, "Love and Justice," June Bingham
W 10-29 Guest speakers: Mary Thomas Burke and Will Hinson

Week 11: Charity/Philanthropy
M 11-3   *SLR* pp. 90–94, "Commitment and Meaning," John W. Gardner; pp. 203–08, "Cultivating Compassion," James A. Joseph
W 11-5   JOURNAL DUE (#2)
          Guest speakers: Rolfe Neill, *Charlotte Observer;* Charles Page, United Way, and Gene Cochran, Duke Endowment

Week 12: Campus/Community Activists
M 11-10 *SLR* pp. 331–42, "Letter from Birmingham Jail," Martin Luther King, Jr.; pp. 108–20, "Diane Nash," Catherine Ingram
W 11-12 Guest speaker: Connie Leeper, Piedmont Peace Project; Bruce Parker, Charlotte philanthropist

Week 13: Grassroots Activism
M 11-17 Guest speakers: Madine Hester-Fails, President of the Charlotte Urban League; Mike Pearson, Sociology Department

W 11-19 Oleen McLeod, Director of Soup Kitchen; Louise Shackleford, Wilmore Center

Week 14: Acts of Caring
M 11-26 *SLR* pp. 95–107, "Reprise: Walking Each Other Home," Dass and Gorman; pp. 209–24, "Who's Helping?" Dass and Gorman, video / discussion
W 11-28 THANKSGIVING BREAK—NO CLASS

Week 15: Global Community
M 12-1 *SLR* pp. 343–61, "From Person to Planet," Dawson Church; "The Blue Pearl," Peter Russell
W 12-3 Follow-up discussion

Week 16: Closure
M 12-8 *SLR* pp. 149–71, "Chapter 3," Paulo Freire
W 12-10 FINAL JOURNAL with volunteer timesheet DUE
CONCLUDING ESSAY AND PORTFOLIO DUE

FINAL EXAM TIME
M 12-15 12:00–3:00PM

Student Name _____ Today's Date _____
Address _____ Phone _____
Agency Name _____ Supervisor _____
Address _____ Phone _____
Days & Hours at Agency _____

List *your* personal goals, objectives, skills to be acquired:

List specific activities and responsibilities at organization:

Plan Approval Signatures

_____   _____   _____
       Student   Agency Supervisor   Faculty Supervisor

1

The Limits of Partnership

> An estimated 11.3 million people are undocumented in the United States.
> —"Major US Immigration Laws 1790–Present"

> Ninety-eight thousand undocumented students graduate each year from high school.
> —Jie Zong and Jeanne Batalova

> Sixteen states and seven university systems offer in-state tuition to undocumented students.
> —"Undocumented Student Tuition: Overview"

> According to ICE, over three million people were deported between 2008 and 2016. In his first two years in office, Trump has deported over half a million.
> —"FY 2016 ICE Immigration Removals"

UNIVERSITIES AND FACULTY OFTEN have lost their students' trust, and for good reason. Academia often fails to act in solidarity with students, particularly those experiencing the effects of white supremacy and anti-immigrant laws and policies. Consider the voices represented in the prologue. Until he became involved with immigrant rights groups, Julio didn't think he could go to college, because of his status. Mohammad was denied admission to a university once admission officials were confronted with his undocumented reality. Once admitted, Tomas finds his university's lack of commitment to its students "embarrassing" when DACA is threatened by a new administration. Claudio talks about how colleges don't follow through with pro-immigrant policies, requiring students to organize and educate their own institutions. As a result, Mohammad states, there's a lack of trust between academia and students. Angelica reminds teachers that students have big concerns other than just completing homework for class—for example, the threat of deportation for themselves and their families. Francis and other student organizers work to stop deportations. These students have done organizing in many different parts of the country, and this book focuses on their efforts in North Carolina and Florida.

This book does not aim to be what Eve Tuck describes as "damage-centered research," the problematic practice whereby scholars "document pain or loss" (413) to advocate for change. Instead, this book is guided by the voices of youth organizers who envision and accomplish the change themselves in an oppressive system. For example, although Mohammad and Claudio point out universities' failures in addressing student needs, they persist and work for immigrant rights on and off campus. They, along with the other organizers quoted in the prologue, have changed much through their rhetorical skills and actions, including gaining access to universities, lobbying successfully for in-state tuition laws in twenty states, pressuring a US president to sign DACA, and stopping some deportations. As Viridiana comments, "I've always believed in the power of our community organized regardless of who is in power . . . ." And Julio adds that his involvement encouraged him to rethink larger issues of justice and "[t]o realize that the whole system was created that way just to criminalize people. . . ." The insights, work, and voices of student organizers, then, guide the two fundamental questions for this book:

1. What is a teacher's responsibility to act in solidarity with immigrant students who are organizing to change anti-immigrant and white supremacist laws and policies? And what are some helpful ways to do so both on campus and in the community?
2. How can a writing teacher's pedagogy center the public-writing classroom more on students' work as organizers and rhetoricians?

In what follows, I argue for teacher responsibility and a pedagogical shift, and I reflect upon how my own positionality as a white male citizen shapes my involvement and limits my perspective. My identity as a teacher was molded by scholarship that reinforced assumptions of white citizenship. This scholarship often assumed students were white citizens who needed to venture out into the community to learn about social injustice. In contrast, working with undocumented students inside and outside the classroom demanded that I rethink my own assumptions and pedagogy. Student organizers were responding to anti-immigrant policies both on and off campus. Also, many undocumented students and students from marginalized communities are taught by white instructors, and there are opportunities, then, for instructors to use their privilege to support the organizing work of these students. So when I write that many organizers don't trust academia, then, I am referring to white faculty like me and administrators who enact white supremacist policies that exclude undocumented students.

This book is mixed with memoir about volunteering and working with immigrant rights groups (2007–2020) and how those interactions with students changed my pedagogy. As I discuss my own experience, my goal is to displace my own centrality and foreground those student organizers and how they can better inform the field's teaching practices. Other writing teachers likely will answer these questions differently based upon their own identities and experiences. The following chapters highlight different organizations led by students in the immigrant rights movement, and unless otherwise indicated, "organizer" refers to student immigrant rights organizer. This chapter, then, reflects the need to unlearn disciplinarity and begin to address the concerns of students.

TRAINING TO BE A COMMUNITY PARTNER

My graduate school education (1995–2002) reflected the discipline's current and ongoing emphasis on community partnerships and assumed identities for teachers and students. This scholarship often explored two questions: (1) As students complete a community project and write about their service-learning experiences, how can we encourage them to reflect upon their personal experiences, see the significance and injustice of larger social structures, and become more active citizens? (2) In a partnership between the university and community, how can we as writing professors work *with* a community rather than engage in hierarchical service work? While these questions guided much of my graduate school training, they did not address the perspectives of many students I have worked with since that time. For example, many students are unable to become citizens, and classroom practices must respond to that reality. As Sara P. Alvarez and Amy Wan note, "Unlike the imagined and flexible boundaries of an uncritically invoked global citizenship, transnational students are impacted by governmental citizenship boundaries and those created by the racialization and hierarchization of language practices" (214). Community-writing scholarship, then, has largely ignored the lived realities of the growing number of transnational students in the writing classroom.

One much-discussed article, published in 1994, Bruce Herzberg's "Community Service and Critical Teaching," argues that his students can find value in their individual service projects, but they had difficulty connecting their projects to larger social issues. As his students tutored adult learners at a shelter and reflected upon the experience, Herzberg comments that they were "immersed in a culture of individualism," and very few of his students understood how "social institutions affect our lives" (317). Herzberg contrasts his students' lives at the campus with those of the shelter residents:

> At the start, the students were naturally apprehensive about tutoring adults in a shelter. Most of them had done some volunteer work before, but not in settings like that. They were nervous when we actually went to the Pine Street Inn. We left Bentley's clean, well-lighted suburban campus and drove the ten miles into Downtown Boston after dark, parked under the expressway, and went past a milling crowd of men into a dreary lobby. (310–11)

As they leave the college campus and volunteer at this shelter, Herzberg wants his students to change their viewpoints: "How do my students abandon their comfortable belief in equal opportunity and meritocracy?" (314). Therefore, service-learning courses like Herzberg's want students to reflect upon individual volunteer experiences and think about larger social issues. In this article, Herzberg's students are depicted as privileged students who need a transformation instigated by this service-learning experience. *Writing the Community: Concepts and Models for Service-Learning in Composition,* edited by Linda Adler-Kassner, Robert Crooks, and Ann Waters, continues this conversation with a collection of essays about the possibilities for service-learning and the teaching of writing, particularly in terms of what students will learn. In service-learning/compositions courses, students can write for, about, or with the community (Deans, "Writing Across the Curriculum"). And one essay, by David Cooper and Laura Julier, proposes writing projects that connect with "effective citizenship" (92) and how the "average citizen" (85) can become a more active participant in their community.

In designing courses that could help students learn and become more "active" citizens, scholars critique the complicated relationship between the university and the community. For example, Aaron Schutz and Anne Ruggles Gere emphasize that universities and community groups should be equal partners as they connect the personal with the public. And in regard to these partnerships, Ellen Cushman discusses the problems of universities being like ivory towers with separations between themselves and communities. She calls for writing teachers to consider how to be "an agent for social change," and in this role, "[p]reparing students for greater civic participation . . . " (12). Therefore, this kind of service-learning work gives teachers and students an opportunity to learn something as they help other people gain "empowerment" (16). Cushman adds, "Said another way, activism starts with some kind of identification with people outside of the university, an identification that often can flourish in a context where both the scholar and people together assess and redraw lines of power structures between them" (19). In this divide between the university and the community, Cushman notes that she is "[i]gnoring one potential means of access into the community—our students. But then, this assumes that we have solid enough relations with them to be able to follow them beyond the moat surrounding the ivory tower" (22). As a beginning teacher, I did not recognize the absence of students in these conversations about university and community. I likely was envisioning a classroom of students with similar experiences to mine and thereby reinforcing my own privilege as we considered such community partnerships.

The structure of community-university partnerships raises important questions about how the university can ignore community needs and perspectives. In *Tactics of Hope,* Paula Mathieu examines the university-community relationship and describes this "public turn" in composition as she reflects upon her involvement with community-writing projects, including working with street newspapers that people who are homeless can write for and sell too. She discusses how composition's work in the community is guided mostly by *"strategic logics"* whereby the university focuses more on its own strategy and goals rather than working in more equitable "timely partnerships" (xiv). She advocates a "tactics of hope," "to continually seek new ways to listen to the communities around [us]" and be "rhetorically responsive" (20–21). Mathieu's book, then, critiques some of the problems with university-community partnerships and encourages service-learning teachers to work to "[f]oreground the needs and expertise of communities, and seek to highlight—and work within—the possibilities and limitations inherent in university partnerships" (90).

Linda Flower also proposes a relationship that avoids hierarchy and focuses on "[i]ntercultural inquiry that not only seeks more diverse rival readings, but constructs multivoiced negotiated meanings in practice" ("Intercultural Inquiry" 182). As Flower discusses literacy projects where college students and teenagers from the local community gather at a think tank at the Community Literacy Center in Pittsburgh, participants engage in this intercultural dialogue: "What matters is that marginalized participants are not merely objects of study but self-conscious partners in an inquiry, with inside knowledge about issues that concern them" (190). For example, Flower uses an image of a table with chairs around it to illustrate such inquiry: the problem is on the table, and in the seats around the table are various people from different perspectives who have come together to discuss it, including the university student, the teenager involved in the project, community members, and researchers (189).

In examining this university-community relationship, scholars like Steve Parks note how the field often has settled for something less than organizing or activism:

> I want to argue that we have settled for a soft vision of progressive change, a vision that at best produces a hesitant and halting trek across a neoliberal landscape eager to validate our students and our own "protestations" as a sign of rich democratic debate. ("Sinners Welcome" 506)

Parks points out that many of the models for community work like Flower's do not address some of the reasons for social problems like the decrease in government assistance and a greater reliance on "government-business partnerships designed to 'empower' the poor as individuals" (511). Parks raises questions about Flower's model for community work and suggests that we need to engage more in "collective political action" and become an "*activist* English department" (521). He discusses the complex relationship between residents of a community in Syracuse and the interactions with the university and developers gentrifying part of the neighborhood near downtown. Parks then argues that we need to do more than this "soft" version of progressive change—that part of our work needs to be activist and political and about collective action. And that kind of work may diverge from current discussions in the discipline about what service-learning/community-writing work should be:

> I would argue that we must move beyond a volunteerist ethos, where individual students learn to understand the power of their individual rhetorical agency in the context of temporary forums, and move toward a collective voice, premised on coming to understand how community histories can act as

the foundational moment for strategic interventions in power networks. ("Sinners Welcome" 522)

This critique of volunteerism again questions the relationship between the community and the university and asks scholars to consider how they can become more engaged activists within their communities.

Also stressing the importance of activism/organizing, Eli Goldblatt stresses the community organizing lessons from Saul Alinsky ("Alinsky's Reveille" 282). Goldblatt compares Alinsky and his emphasis upon action and social change with the works of John Dewey and Paulo Freire; however, Goldblatt argues that Alinsky's focus on how to organize speaks to social justice issues in ways distinct to the United States (281–82). Goldblatt cautions us that he's "not suggesting that we convert undergraduate tutors into young Alinsky agitators" but for writing professors to "think like organizers rather than academics when we devise models of university-community relationship[s]" (282). This approach focuses on community organizing rather than traditional community service projects; however, the emphasis is more upon teachers being the ones to think like organizers. However, what if your classes include student organizers already doing this kind of work?

My graduate school education did not question how my own perspective as a white male citizen might shape and limit my pedagogy for community work. My training had not asked me to consider how scholars of color might have different orientations toward community work as they confront social inequities in their own lives. For example, in "Chicanas Making Change: Institutional Rhetoric and the Comisión Femenil Mexicana Nacional," Kendall Leon reflects upon how her home community shapes her understanding of community work in ways that did not create a rigid separation between her roles as professor and community member: "The purpose of getting any kind of institutional education was not just about individual status but about how you could leverage what you learned or got access to for the greater good. And while I was still in my neighborhood, I did my best to uphold that part of the deal" (167). Leon's research on the Comisión Femenil Mexicana National (CFMN), a Chicana feminist organization, highlights the ways that "[C]hicanas have incited change by writing, theorizing, and making an identity" (171). Also, Terese Guinsatao Monberg reflects upon her own Filipina identity and discusses how she has been "[v]ery uncomfortable with most of the scholarship on service-learning" (23), particularly in its focus on students with privilege volunteering and not as much on students of color and those representing marginalized communities. Monberg notes, "If students of color are more likely to approach service-learning courses with robust (rather than deficit) views of 'the community,' and are more likely to take an activist stance toward/with their communities (Boyle-Baise and Sleeter), then service-learning paradigms need to shift to more fully engage these capabilities" (41). In *Fashioning Lives: Black Queers and the Politics of Literacy*, Eric Darnell Pritchard connects his own identity and educational experiences as he discusses "literacy normativity" or practices that cause "[h]arm[,] and restorative literacies, which consists of literacy practices that Black queers employ as a means of self-definition, self-care, and self-determination" (24). These examples show how teachers' positionalities can shape their approaches to community engagement and contribute much-needed insight to the field.

In contrast, my preparation often assumed that students were citizens in rather privileged positions, and that they "needed" exposure to real community problems and issues of social justice. These community partnerships were being led and written about by scholars whose positionalities are also very much dominant and privileged like my own. Such a dynamic between teacher and students can affect the writing classroom. For instance, Nelson Flores and Jonathan Rosa build upon the work of Django Paris and H. Samy Alim to show how whiteness can shape not just what we see but how we communicate with one another: "The white gaze is attached both to a speaking subject who engages in the idealized linguistic practices of whiteness and to a listening subject who hears and interprets the linguistic practices of language-minoritized populations as deviant based on their racial positioning in society as opposed to any objective characteristics of their language use"

(151). These kinds of assumptions, in effect, recentered my own positionality as a citizen, and occulted how social justice work is a form of labor grounded in everyday lived realities in oppressive systems.

TEACHING CITIZENSHIP AND SERVICE IN NORTH CAROLINA

I started teaching in a city of banks and shiny new buildings, a future of capitalism, which often ignored a history of class struggle and the civil rights movement. Boasting Bank of America's headquarters, Charlotte, North Carolina, reflects many of the neoliberalist policies you would expect a major banking center would have: a focus on privatization, tax incentives for corporations, and reduced funding for public services. Bank of America's sixty-story tower stands in the very center of downtown/uptown, Trade and Tryon Street, the original Catawba Indian trading path crossroads from which the city grew. The bank had a marketplace in their lobby, and if you bought something from one of the shops, you could get a ride to the top and see the view from the tallest building in the Southeast. But your time at the top was limited—it was only a glimpse from the wealthy perch where bank executives worked. From that vantage point, you could see Charlotte's growth and its desire to become a world-class city. Old historic buildings were destroyed and made into new skyscrapers or parking lots, and construction was everywhere even as NAFTA impacted the state's textile industry: from 1994–2016, more than 348,000 North Carolina manufacturing jobs were lost (Ybarra; "North Carolina Job Loss").

But from this white gaze, it might be difficult to note the history, struggle, and sites of change of this city. Like other US states, North Carolina is a site of settler colonialism and the marginalization of indigenous peoples. Just over a mile from this spot is Johnson C. Smith University, a private HBCU with a history of students protesting for civil rights in the 1960s and also of admitting undocumented students in the 2000s when the state legislature passed anti-immigrant legislation and the North Carolina Community College system at one point banned undocumented students from the classroom. And Charlotte also has been called "The New Latino South," with a 500 percent increase in the number of Latinx residents living in this city from 1990 to 2000 (Kochhar et al.). Also, between 2000 and 2010, the Asian American population in the state increased by 85 percent, which was the largest growth in the South and the third highest rate in the country (Yee).

When I started teaching as a graduate student and lecturer in the English department at the University of North Carolina–Charlotte, my training in the field prepared me to think of community writing only with a partnership mindset and to encourage students to become more active citizens in the community. Then a psychology professor from the honors program, Denny Fernald, and I proposed the idea of a new interdisciplinary writing class grounded in service-learning research like Herzberg's. The course proposal included a service-learning requirement, readings and writings about community, and visits from different nonprofit organizations and local politicians. On October 4, 1996, when Attorney General Janet Reno was visiting campus, I was an MA student and got a chance to speak with her about the idea of such a course. When she addressed the university later that day at the school's fiftieth-anniversary celebration, she challenged the university to start such a service-learning course. In her speech, Attorney General Reno said that if she was able to return to this university fifty years later as a "ghost," she hoped to see that the course I was proposing had been implemented:

> Not Only How to Serve the Community But How to Organize and Build Communities That Can Become Self-sufficient and Insure All their Children and All Their Families Real Equal Opportunity to Participate As Constructive Citizens. (Reno 10–11; caps in original)

We didn't use that long title for the course, but we did like her emphasis on other things besides service: organizing and participating as citizens. So, after this unusual endorsement, as an MA student and then adjunct faculty member, I was able to form a faculty committee to design such an interdisciplinary writing-intensive course, "Citizenship and Service Practicum." We chose the term *citizenship* for the title because we wanted the course to emphasize more than service and reflect on our responsibilities and potential as citizens in the political process. At this moment, we were acting under the assumption that our students were citizens and needed to become active in the community both as volunteers and as voters. I made this assumption largely because of my own identity, whiteness, and cultural understanding of citizenship. For instance, the scholarship of service-learning focused on the need for students to move from being volunteers to participating as citizens in such actions as voting but did not explore the many other privileges besides voting. Our main text was the *Service-Learning Reader,* edited by Gail Albert and published by the National Society for Experiential Education. Supplemented by some outside texts, as indicated by the syllabus on pages 7–11, the course readings discussed some of the different reasons to do community service, questioned the effectiveness of philanthropy, and emphasized the importance of active citizenship. As I look back at the syllabus now, I notice that there are no readings about racism, intersectionality, immigration, gender, or the reasons that millions of people are excluded from being citizens and voting. This absence is quite striking when considering that one of the main topics of conversation in the course (and in the version of it developed for second semester composition) was voting and becoming involved as citizens, as seen in this class activity/discussion prompt:

> Why do you think so many young people choose not to vote? Explain.
> Is this apathy (indifference or lack of interest in politics) a problem? Explain. If so, what should be done?
> **Role-playing:** As a group, write from the perspective of an eighteen-year-old who does not register to vote: Fred e-mails his friend, Sam, with information about how and when to register to vote. Write Sam's response to his friend. What reasons does he give to explain his lack of interest in politics?

The design of such an activity did not acknowledge that citizenship excludes millions of people from voting. This framework keeps my perspective as center by imagining that the only reasons someone wouldn't vote would be apathy or little regard for the democratic process. Such a writing prompt puts the focus on the individuals to act rather than on an unjust system. Such an activity does not acknowledge the ways in which the system disenfranchises people because of their immigration status or experiences through our racialized criminal system. I was assuming that both Fred and Sam are citizens or have the ability to become citizens and register to vote. So these kinds of questions about immigration status were not part of my pedagogy and training.

Based on the scholarship about community partnerships, this course's goal was to encourage students to reflect upon their service-learning project and consider how they could become more active citizens in the community. Following the lead of other community partnership models, the course required each student to complete a practicum log where they listed a contact person and the times that they volunteered for a particular project. At the time, the course seemed successful in the sense that we were able to invite nonprofit representatives to campus and students would sign up to volunteer with different organizations, write about what they learned, and make connections with the readings about larger social issues. Therefore, the course appeared to be accomplishing some of the desired goals for community partnership scholarship. In that course, students and I volunteered at homeless shelters, adult day care centers, and other community sites.

As we became partners with different community groups, I wanted this community-writing course to consider such topics as "class and group conflict," connections between "multiple issues," and a state of being "unblurred by ideological imperatives" (Goldblatt, "Alinsky's Reveille" 280). Students kept weekly journals that reflected upon their projects and made connections between the readings and class discussions. Students wrote essays that invited primary research from their work in the community and included different voices/perspectives. We would draw Flower's table for intercultural inquiry ("Intercultural Inquiry" 189), write the problem on the table, and then imagine different stakeholders sitting around the table and what input they could give in addressing this problem. Also, students kept portfolios where they could look back, reflect, and revise their work throughout the term. One key text was Paul Loeb's *Soul of a Citizen,* which included stories of ordinary people working for change. The title of the book emphasizes that need to connect our community work to our duties and potential as citizens, but what if students are unable to become citizens?

I learned that some of my students were already confronting important social justice issues that directly affected them. For example, one of my students told me about the struggle of some Filipino Americans in seeking citizenship. My student Mark had experienced this struggle himself, as he was born in the Philippines; his father was from the American military and his mother was Filipina. Mark, like many others, had difficulty in claiming citizenship because of immigration law. Mark taught me a lot about the possibilities for a writing course to connect with civil rights, as he was a leader in this movement. So much of my preparation to be a community writing/service-learning teacher had focused on what the college student can learn from a community partner (a nonprofit) or how that college student can become more of an active participant in democracy. Students like Mark were already active in a movement, and they were confronting issues of racism and exclusion that affected their daily lives. Mark's project aimed to connect Filipino children with their American fathers who were US servicemen so they could gain proof needed in applying for citizenship. Through use of the internet, email, and letters, Mark helped others from the Philippines gain citizenship in the United States. In addition, for my class, he wrote a proposal and presented at an academic conference about Filipino Americans. Mark wanted to amend the Amerasian Immigration Act of 1982, which did not grant the same rights of citizenship to those residents from the Philippines as to those from other Asian countries. My preparation as a writing teacher—and the field of writing studies—hadn't fully acknowledged and given space to Mark and other students advocating for change on and off the college campus.

STUDENT IDENTITY, CONTEXT, AND RHETORICAL POWER

For a community-writing course focused on partnerships with non-profits, what if students like Mark and those quoted in the prologue are already addressing social injustices themselves? What if they are organizing for change on campus and in their own communities? Although Parks and Goldblatt make powerful and important points about organizing, the field needs to address more of the concerns and organizing work of these students. For example, Angelica talks about the different identities that undocumented students have and that professors should know about: "You're not just thinking about your grades and school, but you're sometimes worried about coming home and not seeing your parents or your siblings because they might be detained or you yourself could be detained." Also, even though community partnership scholarship in the field poses important questions about student learning and the relationship between the university and the community, Mohammad says that he lost "trust" when academia did not respond to their campaign for immigrant students.

One reason for this discrepancy between much of this service-learning scholarship and student organizers is the lack of attention to students' identities, the contexts in which they are writing, and their own rhetorical power. For example, in *Conciencia Bilingüe: The Multilingual and Academic Writing Practices of Undocumented Immigrant Activists,* Sara del Pilar Alvarez interviews twelve undocumented youth organizers and discusses how their writing reflects what she calls "conciencia bilingüe":

> Conciencia bilingüe, in other words, is a working term for how local and racialized immigrant-generation multilinguals begin to make sense of their bilingual practices and processes—especially as they relate to writing—and how these ongoing reflexive processes may lead them to a sense of ownership and advocacy of these practices as bilingual. (57)

Through her conversations with organizers and close reading of their writings, Alvarez discusses how their rhetorical skills "[c]hallenge monolingual assumptions about linguistic legitimacy and citizenship and should be examined in the contexts of their undocumented and immigrant lived experiences" (4). Organizers comment, for example, how the writing they did for their activism—the public writing they did to advocate for change—was more complex than the kind of academic writing asked of them in the classroom:

> For instance, in cases like Tony's his immigration advocacy work with a national campaign asked that he engage his thousands of followers on social media daily and at least twice a day. For undocumented young adults in the immigrant rights movement, writing then is as vital and ongoing as it has become in most professional work spaces (Brandt, 2015). (144)

Alvarez's important study shows, then, the complex literacies organizers practice with (and through) their writing and the contexts in which they are writing for a public audience.

Similarly, Kate Vieira examines the impact of immigration on people's relation to the US context, how they see themselves, and the papers that "make" or break their Americanness. In *American by Paper: How Documents Matter in Immigrant Literacy,* Vieira discusses two groups in a Massachusetts community she calls "South Mills" for her study and the effect documentation has on their literacy practices and lives. Even though both groups speak Portuguese, their birthplace affects whether they can gain legal documentation to live in the United States. Those immigrants from the Azores, islands over nine hundred miles from Portugal, were able to gain legal documentation because of the 1965 Hart-Celler Act, which permitted family unification. However, immigrants from Brazil who lived in the same town had very few options to gain legal status (10–11). Vieira's book raises important questions for literacy education as it emphasizes and details the impact legal documentation has on people and their ability to pursue educational and career opportunities.

In addition to the impact of immigration papers, scholars stress the role of institutional racism on the writing classroom. April Baker-Bell, Tamara Butler, and Lamar Johnson discuss how many teachers, particularly those who are white and privileged, may be unaware of the impact of racism on their students' lives: "[W]e, as educators, are complicit in some of these acts of racial violence when we ignore the pain and overlook the wounds that Black and Brown youth bear as they sit in our classrooms, trying to listen to us lecture while the viral footage of Black and Brown death is replaying in their minds" (123). One step in being responsible teachers is to practice "critical race education," which requires teachers to think about their own perspectives, consider how their classrooms can respond to issues of racism, and find ways for their classes to enter "serious dialogues about how white supremacy, anti-blackness, anti-brownness, homophobia, and other forms of xenophobia lead to race-based violence" (125).

Because of this ingrained racism, universities are places, as Sara Ahmed discusses, of "institutional whiteness" (33) where academics of color confront systematic racism. Turning to scholarship that discusses race and citizenship status shifts the conversation about community writing and speaks to more student concerns/perspectives. In her introduction to *Vernacular Insurrections: Race, Black Protest, and the New Century in Composition-Literacies Studies,* Carmen Kynard writes that most writing faculty have not been trained adequately, and there is a lack of "focus on students of color" (5). In "From Candy Girls to Cyber Sista-Cipher: Narrating Black Females' Color-Consciousness and Counterstories in and out of School," Kynard compares the work of some academics to the Tuskegee experiment and questions the work of academia, particularly white educators, in making social change: "There was no institutional halt on white faculty chasing and receiving very real, material credentials while working in black communities, all the while ignoring the vanishing of black students at their own school" (42). Kynard's point resonates with Tomas's disappointment about his university's not doing enough to assist students when DACA was threatened and Claudio's observation that some schools weren't granting undocumented students in-state tuition. As universities engage in community engagement projects, they often ignore the students in their own classrooms.

One explanation, then, as to why students have been largely ignored in the scholarship is the problem of white supremacy and its effect on higher education. In his 2019 CCCC chair's address, "How Do We Language So People Stop Killing Each Other, or What Do We Do about White Language Supremacy?" Asao B. Inoue addresses white writing teachers in the audience: "You perpetuate White language supremacy in your classrooms because you are White and stand in front of students, as many White teachers have before you, judging, assessing, grading, professing on the same kinds of language standards, standards that came from your group of people." Inoue says that the solution is not to "soften our hearts," but that to make a better community and classroom, larger change is needed: "The key is changing the structures, cutting the steel bars, altering the ecology, in which your biases function in your classrooms and communities." And besides revising the ways that writing is taught and evaluated, as Inoue argues, we also need to consider the assumptions made about students, their citizenship status, and their relationship to community organizing. For example, a community-writing course based on encouraging students to become active citizens cannot ignore how citizenship excludes people. As Ana Milena Ribero comments, "[C]itizenship in its essence is built on exclusions that are largely based on racialized, gendered, and sexualized identities" (32):

> As the building block of the nation-state—itself a requisite for the workings of neocolonialism and neoliberalism—citizenship helps to delineate and reinforce national borders that constitute global hierarchies of social, political, military, and economic power, hierarchies that disproportionately benefit the Global North at the expense of the racialized peoples of the Global South. (33)

Although the Fourteenth Amendment to the US Constitution maintains that anyone born in the United States is a citizen, Ribero notes that there have been efforts to change this policy to stop citizenship for children whose parents are not documented, including the Birthright Citizenship Act of 2009 (33–34). Although this act was not passed into law, these efforts to stop certain children born in the United States from becoming citizens reflects a racist approach in defining citizenship:

> Although anchor babies supposedly threaten the United States by forwarding the Latinization of the nation—the browning of America—terror babies, believed to be US-born from women sent to the country by terrorist organizations, purportedly pose a violent threat to the nation because of their terrorist connections and the ease of cross-border migration made possible by their *jus soli* US citizenship. (Ribero 34)

As reflected in these racist terms to describe babies, Congress has regularly restricted who can be a citizen. With an economic engine of slavery and exploitation, the United States started by excluding everyone from being citizens except white men in the Naturalization Act of 1790. Although Congress later amended these acts and abolished slavery, we have a history of racist policies including the Chinese Exclusion Act (1882) and other laws that favored Europeans over immigrants from other parts of the world. But even with the 1965 Immigration and Nationality Act (the Hart-Celler Act), and the 1986 Immigration Reform and Control Act passed under the Reagan administration that permitted undocumented people to apply for legal status if they had lived in the United States since before 1982, the immigration system still prevents millions of people from becoming citizens ("Major US Immigration Laws").

Anti-immigrant efforts like Arizona's SB1070 law in 2010 continue this racial profiling by making it mandatory for people who are not citizens to always have documentation on them to show that they can legally be in the state (Ribero 35):

> Every alien, eighteen years of age and over, shall at all times carry with him and have in his personal possession any certificate of alien registration or alien registration receipt card issued to him pursuant to subsection (d) of this section. Any alien who fails to comply with the provisions of this subsection shall be guilty of a misdemeanor and shall upon conviction for each offense be fined not to exceed $100 or be

imprisoned not more than thirty days, or both. ("Arizona's Immigration Enforcement Laws")

Arizona's law dehumanizes people by giving police the power to profile them if they are suspected to be immigrants. Ribero adds, "Citizenship, then, is marked on the body through phenotypical characteristics (e.g., skin color, hair texture) and social traits (e.g., clothing, mannerisms, language use)" (35). Therefore, service-learning scholarship about citizenship must consider Ribero's critical reflection upon what citizenship means and who is excluded.

INTERSECTIONALITY

Multiple factors—including racism, white supremacy, economics, and gender—shape conversations about immigration and the writing classroom. In Mark's project, in which he was advocating for the rights of Filipino children with American fathers, for example, people had different access to citizenship based upon their ethnicity. They needed the resources to connect with their American fathers to apply for citizenship. Plus, the challenges facing students like Mark, one could argue, are a result of US militarism as US forces maintained a presence in the Philippines. Considering such points was not part of my graduate school training. One theoretical tool, then, in addressing how these different factors influence each other is intersectionality. As Patricia Hill Collins and Sirma Bilge discuss, injustice is "[s]haped not by a single axis of social division, be it race or gender or class, but by many axes that work together and influence each other" (2). Along with the Combahee River Collective and its statement that discusses "the intersection of multiple oppressions, including racism and heterosexism" (Anders), professor of law Kimberlé Crenshaw is credited with first using the term *intersectionality* to discuss the "intersecting patterns of racism and sexism" that can affect black women and other women of color with legal discrimination (1243). For example, Crenshaw discusses the requirement in the Immigration and Nationality Act that women stay married for two years to an American citizen before qualifying for a green card. If a woman found herself in an abusive relationship, it would be difficult to leave that marriage because doing so would jeopardize the possibility of a green card and citizenship. Therefore, issues of women's and immigrant rights intersect in this example. The Immigration Act of 1990 tried to respond to this problem by making it possible for women to report domestic abuse without affecting their chances for citizenship (Crenshaw 1247). However, even with this change, there are many other social factors to consider for women from marginalized groups: "Those immigrant women least able to take advantage of the waiver—women who are socially or economically the most marginal—are the ones most likely to be women of color" (1250). The law is more likely to help those women who have access to resources—lawyers, doctors, and psychologists—to gather evidence for their cases, and less likely to help those women without access to these resources or fluency in English. Women who are able to benefit from this change in the immigration law are more likely to have more economic resources and other privileges.

Racism plays a significant role in the conversation about who should be legalized as an immigrant. For example, many immigrants from Haiti are affected by a different immigration policy, TPS (Temporary Protected Status), and their rights as immigrants are sometimes left out of the conversation regarding Dreamers and DACA. And as noted by NYU Law and Black Alliance for Just Immigration's study, "Although African and Caribbean immigrants constituted only a small percentage of the immediately eligible population for DACA, the rates of application accepted and status approved for Black immigrants are lower when compared to all top 25 countries listed by USCIS" (17).

In addition, many students do not qualify for DACA based on a variety of factors, including at what age they came to this country. As the immigration system discriminates, some corporations profit from mass incarceration, ICE arrests, and detention centers, and this prison economy directly affects students and their families. According to the Migration Policy Institute's analysis of census data from 2012 to 2016, an estimated 11 million immigrants are undocumented in the United States, including over 2 million young people. People migrating from Mexico represent 53 percent of this group, 16 percent are from Asia, 14 percent Central America, 6 percent South America, 5 percent Europe/Canada/Oceania, 3 percent Caribbean, and 3 percent Africa ("Profile of the Unauthorized Population: United States"). Although nearly 750,000 gained DACA from 2012 to 2017 ("Consideration"), undocumented students pursue their degrees without permanent status and with the threat of deportation for themselves and their families. In this uncertainty from 2008 to 2016, over 3 million people were deported (see Figure 1.1). The Obama administration stated that they prioritized the deportation of criminals and created the DACA program, which will be discussed more in the next chapter. However, a *New York Times* 2014 study shows that two-thirds of those deported were undocumented people arrested for nonviolent offenses like driving with an expired license (Thompson and Cohen).

Intersectionality, then, can help address the reasons our government would deport over 3 million people between 2008 and 2016. Such a system is a money-making business with neoliberal policies that affect the most marginalized and disenfranchised in our communities. For example, Collins and Bilge connect the mass incarceration of people in prisons and detention centers to the ways that corporations try to take away the rights of workers. Therefore, corporations gain more power as many workers lose the ability to resist

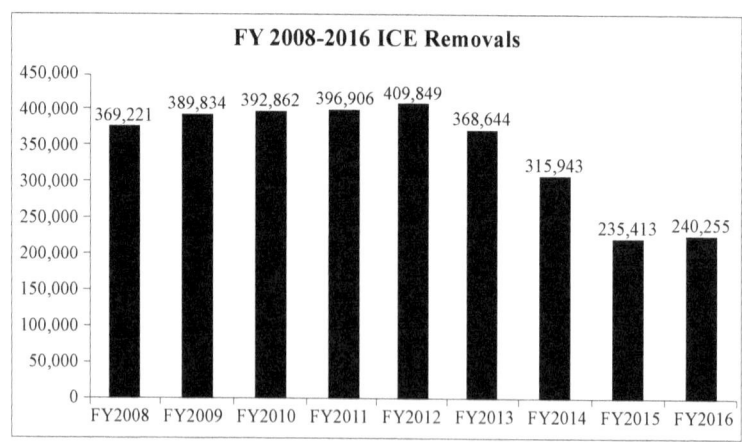

Figure 1.1. ICE removals for fiscal years 2008–2016. (Source: ice.gov.)

and have a greater likelihood of being incarcerated. The neoliberal state, then, has decreased regulations on corporations but has escalated the "securitization" or the control of people's lives (Collins and Bilge 155–56). There are many examples of this control, including racial profiling by the police, laws limiting the ability to protest, and the incarceration of more and more people of color. Although there has been a slight decrease in prison populations due to some states changing their sentencing policies (Gelb and Stevenson), the United States continues to be the number one country in the world in imprisoning its citizens. According to the Sentencing Project, this increase in incarceration has happened over the last four decades, with the number of people behind bars multiplying by five. The United States has 2.2 million people imprisoned ("Trends" 2). And as Michelle Alexander writes in *The New Jim Crow*, "Mass incarceration has been normalized . . . " (181), and African Americans are sentenced to jail "at more than 5 times the rate of whites" ("Criminal Justice Fact Sheet").

In addition to the 2.2 million people in prisons, every day at least 34,000 immigrants are required to be behind bars according to legislation passed by Congress. Detention centers (or prisons for immigrants) also have been normalized. In 2009, with a Democratic majority, Senator Robert Byrd (D–West Virginia) introduced a provision into a congressional bill that mandates that a certain number of undocumented immigrants be arrested and housed in detention centers (or prisons). The bill says that this detention center system "shall maintain a level of not less than 33,400 detention beds," funded by "not less than $2,545,180,000 [for] detention and removal operations" (United States, Congress, PL 111-83)). ICE has used this bill as a mandate that beds be filled with immigrants. There are 250 detention centers, mostly run by private corporations, holding immigrants at a cost to taxpayers of $120/day each ("Immigration Detention 101"). Some immigration-rights activists and organizers point out that private corporations like GEO Group have made campaign contributions to politicians, both Democrat and Republican, who vote on immigration legislation. For example, the last two congressional representatives in the district where my university in Miami is located and also where a detention center is maintained both received campaign contributions from GEO Group ("Influence and Lobbying"). The first was a Democrat and the second was a Republican. Therefore, one reason we have so many immigrants being arrested and detained is that corporations are able to make so much money from this business. Every year, private corporations earn $2 billion on these detention centers ("Immigration Detention 101"). In Chapter 4, I expand more on detention centers when describing a community project of visiting detainees. To distract the public from the effects of neoliberal policies, politicians often treat refugees and immigrants as criminals or possible terrorists. President Trump's executive orders illustrate this attitude: build a wall to stop people from coming into the country, imprison them, and deport them.

In addition, undocumented immigrants can be issued ITIN (Individual Tax ID) numbers so they can pay income tax. According to a report from the Institute on Taxation and Economic Policy, undocumented immigrants pay billions in taxes:

> Collectively, undocumented immigrants in the United States pay an estimated total of $11.64 billion in state and local taxes a year. . . . This includes more than $6.9 billion in sales and excise taxes, $3.6 billion in property taxes, and just under $1.1 billion in personal income taxes. (Gee, Gardner, Wiehe 2)

In addition, studies estimate that undocumented immigrants contribute $12 billion a year to Social Security, even though they are not eligible for such benefits (Goss et al. 3). Immigrants, then, contribute by paying taxes but they are denied any of those benefits because of their status. Government legislation regularly denies rights to immigrants, including the 2020 stimulus bill during the coronavirus pandemic that excludes undocumented immigrants from relief. Therefore, this immigration system profits on excluding people from their full rights. Laws and policies marginalize groups based upon their identities, and such exploitation reflects a neoliberal system that profits from mass incarceration. University classrooms can reflect these policies like excluding immigrant students or charging them higher tuition, and teachers' pedagogies need to challenge such marginalization of students.

PEDAGOGICAL SHIFT

As teachers, we need to build trust and better listen to the struggles that confront students who are undocumented. As Kynard argues, we need to examine how our research and teaching reflect our principles of community work. As seen in the prologue, Mohammad and others say that they've lost trust in academia, particularly when teachers have been unresponsive to immigrant student needs. In *Community Literacies* en Confianza: *Learning from Bilingual After-School Programs,* Steven Alvarez discusses the importance of trust between K–12 teachers and students and uses the term *confianza.* As Alvarez explains, "In English, *confianza* translates literally as 'confidence,' but in practice *confianza* means a reciprocal relationship in which individuals feel cared for" (4). To achieve such a relationship, Alvarez advises teachers to have "openness to students' complete linguistic repertoires" and focus on the importance of "local communities" as seen with successful after-school programs for bilingual learners. By listening and learning from students in the classroom, by developing this community literacy in K–12 and at the university, teachers can build the trust that often has been absent.

Even though many students are academically successful, there are other social factors that affect their studies. In the surveys of DACA recipients, Roberto Gonzales and Veronica Terriquez found that although DACA benefits many students, it does not remove the "threat of deportation" affecting their family members (1). Nearly all (94 percent) of those surveyed said they would like to become citizens if they could. Undocumented students encounter higher levels of stress and often feel isolated because of their status (Gonzales et al. 2). Students learn of their status at different moments in their lives (2). Although many undocumented students succeed, their status often can be a cause of great pain. Joachín Luna, an eighteen-year-old Texas high school senior, took his own life in November of 2011 as he struggled with high levels of stress associated with his status and inability to attend college (Logan). This incident motivates many organizers to help students like Joachín, and it should continue pushing teachers to incorporate activist work for undocumented students in their classrooms.

Although many service-learning scholars point out the separation of the university and the community, it is important to note how some students may not find it a safe place or an ivory tower. Besides the practice of universities discriminating against undocumented students, there is a history of policies that marginalize people:

> It is undeniable that schools have never been unilaterally safe spaces or even places of sanctuary. The examples abound through the time line of the nation. From the US Indian Bureau of Education that sought to strip Indigenous culture from sovereign Native peoples (Deloria, 1969), to the outlawing of literacy and schooling for enslaved Black peoples (Cutter, 1996), to the sequestered, substandard English-only mandates that have not so subtly told immigrant populations that they would only be liminally welcomed if they could approximate the practices of US-born monolingual students who grew up speaking standardized academic English. (Patel, "Immigrant Populations" 524)

Before Trump's policy of separating immigrant families requesting asylum at the border in 2018, previous administration's policies also criminalized immigrant children. For example, there have been widespread raids conducted by ICE imprisoning children who are undocumented ("Love Not Raids"). In North Carolina, high school senior Wildin Acosta was arrested in 2016 on his way to school, and there was subsequently a 20 percent drop in school attendance in Durham because of the fear immigrant students would be arrested (Boone). Also in 2016, seven-year-old Alisson was held for over six months in Berks Detention Center in Pennsylvania (Cambria). And some undocumented college students worry about being arrested by ICE on their way to class if their universities must follow the law, a point raised by Tomas about his university's response to

DACA being threatened: "FIU will always be a welcoming place for undocumented immigrants as long as FIU is in compliance with federal law." But the law often means arresting people because of their identity and status. Leigh Patel adds, "If schools are to be sanctuaries for immigrant populations, then they must dispense with the idea that these populations are less than their US-born counterparts. They must be respected and treated with respect for their own full humanness, not as prospective citizens on a path of assimilation" (528).

The community-engaged writing teacher, then, often has had an implied identity as a white citizen. And because of this assumed role, this pedagogy lacked a critical analysis of how white supremacy and anti-immigrant ideas were affecting the classroom and community. And so much of this pedagogical approach assumed that students were citizens, and that we need to encourage students to become more active citizens. This community-engaged teacher prioritized partner needs over student concerns. This pedagogical approach organized the structure and nature of students' community work and what they should learn. This approach failed to acknowledge the rich rhetorical skills that many students possess in challenging racist, neoliberal policies. And this disciplinary role shaped my initial pedagogy when teaching community writing. Although much scholarship acknowledges that university-community partnerships can be problematic and exploit marginalized communities, implicit in these partnerships is the image of a college student volunteering with a community agency and the faculty member helping to facilitate this relationship. Such a framework can overlook the ways in which many students were responding to an exploitive neoliberal system.

Students helped move me out of that role into a different kind of work for students like Mark and the writers described by Sara P. Alvarez. Also, the scholarship of Kynard, Ribero, Vieira, Inoue, and others raised important questions about institutional racism. With millions of undocumented people prevented from becoming citizens, the community partnership model didn't fit. There were issues directly affecting students, and some students had started to organize to change anti-immigrant and racist policies. As Alvarez discusses, undocumented students were organizing against the racist policies affecting their ability to attend school and the futures of their families. They were challenging a system in ways that many service-learning projects were not. Their voices and ideas often were not part of the curriculum. And although not all of the students in our classrooms are confronting these issues, we do not always have to travel off campus to meet organizers working for social change: many organizers are at the desks right in front of us in the classroom.

Our field has a rich history of scholars advocating for social justice and for pedagogies focused on community-based writing and service-learning, but this book proposes a different framework, a reimagining of what community writing and engagement is needed. How can we create an atmosphere in the writing classroom and writing center that respects all students, including those who are undocumented? What can we do on our campuses to address the unequal status of undocumented students? How can our assignments invite students to become engaged with this issue and others that affect them in their writing? These are some of the questions that guide the remaining chapters.

THE CHAPTERS THAT FOLLOW

The chapters that follow attempt to continue the conversation started by Alvarez, Vieira, and other scholars. Chapter 2 focuses on the rhetorical skills that immigrant rights organizers often use to stop deportations. The chapter begins with a story about a campaign to stop a student's deportation and how a group called the North Carolina DREAM Team was able to stop this student's deportation. Petitions and op-eds became tools in a network of action to keep a family together.

Chapter 3 begins with a protest for immigrant rights that took place in Charlotte one year before the Democratic National Convention. The experience of having student organizers stay in my home, be arrested at a protest, and then continue their work once freed shows the complex ways that they advocate for change. This chapter discusses how their advocacy work can offer a new lens for the public-writing classroom.

Chapter 4 discusses off-campus projects, including a visitation program at a detention center near my university, writing letters to detainees, and campaigns to stop deportations. The chapter focuses on a campaign to stop the deportation of a father that evolved into a letter-writing project for those detained.

Chapter 5 concludes by discussing some guiding principles for this new pedagogical framework. In addition, I am including a revised syllabus of the community-writing course that I'm teaching now (see pages 143–50), which contrasts with the course discussed in this first chapter.

2

Petitions to Stop Deportations

> It was a nightmare coming from the police department to my brother's empty room, knowing he was spending the night in a jail cell. This was the first of three sleepless nights I spent wondering when I would see my brother again, and praying he would not be transferred to a detention center in Georgia. . . . The fear that I allowed to rule me began to dissipate. I would no longer remain silent. I would no longer encourage my brother to take a voluntary departure. It was time to share our story; it was time to speak out, to break the shackles of fear we allowed to enslave us. Only with courage will we have an opportunity to help our community, to ask for accountability, and to point out the discrepancy between politicians' words and the actions of local governments against undocumented youth.
>
> This is why I am coming out—to share my brother's story, to share my story, and to be a voice who encourages others to come out of the shadows.
>
> —Angelica Velazquillo, "Fighting Together"

ON THE NORTH CAROLINA DREAM Team website a few weeks before her brother's trial, Angelica writes about the decision to go public with her undocumented status. Angelica's writing reflects many of the reasons undocumented students decide to go public: they are responding to an oppressive immigration system. Indeed, after feeling "betrayed" by a country that would imprison and threaten to deport her brother, Angelica connects with a group in North Carolina that works to stop his deportation.

In their work for immigrant rights, student organizers confront an immigration system based in white supremacy, and resisting such racist policies requires complex rhetorical moves. Sara P. Alvarez points out that these students "[a]re in a seemingly constant battle of fighting to attain basic rights, like pursuing education, but also realizing that their constant struggles in seeking citizenship as non-white people have long histories in their US context" (103). As they respond to the law's requirement that someone be a benefit to the community, organizers use petitions and other public writings, which become part of a network of action, based on the belief that everyone deserves rights. This chapter, then, discusses student organizers' framing of coming-out stories, particularly in their nuanced use of Americanism/nationalism and the complex identities at work. It concludes by reflecting upon how this important work has relevance for the community writing classroom.

To do this work, the chapter focuses on Erick, Angelica's brother, who was facing deportation, and the youth organizers who rallied to help him. Angelica was a student profiled by the Hispanic Cultural Center of Charlotte, where I volunteered from 2007 to 2008. As we prepared a college fair for immigrant students, this organization created videos of immigrant students and their stories of going to college. Angelica also helped with a street theater project a group of us created in the summer of 2010 in response to the Arizona SB1070 anti-immigrant legislation and the appearance of copycat bills across the country, including in North Carolina. This chapter aims to centralize Angelica and her family's experiences as they cope with deportation, because it shows how a youth-led organization, the North Carolina DREAM Team, used writing and activism to help. Such work reflects the END (Education Not Deportation) campaigns taking place in communities across the country.

FRAMING PETITIONS WITH AMERICANISM: "EVERYONE IS A LOW PRIORITY"

Organizers use nuanced nationalistic language to respond to an oppressive immigration system. This rhetorical deployment of Americanism makes it possible to argue that everyone is exceptional and everyone deserves rights. Mohammad, one of the organizers in DreamActivist and the National Immigrant Youth Alliance, stresses the importance of arguments based on what has been written:

Always ask for what is already promised to you on paper. Because it's easier to hold people accountable to, but you just ask for what the Obama administration is already promising you that they'd do . . . so my interpretation of that was just sort of like our low priority memos [for deportation]. It's the same thing. You know, yes, they say low priority [for deportation] is people XYZ, but they also say if it's in the public benefit [that someone is not deported]. So in our eyes, everyone is a low priority. It's just the matter of the community actually holding them accountable to what they promised you on paper . . . . —Mohammad

By focusing on what is said on paper—what is promised by the law—organizers can use that language and argue that everyone is an exceptional community member and represents "the public benefit." So although the law discriminates against people because of their status and race/ethnicity, there also is the opportunity to persuade others that a person is a positive addition to the community and cannot be separated from being "American" (even if they may not identify as American). The fact that these organizers must argue for their worth to the community reflects unjust, racist laws, but this public sharing of stories through petitions, rallies, and vigils challenges white supremacist ideas embedded in the public discourse about immigration.

Such a strategy, then, is responding to white supremacist ideas about who is deserving of citizenship and who is not. In "Illegal," Amanda Espinosa-Aguilar discusses the words *illegal* and *immigrant*. An immigrant can be a citizen, a permanent resident, someone with a student visa, or someone with no visa, but the language of white supremacy often questions all immigrants' legality, identity, and worth. Espinosa-Aguilar then continues her examination of the terms *citizen* and *immigrant:* "In today's political climate, these words are understood as opposites: the first implying a native-born person, the second meaning an alien" (95). This divisive rhetoric of immigration, then, separates people into native-born and the other. Evidence of this language is seen in laws like the Illegal Immigration Reform and Immigrant Responsibility Act of 1996. Section

287(g) has been criticized by many immigrant rights organizers, because it permits police officers to become involved with immigration law and inquire about citizenship status. Therefore, if the police suspect someone is an immigrant, they would be able to enter their names into a federal database to check their citizenship status, and they can keep them in jail until ICE can send them to a detention center. Not all communities participate in these agreements as it is a local decision whether to cooperate or not; however, a routine traffic stop could lead to someone being deported, and it's difficult to separate the issue of race from such a process. Such laws reflect a dominant public discourse that treats every immigrant as the other and as a criminal. In a 2013 study of hundreds of students from Los Angeles, Washington State, New York City, and Boston, respondents discussed "intense feelings of isolation and hopelessness derived from the extreme concealment, self-censure, and hyper-awareness about others discovering 'who they really are'" (Gonzales et al. 12). Anti-immigrant policies, then, greatly affect the lives of students and their families across the country.

The United States has a history of excluding nonwhite people from citizenship (Ribero); therefore, crafting petitions to respond to such a system is a challenging rhetorical task in how to frame the argument. As Claudia Anguiano notes in her study of the DREAMer movement, one of the first rhetorical moves was "to shift the negative associations with the notion of *undocumented* to positive" (100). Organizers find that it can be rhetorically effective to argue that someone is a positive community member and that someone embodies the ideals of America while at the same time redefining or challenging Americanism. According to historians Michael Kazin and Joseph A. McCartin, "'Americanism' has two different meanings. It signifies both what is distinctive about the United States (and the colonies and territories that formed it) and loyalty to that nation, rooted in a defense of its political ideals" (1). As the language of a petition invokes Americanism, the narrative often becomes one of American individualism and exceptionalism. As Roberto G. Gonzales explains this rhetorical act, "The framing of undocumented youth as innocent children or as truly American has proven such a successful strategy for the promotion of their deservingness that it has become the basis for this group's full legal inclusion" (175). But as Gonzales and student organizers point out, this kind of "framing" can exclude other immigrants if an argument implies that other immigrants are not as American, including parents who may not be defined as "DREAMers." Organizers avoid such framing as they compose their narratives.

In this advocacy work, the writing of petitions reflects an intricate relationship with home. Alvarez comments that undocuactivists can be "in constant friction with the boundaries of the state they call home" (102–03) and "[o]ften contest nationalist ideologies of belonging" (104). As she discusses what she finds distinctive in their writing—what she calls "conciencia bilingüe" (57)—Alvarez highlights the complexity of their identity:

> (1) They are Americans "without papers"; (2) They speak English, but also seek to sustain the languages tied to their ethnic communities; (3) They work hard and want an education, but there is legislation that prevents them from accessing higher education; (4) They navigate and graduate from a difficult—nearly impossible—higher education system in which they must pay their tuition on their own, but they cannot obtain jobs. (103–4)

One undocumented activist interviewed by Alvarez comments that she does not consider the place of her birth as her hometown but sees the place where she grew up and the community she knows as home. However, Alvarez notes, "Sandra's description of hometown would make her the bicultural American that she appears to be, but it is important to remember that she is not American" (94). Therefore, this kind of writing often reflects a complex identification of home.

For example, the North Carolina DREAM Team helped a high school student facing deportation in 2011 and used the following petition:

The Petition

To Assistant Secretary of Homeland Security John Morton and Secretary of Homeland Security Janet Napolitano:

We, the undersigned, write to humbly request that you take immediate action to stop the deportation of Rodrigo (A# XXX-XXX-XXX).

Rodrigo was brought to the United States when he was only ten years old. Originally from Mexico, for the past six years he has made Charlotte, North Carolina, his home. Now sixteen years old, Rodrigo finds himself fighting his deportation to a country he no longer calls his home.

On January 3, 2011, Rodrigo was accused of shoplifting at his local mall. Since North Carolina is one of only two states that prosecute sixteen- and seventeen-year-olds as adults, Rodrigo, despite being sixteen, was processed through the 287-g program. Since that day the criminal charges have been dropped, yet Immigration and Customs Enforcement still wants to deport him to a country that is no longer his home. Rodrigo is nothing but a normal high school student with strong ties to his school and community. He fears being separated from his parents and brother. Please take immediate action to stop Rodrigo's deportation.

Rodrigo attended Montclair Elementary and Sedgefield Middle School, and is currently a sophomore at Harding University High School in North Carolina. He was an outstanding student with grades above average, until his life took a turn for the worse the day of his arrest. In the weeks following, Rodrigo began to suffer from insomnia because he had little to no knowledge about how the judicial system worked. He didn't know what would happen next and was terrified of being deported and separated from all he knows and loves.

Rodrigo wants to pursue the American dream. He dreams of graduating from high school in Charlotte and going to college to study international relations and franchise management. He and his family attend St. Gabriel's Catholic Church in Charlotte regularly. He has been a Boy Scout for the last three years, where he has learned values of honor and duty. As a Boy Scout, he volunteers to help coach soccer with kids ages 6–10. Rodrigo wants to continue living his life in Charlotte and contribute to his community.

Rodrigo would qualify for the DREAM Act, a narrowly tailored bill that majorities in both the House and the Senate voted to support this past December. Both President Obama and Secretary of Homeland Security Janet Napolitano have stated that DREAM Act–eligible youth are not a priority for deportation. In a recent announcement, Secretary Napolitano stated new guidelines for prosecutorial discretion. According to these guidelines, Rodrigo is not deemed a priority for removal by DHS and merits a favorable exercise of discretion. Rodrigo exemplifies what it means to be an American and should be allowed to stay in the United States to live his American Dream. Education is extremely important to Rodrigo, and his deportation would mean the end of his educational goals. Rodrigo wants the opportunity to finish high school and pursue his dreams just like the rest of his classmates. Please help keep Rodrigo in the country with his family and supportive community.

We, the undersigned, urge you to take immediate action to stop Rodrigo's deportation.

The language of the petition emphasizes American identity. Rodrigo is described as "nothing but a normal high school student with strong ties to his school and community." The petition includes the various local public schools that he has attended and comments on his good grades. The petition includes details about his time with the Boy Scouts, volunteering, and his religious affiliation. At the same time, his story is contextualized by discussing stated government policies; according to the Obama administration, "DREAM Act eligible youth are not a priority for deportation." In other words, the government has promised not to deport students like Rodrigo. The petition concludes with discussion of his desire to live the "American Dream" and pursue education as he stays with his family. This petition was also part of other actions, including a media campaign in newspapers, radio, and television. In addition, there were rallies and a discussion about his case after a theatrical production about immigration. When Rodrigo was asked to go to the immigration office, he was required to check in and show proof he had bought a ticket to Mexico for his scheduled deportation. After he entered the facility, officials likely saw the crowd gathered outside, including a local radio station covering the event. His deportation had been deferred and he was able to stay in the country. Invoking Americanism in this petition was successful when combined with these other actions. Such an action emphasized Rodrigo as emblematic of the American dream but also publicized the inconsistencies in American immigration law and its enforcement by ICE.

COMING OUT OF THE SHADOWS

Besides composing petitions, organizers also share personal stories through rallies, vigils, and online platforms. During team-building Face to Face events, members discuss strategy, know-your-rights trainings, and other rhetorical skills. One activity, called the "Story of Self," focuses on how to share your personal story in a public space. To *come out of the shadows,* many students share their own personal stories at on- and off-campus events, at rallies, and through writing. In workshops, the presenters discuss how to structure such stories, particularly focusing on how a person can frame their experience—the challenge confronted, a choice to be made, and the outcome. This approach may resonate with other "story of self" trainings for advocacy groups whereby people structure personal stories in such a way that they connect with an audience's emotions and also provide analysis for a larger social issue. Student organizers in the immigrant rights movement often invoke and challenge American identity through such stories of self as seen in published texts like *Undocumented and Unafraid*. Genevieve Negrón-Gonzales connects these stories of self to the act of testimonio:

> Testimonio is an important site for the reconfiguration of this punitive framework. Testimonio is a practice of "documenting silenced histories" (Latina Feminist Group 2001), a way

of telling one's story in one's own words in order to make meaning of it and reclaim its power. Testimonio as a written form has a long history in resistance movements in Latin America, and it has been utilized widely in the undocumented student movement to challenge fundamental public notions of what an undocumented person looks like (Negrón-Gonzales 2014). ("Undocumented Youth Activism" 102).

Such complex storytelling, as Mohammad comments earlier, can be an "energizing, powerful, therapeutic thing" for undocumented people. In "Undocumented Identity Storytelling: (Re)framing Public Relations," Anna V. Ortiz Juarez-Paz discusses the ways in which undocumented youth share personal stories to connect with one another and challenge the system:

> The USM [Undocumented Student Movement] has created a culture in which an immigration story is something powerful, a tool used to communicate resistance, perfectly normal and even necessary to share with friends and strangers. This culture that embraces said stories is at the base of their resistance against marginalizing processes and against structures that attempt to erase their humanity. (171)

Ortiz discusses her findings based on seventeen interviews and two years participating in the movement, including time spent at the US/Mexico border. She comments that storytelling can "build solidarity" (171) among the group and "frame the USM as a human rights movement" (175). The stories become more than just helping one group gain status: "What was once a movement to pass the DREAM Act, has now become a movement seeking a path to citizenship for all, not just students" (175).

A common refrain at rallies and one that is written on signs and t-shirts is "to come out of the shadows," and several scholars have compared the LGBTQ+ movement and the undocumented youth movement in sharing these coming-out stories. For example, in *Identity, Social Activism, and the Pursuit of Higher Education,* Susana M. Muñoz comments, "While both the LGBTQ population and undocumented immigrants share similar risks and consequences for disclosure, each group brings differences in how members came to know their identities" (56). Muñoz mentions that revealing that you are undocumented is not something you usually have to reveal to your family and includes a network of support in the family. Coming out as gay, though, "[m]ay risk the loss of a relationship with an immediate family member as a result of their disclosure, which creates differentials within their support networks" (56). However, organizers also note how these two movements intersect. In an op-ed, "How Queer Undocumented Youth Built the Immigrant Rights Movement," Prerna Lal and Tania Unzueta, two leaders in the immigrant rights movement, emphasize the significant number of immigrant leaders who identify as queer and the different strategies they use as community organizers: "From our lived LGBT experiences, we knew that the way to formal equality for undocumented immigrants was to use our stories as our weapon, to 'come out' as undocumented, just as we had come out as gay, lesbian, or transgender." The National Immigrant Youth Alliance (NIYA) started using the term *undocuqueer* to come out as both undocumented and queer. And Lal and Unzueta conclude that when talking about the immigrant rights movement of the last decade, "queer undocumented youth built it" (Lal and Unzueta). This movement reflects an intersectional approach in their work for both LGBTQ+ rights and immigrant rights. And in this movement, "coming out" in a public space often means taking a risk as someone finds support and strength from a group.

One of the first nationally publicized sharings of stories took place in 2010 when four students from Miami Dade College walked fifteen hundred miles from Miami to Washington DC to tell their stories about the challenges facing undocumented students and families. The trip was called the "Trail of Dreams," and the four students, Carlos, Gaby, Felipe, and Juan, told stories about the pressures facing undocumented families. This walk to DC received national media coverage. At stops in different cities, Gaby Pacheco, for example, talked about what it was like to see immigration officials raid her family's home (Hutchinson, "Story Time in Arizona"). In "Trail of Dreams," Pacheco writes about her story and her family's story:

Every year my family wavers between feeling depressed and fighting to stay. My family received a final order to leave the country in 2009.

Living in the shadows was safer, but because of my public fight, they now live in a dangerous light. I believe that being undocumented means we need to take risks and lift our voices instead of settling for a life full of uncertainty. I have to remind myself that it is an oppressive, broken system that forces us to make these difficult and heartbreaking decisions. (57)

Undocumented and Unafraid: Tam Tran, Cinthya Felix, and the Immigrant Youth Movement, part of a three-book series about undocumented youth published by the UCLA Center for Labor Research and Education, includes other powerful stories of youth advocating for change, including those of Tam Tran and Cinthya Felix, two initial leaders who advocated for the DREAM Act. Tran shared her story before Congress in 2007, and three days later, ICE "[s]taged a predawn raid on her family's home in Orange County and took her parents and brother into custody" (Wong and Ramos). She was able to organize and gain their release, but sharing a story even on Capitol Hill can be a significant risk.

Other undocumented students have told their stories before Congress, including Marie Gonzalez, whom I interviewed in 2008 as I was writing a play about DREAMers (discussed more in Chapter 5). Marie came to the United States when she was five years old. While she was in college, her parents were deported to Costa Rica. She became an activist for the DREAM Act as she attended Westminster College in Fulton, Missouri, majoring in political science and international business. In 2007, she testified before Congress:

> My family is originally from Costa Rica. I was born in Alajuela, Costa Rica, but have been living in the United States since the age of five. My parents, Marina and Marvin, brought me to the United States in November of 1991. Having come over legally, their plan was to become US citizens so we could one day all benefit from living in the land of the

free. We sought to live the "American Dream"—the promise of a better education, a better life, and altogether a better future—what any parent would [want] for their child. . . . I can personally attest to how life in limbo is no way to live. Having been torn apart from my parents for almost two years and struggling to make it on my own, I know what it is like to face difficulty and how hard it is to fight for your dreams. (United States, Congress, House)

After speaking out and advocating for the rights of undocumented students, Marie was able to receive a special visa sponsored by Senator Richard Durbin of Illinois and complete her studies and graduate. However, many students live a "life in limbo" because achieving citizenship can be impossible.

Besides rallies and testimony in Congress, organizers use online platforms to share stories. In "DREAMing Citizenship," Liana Gamber-Thompson and Arely Zimmerman discuss the ways that these stories can be posted online: "Sharing one's story involves high risk, and thus doing so fosters an ethos of trust, mutuality, and reciprocity that contributes to a sense of collective identification both in online and offline spaces." Gamber-Thompson and Zimmerman point out that such online work is not "slacktivism," which often can be seen as requiring less commitment and being less effective. To share a video of a coming out story is a risk but can have a powerful effect. In addition, the sharing of the story and the petition is combined with action, as Mohammad stresses:

And then we found . . . stories of like one person that specifically had like a heart-wrenching story of not being able to go to college and then her sister was sick, and these sorts of things, and so we sort of crafted this story of hers and put it in the email and then we just sent it to all the professors—in our minds thinking that you know these are folks that are respected, and if they are to reach out and understand the issue, then it will change. . . . [I]t was this very naive notion of like, "Oh, if people just knew our stories, then things would change." That's the only thing that's lacking. People just don't know our stories. So that was sort of the first campaign and the DREAM Act failed in October 2007. And after it failed, a lot of us who were in the online forum, we sort of were trying to push other people to do more. . . . Let's be more active in actually changing things. And so that's how we started DreamActivist was we wanted to have a space for community for dreamers, but we also wanted to be activists.

Mohammad points out, then, that the movement changed from just the sharing of stories to activism. The stories themselves couldn't create change unless they were organized and acted upon. Therefore, organizers share stories and compose petitions by deploying a set of complex rhetorical moves. Stories can emphasize how a person benefits the community and reflects the ideals of the American dream. At the same time, though, the story is shared in ways that challenge an oppressive, racist immigration system. Just writing the petition, or sharing the story, is not enough. A network of action is required to elevate the case in the public eye and garner community support.

ERICK, ANGELICA, AND THE NORTH CAROLINA DREAM TEAM

When her brother was arrested, both he and Angelica seriously considered leaving the country. Lawyers and one of the local nonprofit immigration groups told them that they didn't have a chance to fight his deportation, and even though they both would have qualified for the DREAM Act, it didn't matter since it had never passed. According to this thinking, Erick was going to be deported, and so Angelica and her brother were preparing to leave. It seemed as if there was no other option.

Then Angelica learned about a rally for undocumented youth ninety miles away in Greensboro. She was invited by one of the members of the North Carolina DREAM Team, a group of undocumented youth and students challenging the anti-immigrant laws in our state. I had read about the DREAM Team in the newspaper when they went on a hunger strike outside Senator Hagan's office in Raleigh in support of the DREAM Act. I contacted them about joining a rally that summer in Charlotte against the Arizona SB1070 law and told Angelica I was impressed with their skills as community organizers.

But when Angelica called me and asked whether I thought she should go with one of them to the Greensboro rally, I was hesitant to answer. Because of citizenship and privilege, I am not risking so much when I go to a rally, do street theater, or express my viewpoint in a public forum. But for Angelica and others, it is a big decision to go to such a rally, and it made a significant difference in her life, as she comments in the prologue. As discussed by Ortiz, Anguiano, and others, participants in a coming-out rally often discuss their own personal stories and how anti-immigrant policies affect their lives. Even though many youths are advised to be quiet and avoid publicity, many students and organizers argue that speaking out is important and necessary to regain power in your community. At the rally, the North Carolina DREAM Team learned about Erick's situation and started to organize a campaign to stop his deportation. The group took the lead and created this petition:

STOP ERICK'S DEPORTATION!

Erick's future will be decided in a few days. On July 19th, an immigration judge will decide if Erick can stay home in the US. Please take action now to stop his deportation: Sign the petition and make the calls!

Erick came to the United States when he was only two years old. Now twenty-two, he has lived in North Carolina for the majority of his life. One night driving home from the gym, Erick was pulled over in Matthews, North Carolina, for driving with his high beams on. He was arrested and spent three days in jail.

On July 19, a judge in immigration court in Charlotte, North Carolina, might send him back to a country he doesn't remember. Erick is an athlete and an aspiring nutritionist; he has every desire to stay and live in the United States as the American he already is. If deported, he will be sent back to a country he hasn't been to in twenty years!

PLEASE FORWARD THIS PETITION AND ACTION ALERT TO 5 OF YOUR FRIENDS!

1. Call Senator Hagan (202-224-6342)

Sample Script: "Hi, I was calling to ask that Senator Hagan introduce a private bill for Erick (A# XXX-XX-XXXX). Erick has been living in the United States since he was two years old. If deported, he will be returned to a country he hasn't been to in twenty years. Erick wants to contribute to this country as a nutritionist. Please introduce a private bill for Erick."

2. Call DHS—Janet Napolitano (202-282-8495) and ICE—John Morton (202-732-3000)

Sample Script: "Hi, I was calling to ask that Erick's deportation be deferred. Erick (A# XXX-XX-XXXX) has been living in the United States since he was two years old. If deported, he will be returned to a country he hasn't been to in twenty years. Erick wants to contribute to this country as a nutritionist. Don't deport Erick."

3. Sign the petition to your right and ask all of your friends to sign it! Together we can stop Erick's deportation; please take 5 minutes and complete these 3 easy steps!

Your Contact Information
First Name*
Last Name
Email*
Zip*
* Required information
The Petition

To Senator Kay Hagan, Assistant Secretary of Homeland Security John Morton, and Secretary of Homeland Security Janet Napolitano:

We, the undersigned, write to humbly request that you take action to immediately stop the deportation of Erick (A# XXX-XX-XXXX).

Erick came to the United States when he was only two years old. Now twenty-two, he has lived in North Carolina for the majority of his life. Despite having lived in the United

States for twenty years and considering this country his home, Erick finds himself fighting his deportation to a country he no longer remembers.

One night, driving home from the gym, Erick was pulled over in Matthews, North Carolina, for driving with his high beams on. After he told the officer that his ID was in his gym bag, the officer searched his car. Upon finding it and seeing a surname, the officer assumed Erick was giving him false information. He was arrested for driving without a license and giving fictitious information to an officer. He spent three days in jail before his family was able to pay his immigration bond. Erick left humiliated, being treated like a criminal.

On July 19, a judge in immigration court in Charlotte, North Carolina, might send him back to a country he doesn't remember. Erick is an athlete and an aspiring nutritionist; he has every desire to stay and live in the US as the American he already is.

In North Carolina, undocumented immigrants can no longer get drivers' licenses. The people who do have them will soon see them expire and will be unable to renew them, leaving them vulnerable to dragnet programs like 287(g) and Secure Communities. Despite the memo by DHS Assistant Secretary John Morton, there are no guarantees that ICE field offices will stop putting undocumented youth in deportation proceedings. That is why you need to take action.

Erick would qualify for the DREAM Act, a narrowly tailored bill that majorities in both the House and the Senate voted to support this past December. Secretary of Homeland Security Janet Napolitano and President Obama have both stated that deporting DREAM-eligible youth is not a priority. We ask that you immediately take action to stop Erick's deportation so he can continue to contribute to his community.

If deported, Erick would be returned to a country he no longer considers his home. Please take action to stop his deportation.

We, the undersigned, urge you to take immediate action to stop Erick's deportation.

A student-led campaign started, and organizers asked for signatures on a petition to stop Erick's deportation. A petition was chosen because it can be used in activating a network of action and encourage a larger number of people to speak out on this issue. For example, Angelica, Erick, and I set up a table in the Charlotte arts district, NoDa, and encouraged people walking by to sign the petition or access it online. When people heard Erick's story and met him in person, most signed. Most people were surprised and shocked that the government would want to deport someone who had lived in the United States since he was two years old.

Signing the petition, then, sent a message about Erick and immigration policy to decision makers. Also, the petition asked for other actions: telephoning US Senator Hagan and contacting the Secretary of Homeland Security, Janet Napolitano. Different audiences could do different things. Senators could create a private bill to help Erick, and ICE had the discretion to drop the case. And the final part of the petition gave background on the North Carolina Driver's License Law and the DREAM Act. The petition places Erick's case in a political context: "Secretary of Homeland Security Janet Napolitano and President Obama have both stated that deporting DREAM-eligible youth is not a priority" yet such deportations are continuing. John Morton, the Director of ICE under President Obama, issued a memorandum in June 2011 that stressed the role of prosecutorial discretion and advised that ICE would not target low-priority cases, including students, for deportation (Memorandum). In his memo to ICE, Morton lists several different factors to consider when dropping a deportation case, and two of those include when someone came to the country and their educational pursuits:

- the circumstances of the person's arrival in the United States and the manner of his or her entry, particularly if the alien came to the United States as a young child

- the person's pursuit of education in the United States, with particular consideration given to those who have graduated from a US high school or have successfully pursued or are pursuing a college or advanced degrees at a legitimate institution of higher education in the United States

Also, one other factor would be "the person's ties and contributions to the community, including family relationships." The memo then concludes by saying ICE should drop such low-priority cases as quickly as possible. Such a memo is problematic in the sense that it creates categories of immigrants and prioritizes some over others. However, even though this was the official memo, many ICE offices were not enforcing this policy, and they continued to deport students like Erick.

Petitions like those created by the North Carolina DREAM Team show the complex rhetorical moves and labor used by organizers as they refused to be told that nothing could be done. Even though lawyers and a nonprofit organization told them the case was hopeless, they persisted. They purposefully "came out of the shadows" and challenged federal immigration policy by their petition, television and newspaper interviews, and pressure on ICE to enforce the Morton memo. In these contexts, everyone is exceptional. Everyone deserves freedom. And everyone has something to contribute to the American dream even if we might challenge the traditional narrative of that dream. Even though the invoking of Americanism can be problematic, if done correctly it can be effective in a campaign to stop a deportation. Erick's petition, for example, emphasizes that the United States is his home and reflects on what it means to be an American: "Erick is an athlete and an aspiring nutritionist; he has every desire to stay and live in the US as the American he already is. If deported, he will be sent back to a country he hasn't been to in twenty years!" There is an ethical dimension, then, to the invoking of Americanism.

Therefore, this petition reflects the rhetorical skills needed in challenging nativist discourse and resisting a system that treats immigrants as criminals and prevents them from becoming citizens. Although organizers may not identify with the term *American*, the writing emphasizes the ties that the person has with the community, their American dreams, and their good work as a community member. At the same time, though, organizers are precise in their language so that it doesn't treat one immigrant as American and another immigrant as less American. Their writing, then, reflects a complex identification of home (S. P. Alvarez). Petitions and other narratives can make an argument that the United States is home even if a person's identity connects to more than one community or place.

VIGILS, PR, AND COURTS

The story of Angelica's brother continued to be publicized in the weeks before the trial as the DREAM Team organized a vigil at a Catholic church downtown, wrote press releases, and contacted the media. At the vigil, individuals stood up in front of the pews and explained why deporting this college student was wrong. People were encouraged to light candles and also to make phone calls to ICE and Congress. The local newspapers and television news covered the story in Spanish and English and interviewed Erick too. The campaign generated more than one thousand calls and emails to ICE, and the petition received close to three thousand signatures in support of Erick (Ordoñez). Sometimes media campaigns like this one (often called END campaigns to stop a deportation) can be successful in raising the profile of a case so that the public can speak out in support of someone (as discussed more in Chapter 4).

Erick's lawyer was not convinced that all this would make a difference, but the North Carolina DREAM Team persisted. When the group accompanied Erick into the courtroom in July 2011, a lot was at stake. If the judge ruled against him, Erick would be deported to a country that he did not know and separated from his family. The decision was also determined by the discretion of ICE—whether they wanted to follow the Morton memo or not. Fortunately, his deportation order was dropped and he was able to stay in the country and continue with his studies (Coscia; Hutchinson, "Help Students"). After the group left the court, there was a press conference outside with people holding signs like "Education for everyone." As the news reported this story and all of the community support, the profile of Erick's case was raised, and many felt that effort made the difference, particularly since three million other people were deported from 2008 to 2016. After the campaign to help Erick, the group continued to work with other students in similar situations, including high school students. But even with this victory, Erick's status had not changed. He was still subject to arrest and deportation at any time unless the law was changed (or until DACA was approved, as discussed in the next chapter).

As organizers stop deportations, people's status usually is still in limbo. Kate Vieira's work in *American by Paper* shows how a piece of paper—a legal document—greatly determines a person's ability to stay in the country and the opportunities they will have, including a sense of belonging and a literacy determined by citizenship status. As she discusses the different experiences of Brazilian and Azorean Americans living in a Massachusetts town, those with legal documents gained more access: "Papers allowed Azoreans and Azorean Americans a kind of mobility often denied the undocumented: as citizens or permanent residents, they populated the immigration office, hospitals, police force, schools, and banks" (45). Vieira notes that legislation like DACA (which focuses on younger people who came to the United States before they were sixteen) can create distinctions between different immigrants: "As this policy, or any future policy, is put into action, transnational migrants will be learning literacy from their particular state-defined positions, with their attendant rights and restrictions. Some will write to attain papers under new legislation, or to help family members attain papers. Others will write with the knowledge that they are, again, left out of the bureaucratic net of the nation state" (152).

Student organizers often resist these categories. Angelica, for example, doesn't identify with the term *DREAMer*, because she feels it "classifies and labels a group of young adults who are seen as worthy of a more humane treatment than our parents." She came to the United States when she was four years old. Angelica is proud of her parents and doesn't want to "criminalize" them. She notes that students have "multiple identities": "You're not just a student, but you're also someone who doesn't have documentation, or you might be part of a mixed-status family—then you have additional worries. You're not just thinking about your grades and school, but you're sometimes worried about coming home and not seeing your parents or your siblings because they might be detained or you yourself could be detained. . . ." As Muñoz notes, "The notion of the 'perfect DREAMer' perpetuates the assumption that only those with high scholastic abilities or those who most resemble assimilationist perspectives of 'American' values are most deserving of legal status" (83). But in her study of activists in the movement, Muñoz comments that many started to see "[t]hat activism is no longer about them or the DREAM Act; activism has become a much broader issue" (84). Student organizers, then, are not just focused on passing the DREAM Act or legislation that would help only their status; they are organizing with their communities to work for justice for all those who are exploited by anti-immigrant policies. In addition, they are building alliances with other groups, including those focused on issues of racial justice, worker's rights, and environmental concerns.

Discussing identity and this complicated use of Americanism can connect with other aspects of writing and identity in the classroom. In my classroom in Miami, for example, where students often identify themselves as Venezuelans, Colombians, Cubans, or Haitians, some students question why "American" refers only to people in the United States when there are also North, Central, and South America. These discussions about identity connect with students' relationship with language and writing. The use of "American" as representing the United States—and also white and monolingual identities—excludes translingual students from different backgrounds. As Eunjeong Lee and Sara del Pilar Alvarez argue, "The monolingual ideology and the corollary racialization of students has . . . been also (re)produced through the limited conceptualization of language ownership—more specifically, the ownership over English, along with the question of who the writing classroom sees as the owner of English and how" (7). And it's difficult to generalize about the estimated 11 million immigrants who are undocumented in the United States. According to PEW

Research about population changes from 2009 to 2015, an estimated 5 million undocumented people were born in Mexico and 5.7 million were born in other countries, including an increasing number of immigrants from Asia and Central America (Krogstad et al.). These kinds of identity questions can strike a chord with some of the most basic assumptions about the nation-state and what it means to be a citizen.

Also, how and when people identify themselves as undocumented can vary. One student, Julian, compared learning about his status to "awakening to a nightmare" (qtd. in Gonzales and Chavez 262). Discovering the limits of their status can affect their lives greatly:

> In school they are told that if they work hard they can attain their dreams. But when their peers begin to move through important rites of passage—taking their first jobs, getting their driver's licenses, and applying to college—their inability to join them sets off a series of discoveries about what it means to be undocumented. In addition to the onset of multiple exclusions, their lives are fraught with feelings of fear, anxiety, uncertainty, and guilt. (Gonzales et al., 2)

Therefore, students learn of their status and its significance at different life moments. As he discusses in his book *Dear America: Notes of an Undocumented Citizen,* Jose Antonio Vargas didn't know his undocumented status until he was sixteen, when he tried to get a driver's license and the DMV rejected his paperwork. Vargas, the Pulitzer Prize–winning *Washington Post* columnist who also is undocumented (and was the keynote speaker at the 2017 CCCC in Portland), started a nonprofit called "Define American." His group's writings, films, and presentations reflect upon such questions of identity.

CONNECTIONS WITH THE COMMUNITY-WRITING CLASSROOM

One of the first fliers I created to advertise my 1997 course based on community partnerships used an image of two college students in cap and gown standing at the beginning of a road that connected to downtown Charlotte. The flier asked, "Want to Be a Roads Scholar?" As evident in the syllabus that begins this book, this course, grounded in community partnerships, pushed forward a volunteer approach to community change whereby students would venture on this road into the community, learn about social injustice, and try to make a difference. The course aimed to connect individual service projects to larger social questions of justice (Herzberg). And another key goal for such a course was Linda Flower's model whereby "marginalized participants" join the conversation as "self-conscious partners in an inquiry" (190). In contrast, the rhetorical moves of student organizers discussed in this chapter challenge many of the assumptions of such a community partnership course.

First of all, student organizers do not need to become volunteers in order to encounter injustice. They are responding to an oppressive, racist immigration system that affects both their lives and their families'. This system can arrest them, imprison them, and deport them. On the college campus itself, universities can reflect such anti-immigrant policies by banning undocumented students, charging them higher tuition, or refusing to be sanctuaries free from ICE. Instead of traditional volunteering, organizers are involved with advocacy work that directly affects themselves and their families. And in doing this work, student organizers use a variety of rhetorical skills to advocate for change.

As discussed in this chapter, student organizers are not partners but leaders as they share their own personal stories in events called "coming out of the shadows." They connect their own personal experiences with larger social issues like the effects of anti-immigrant laws. And in sharing these stories, they deploy complex rhetorical moves like invoking Americanism/nationalism as they challenge a system based on white supremacy. In stopping deportations, for example, organizers answer the law's request for proof that this person is in the "public benefit" and compose arguments to plead each person's value to the community.

In addition, the petitions to stop the deportations of Rodrigo and Erick show the network of actions required to elevate these stories in the public eye. Organizers contact the media (newspaper, television, and radio), they use the internet to share petitions, they plan vigils and rallies, and they create pressure on decision makers to follow edicts like the Morton memorandum. And as they complete this sophisticated rhetorical and advocacy work, they are negotiating a complex sense of identity with a place that is home but does not treat them as residents or citizens.

The work of student organizers should lead to a change in "community-partnership" pedagogy. In *Decolonizing Educational Research: From Ownership to Answerability,* Leigh Patel comments on the ways that DREAMers organize and challenge traditional education:

> To impact policies, they have formed multiracial, multiethnic activist groups and have used various public actions, such as rallies, to both educate and shift the opinions of various stakeholders. Within their meeting spaces and in public demonstrations, undocumented youth engage in pedagogies and research those pedagogies out of answerability to changing social contexts. I offer these extra-educational examples not to barter in tacit anti-intellectualism or to imply that deep, rigorous, discipline-specific study is unimportant, but to promote a radical reconfiguration of being and being-in-relation-to knowledge and learning, to foreground how fundamental a shift and re-setting should be undertaken to strip off the layers of the colonial view of education. (81)

Patel highlights the ways in which undocumented youth have developed their own "pedagogies" that are resisting anti-immigrant policies of universities and the government. Patel comments, "Answerability means that we have responsibilities as speakers, listeners, and those responsibilities include stewardship of ideas and learning, ownership" (74). In this form of literacy work, these student organizers are responsible to one another and to their communities as they advocate for immigrant rights. She compares their approach to teaching as an example of the "radical" change needed in education—a change that challenges a "colonial view." A course based more on student organizing voices may challenge, then, some of the disciplinary identity of community writing courses within English departments. Rather than focusing on individual volunteer projects, much of this new work is focused on collective organizing. And such organizing work is political but not partisan—as Julio comments, "The same party that said that they support us was the one who was deporting us." As both political parties support increased incarceration that disproportionately affects students of color and their families, and as the United States continues to be the nation that imprisons more of its people than any other, writing pedagogies need radical transformation.

Instead of just traditional volunteer work, a community-writing class can make more central to its curriculum and assignments the value of student organizing expertise, and by doing so transform the community-writing classroom. For example, Romeo García comments, "So many academic stories are the stories white folks tell each other, stories that echo traditions of savior or progress narratives" (12). Although rhetorical listening is supposed to practice a "stance of openness that a person may choose to assume in relation to *any* person, text, or culture," particularly in understanding how people may identify their gender and race (Ratcliffe 17), García points out the advantages of a different kind of listening—community listening—that values the "lived experience" of people (13). He compares the way listening often takes place in the classroom and the way it takes place in community:

> Then and now, academic or rhetorical listening is characteristically reflective of a colonial unconsciousness. Community listening, rather, encourages a type of responsibility and justice that does not function from the "right to speak" for (Alcoff) or to eavesdrop upon the subject, but rather from an understanding that students, while already shaped by language, are also shapers of language, discourse, and modalities of agency. (13)

García points out how one of his former professors dismissed his thoughts on the borderland, and the only way the professor would acknowledge him is if he "spoke in and on [the professor's] terms" (13). We should avoid such a "colonial unconsciousness"; writing classrooms need more community listening to student perspectives.

Listening more to students in such a movement can change the writing classroom. Rather than focusing only on what we can learn from a nonprofit organization, or a community agency where we are volunteering our time, we can also focus on the social justice issues that directly affect students in the classroom. Students can learn, for example, from the rhetorical skills of organizers in the immigrant rights movement. For instance, the syllabus can include published writings of student organizers. Students can give input on what should be added to the reading list and which guest speakers should visit and discuss how they use writing/rhetoric to advocate for change. Writing assignments can expand from traditional service-learning reflective assignments, including an innovative use of the op-ed (discussed in Chapter 3). Such a new framework is not a rejection of all community partnerships or traditional service-learning; however, such a new approach is a step toward transforming the classroom into a space more responsive to student concerns. The community writing classroom can focus on the actions that student organizers take to challenge injustice in their own communities. Those leaders may already be in the classroom, or they can be invited to visit and to share their expertise and rhetorical skills. For this kind of classroom, community listening is key—listening that values students' use of language and perspectives.

Finally, as Mohammad points out, stories alone don't change policies: "Things don't change because people want to change; things change because you force people into having no other option but creating change. And so that's when we sort of learned more about civil disobedience. . . ." For example, when Mohammad and other organizers shared their stories with faculty members from many different universities, no change happened. In order for policies to change, action is also required, which can include protests and civil disobedience. The next chapter focuses more on how writing combined with civil disobedience can be a necessary step in advocacy work, particularly when sharing stories and organizing lobbying campaigns aren't enough to create change. And the ways in which student organizers use writing as a tool in such advocacy work can offer a new lens for the community-writing classroom.

3

A Collective Lens for the Public-Writing Classroom and Op-Eds

> An Undocumented Immigrant Speaks Out
> By Angelica Velazquillo
>
> I am an undocumented immigrant. This month, I and nine other undocumented young people were arrested in Charlotte, North Carolina, after staging a sit-in that stopped traffic at a busy downtown intersection.
>
> Our goal is education, not deportation, for undocumented students.
>
> Ours is a movement that started in Arizona and then spread to California, Georgia, and North Carolina. This movement is not going away.
>
> Although President Obama has promised change, his administration is deporting people at a faster rate than the Bush administration did.
>
> We are tired of waiting for change. We are tired of seeing families torn apart. So we took action.
>
> When my family moved here, I was 4 years old, and my brother was 2. When we got older, we realized that going to college and living as everyone else does would be difficult. I graduated from college, but my brother hasn't been able to complete his education.

Portions of Chapter 3 were published in "A Collective Lens for the Public Writing Classroom: Undocumented Student Organizing," *The CEA Critic,* vol. 82, no. 2, July 2020, pp. 118–38. Copyright © 2020 The College English Association. Published by Johns Hopkins University Press. Reprinted with permission.

In many states, including mine, more anti-immigration laws are being passed.

So we spent three days in jail to challenge a system that has deported nearly a million people in the last three years. We were willing to be sent to a federal detention center, but because of all the publicity surrounding our protest, we were released. I guess officials want to pretend nothing happened.

Although we still face criminal charges, the government has dropped our deportation orders. This, however, prevents us from challenging our immigration status and applying for work permits. Despite our academic accomplishments, community involvement, and all our hard work, we have been left in limbo again.

Some say we are not Americans. But our civil disobedience shows how much we love this country and how American we are. Like the activists of the civil rights movement, we are standing up for our ideals, and we are willing to sacrifice.

We want to be citizens. We want opportunities, not deportations.

Angelica Velazquillo is a graduate of Belmont Abbey College, near Charlotte. She wrote this for the Progressive Media Project, and it was distributed by McClatchy-Tribune Information Services.

After the campaign to stop her brother's deportation discussed in the previous chapter, Angelica discusses why she and nine other undocumented young people decided to practice civil disobedience in downtown Charlotte, North Carolina, on September 6, 2011. In the op-ed above, she places her argument in the context of movements across the country challenging the record number of deportations during the Obama administration. Students are blocking intersections and being arrested so they can be heard and change an immigration system. Throughout the United States, they organize for classroom access, in-state tuition, and the end to deportations. They often form intersectional alliances with other groups advocating for social justice issues like a living wage, the rights of farmworkers, and an end to the school-to-prison pipeline. Angelica includes part of her own personal story and links civil disobedience to something very American: "Like the activists of the civil rights movement, we are standing up for our ideals, and we are willing to sacrifice." By confronting a system that questions their right to live in the United States, these students' activism questions the "legitimacy" of unjust laws (Negrón-Gonzales, "Undocumented Youth Activism" 99). This protest connects to others around the country that escalated into the next summer, putting pressure on President Obama to sign DACA before the 2012 election.

Student organizing in the immigrant rights movement can offer a new lens for the public-writing classroom, particularly in how writing can help form publics for short-term campaigns and also for long-term community organizing. In essence, organizers' collective work as rhetors makes it possible for them to enter a public discourse that tries to exclude them. Thus, they form a more inclusive public sphere. Such rhetorical activism requires collective effort rather than just one individual voice as they must combine writing and action to respond to institutions that often do not listen to their perspectives. In addition to the use of stories and petitions, as discussed in the previous chapter, organizers also practice civil disobedience to create a space for their concerns to be amplified. Civil disobedience in this context may mean conducting a sit-in, blocking street intersections, and planning to be arrested to challenge unjust laws.

This chapter argues for a writing classroom that focuses more on student organizers, a classroom where sometimes those students must work collectively to practice civil disobedience and construct a public sphere. First, this chapter discusses the need to construct a public sphere and the risks of going public. Student organizers in the immigrant rights movement use a variety of tactics to reconstruct and enter this public sphere by holding sit-ins and other modes of civil disobedience. The chapter focuses on one particular protest in Charlotte in 2011 that Angelica describes in her op-ed. In this protest, students, community members, and faculty members gathered at an intersection to protest anti-immigrant policies. In this short-term campaign, organizers joined for a moment that would be followed by many other actions in a long-term campaign. By discussing this protest in the context of other such protests, the chapter argues for a different public-writing classroom framework. I argue that, when a writing teacher assigns typical public-writing assignments, such as petitions, op-eds, and other community-based writing assignments, the perspectives of student organizers can help transform those writing assignments for the course. But to benefit from these organizers' insights, ultimately, I argue, the writing teacher likely will need to redefine their role within this new pedagogy.

PUBLIC WRITING: GOALS AND POSSIBILITIES

One standard assignment included in my first community-writing courses was the "writing to change" paper. This writing task asks students to write a proposal for change or to write an op-ed or letter to the editor. Often the proposal grew out of their involvement with their community projects. In this assignment, the public often is an imagined audience of institutions—government leaders, newspapers, or university leaders. The writer is addressing their elected representative, their city or campus newspaper, or the university president. Also, in composing this proposal for change, the writer acts individually, perhaps in the role of the good citizen who is part of this public sphere. However, the challenge to such an assignment is that the institutional audience may not be receptive. Also, even if the writing is full of great arguments and composed with appropriate style, many writers, particularly those who are not viewed as citizens or part of the public sphere, are excluded.

The challenges of this writing assignment reflect how the public sphere is often "fragmented" and that to participate in public discourse requires "constructing a responsive public" (Wells 328–29). In her often-cited 1996 essay, "Rogue Cops and Health Care: What Do We Want from Public Writing?," Susan Wells explores how we define public writing as she reflects upon Jürgen Habermas's definitions of the public sphere. She wants more students to be able "to defend themselves in bureaucratic settings" and argues that "we need to build, or take part in building, such a public sphere; that the public sphere is always constructed; and that it cannot, in our society, be unitary" (326). Wells emphasizes, "All speakers and writers who aspire to intervene in society face the task of constructing a public sphere" (329). And she argues that the problem with the way public writing is taught is that "[t]he writing classroom has no public exigency . . . " (338) and suggests that creating a zine or "church bulletin" might be more "useful" than traditional writing assignments (340).

Wells begins her essay discussing a news story she read in the *Philadelphia Inquirer.* A Temple University student, Arthur Colbert, was attacked by the police: "He was beaten; a gun was pointed at his head. Colbert spent the rest of the night at the 39th District Headquarters on Hunting Park Avenue, being questioned, slapped around, and threatened" (325). Wells then explains that Colbert filed a three-page citizen's complaint about the police violence, which made a large impact:

> The officer in charge was impressed: unlike other complaints against these policemen, Colbert's was "coherent and concise, loaded with details." The subsequent investigation uncovered (eventually) a pattern of frameups, bribes, and abuses of power by the Philadelphia police; it led to charges, suspensions, transfers, and other reforms. (325)

At first when reading about Colbert's effective complaint, Wells wonders if he learned such writing skills from the courses he took at Temple University, where she teaches, but she adds, "My triumph settled down with my next cup of coffee—Colbert's complaint had been the twenty-third filed against these cops, and the Rodney King incident probably prompted the department's investigation" (326). What's particularly noteworthy for the purposes of this chapter is that Wells's essay about public writing begins with discussing a piece composed by a student—a complaint against the police—and how it made a difference. Yes, there were twenty-two other complaints, but who made those? Were they random complaints or an organized effort? Because Colbert's complaint was not a singular complaint—it was accompanied by many other voices—that collective effort did not make it less noteworthy. In fact, such public writing points to the power of collective action to be heard in the public sphere—a point not explored further in this landmark essay.

One task, then, for public writing is to find ways to construct a public sphere. As Laurie E. Gries argues, "[s]tudents come to understand community as an emergent, unfolding phenomenon that is constantly assembling and reassembling. . . ." When we write, we do not do so as individual actors; we need "[t]o think about community as collective action . . ." (335). Gries's course, for example, asks students to "[pay] close attention to how various groups deployed visual rhetoric, image events, and other creative tactics to accomplish a variety of campaign goals" (340). As Gries's students apply these ideas to on-campus projects, she notes:

> In order to take themselves seriously as responsible rhetorical beings, students must come to believe that they are viable agents in this complex, organic process—as citizens constantly assembling in response to various concerns but also as assembling beings—as rhetors with the ability to assemble and distribute discourse that can, in turn, assemble and reassemble bodies around a shared concern. (336)

Gries mentions examples of campus projects, including the presence of feral cats on campus, Adderall abuse by students, and LGBTQ+ rights and representation. In this work, students can make connections between writing and forming community: "As a composing practice, writing to assemble publics is a big rhetorical responsibility that demands effectual rhetorical designs, diverse socio-material entanglements, and deep sociopolitical-ethical considerations . . ." (351).

In addition to the goal of helping students participate and construct a public sphere, other scholars explore the risks of going public. Scott Sundvall and Katherine Fredlund, for example, discuss activism in their public-writing courses. In one course, Sundvall's students started a campaign against wearing fur and the students spray-painted a hashtag throughout the university campus, photographed it, and then displayed the images through social media.

Sundvall reflects upon this use of civil disobedience—spray-painting on public property—and comments that the students had read essays in class about civil disobedience, but the application of such civil disobedience raised questions. Both instructors are concerned about their students' well-being and the risks they may be taking by practicing civil disobedience or going public with their points of view: "The failure then, perhaps, was that the reality of civil disobedience they read about and saw on screen did not translate to their own lives. They felt somehow removed from the often violent, punitive, and at times life-altering consequences of such methods." Sundvall and Fredlund, then, see a gap between what students read about civil disobedience in their classes and the implementation of it in their own community. And in addressing this gap, scholars point out faculty's responsibility to help students learn effective use of rhetoric and activism. Similarly, Gries notes examples of student activism, including those students responding to the shootings at Marjory Stoneman Douglas High School in Florida: "[W]e might be concerned with where students are learning the rhetorical arts of activism and wonder, as Valdivia suggests, about our own responsibilities in teaching students effective civic organizing practices" (330).

The work of student organizers can help address the gap between theorizing about activism and applying it in the public sphere. Students may be writing and acting upon issues that have an impact on their lives, and those issues may have a different weight for instructors' lives, depending upon their positionalities. For example, as Laura Wildes-Muñoz describes in *The Making of a Dream,* there is a rich history of undocumented youth advocating for immigrant rights. In 2006, for example, coalitions of groups formed massive protests around the country against the proposed Sensenbrenner bill that would make not having a valid visa a federal crime and anyone aiding someone who is undocumented chargeable with a felony (Wildes-Muñoz 58). After millions of people took to the streets to protest in 2006, the Senate did not pass the bill. And since those demonstrations, personal stories, social media, and direct action show the many risks that immigrant organizers have taken to challenge anti-immigrant policies—with tactics and strategies changing over the last decade. For example, in "Undocumented, Unafraid and Unapologetic: Re-articulatory Practices and Migrant Youth 'Illegality'," Genevieve Negrón-Gonzales discusses the ways in which undocumented youth from the DREAMer movement started to use civil disobedience to advocate for change on May 17, 2010:

> [U]ndocumented youth staged a sit-in at Senator McCain's Arizona office calling for an end to the criminalization of immigrants and the passage of the DREAM Act (Preston, 2010), triggering deportation proceedings for many of them. Months later, undocumented students in Georgia risked deportation by occupying a downtown intersection in a daring act of civil disobedience protesting the passage of repressive statewide legislation (Brumback, 2011). Young people risking deportation as political strategy was unimaginable a decade ago; today it is a cornerstone of this movement. (263)

When the students conducted their sit-in at Senator McCain's office, they were dressed in "graduation caps and gowns" as "outside . . . 50 supporters gathered to show their support" (Galindo 596). The timing of the event coincided with an additional lawsuit against Arizona's anti-immigrant SB1070, as well as the fifty-sixth anniversary of the *Brown v. Board of Education* Supreme Court decision (597). In the planning of actions, organizers often make connections with important dates in the past and future, such as a landmark Supreme Court decision for equality in education, to amplify how their organizing connects with other social movements. In addition, a letter writing campaign was started after the sit-in to bring attention to the DREAM Act. One of those students in Senator McCain's office was Mohammad, who was interviewed for this book. He wrote a public letter about the action:

> Dear Mr. President,
> My name is Mohammad Abdollahi and I am an undocumented immigrant. Two months ago I made history.

> On May 17, according to the *New York Times,* I become one of the first undocumented students, along with two others, to "have directly risked deportation in an effort to prompt Congress to take up [the DREAM Act]." Risking deportation was no small act for me. Not only did I risk being forcibly removed from [the] United States, the only country I know as my home, to Iran, where I don't know the culture or the language, I also happen to be gay. In Iran, people like me are tortured and executed. I am still at risk of deportation and execution, right now, and I will continue to be at risk until the DREAM Act is passed.

Mohammad's letter is an example of writing combined with action helping to construct a public space. Like Arthur Colbert's complaint about the police described in Wells's essay, Mohammad's letter is part of a network of action and other writings. Other writers who participated in the sit-in wrote letters too, which were published. In Mohammad's letter, he refers to a *New York Times* story that was an example of the national press coverage about the sit-in. As Mohammad and four others risked deportation, they were placing pressure on Senator McCain to vote for the DREAM Act, something that he had supported in previous years. However, in this letter to the president, Mohammad addresses an audience whose political party (the Democrats) controls both houses of Congress. The stakes are raised in this piece of writing by pointing out that the writer is gay and if deported, he could be "tortured and executed" in Iran. Unlike the spray-painting example from Sundvall and Fredlund's essay, Mohammad and other students are well aware of the risks for participating in civil disobedience.

When organizers complete such actions, there is a common refrain: "We are undocumented, unafraid, and unapologetic . . . " (Negrón-Gonzales, "Undocumented, Unafraid" 263). Negrón-Gonzales compares the ways in which undocumented youth use civil disobedience to a counternarrative—or what she calls a "counter-spectacle":

Civil disobedience is a campaign tactic in which protestors disrupt the normal functioning of daily life in order to call attention to their plight, but it is also a counter-spectacle that weaves a different narrative about unjust laws and the place of undocumented young people in challenging these laws. ("Undocumented Youth Activism" 101)

Such events often use the imagery of the students wearing the graduation caps and gowns that they wore in the sit-in for Senator McCain's office and even having "'pop-up' graduation ceremonies that are integrated into larger public actions such as protests, press conferences, and rallies" ("Undocumented Youth Activism" 99). Thus, these graduation protests take the trappings of academia "[a]nd reappropriate them as symbols that challenge their traditional association to new beginnings, hopes, and bright futures" ("Undocumented Youth Activism" 99).

By engaging in such acts of civil disobedience, as René Galindo comments, "[u]ndocumented students asserted that their cause was the cause of civil rights and not of the illegality ascribed to them" (604). These protests "[f]ormed a counter-public whose aim was to make undocumented immigrant students visible and bring national attention to their plight" (Galindo 607). The organizing of the immigrant rights movement, then, uses complex rhetorical moves in public writing and protest so students can be heard in the public sphere, and in doing so, they are taking important risks. The op-ed of Angelica's that begins this chapter articulates some of the reasons for taking such risks, and the protest she describes was one example of other actions across the country.

CHARLOTTE PROTEST, SEPTEMBER 6, 2011

After the successful campaign to stop the deportation of Erick (a college student who was arrested for driving with an expired license, as described in Chapter 2), I maintained contact with organizers from the North Carolina DREAM Team. At the beginning of the fall semester in 2011, Angelica (Erick's sister) said some students and organizers from different parts of the country needed a place to stay as they organized a protest, and so I offered my home. At first, it was a couple of people, but then the numbers quickly grew. By the following week, there were over a dozen people staying in extra beds and sleeping bags, preparing for a protest at Central Piedmont Community College (CPCC). They planned. They organized. They consulted with lawyers. In preparation for the event, student organizers made YouTube videos in the den, filmed against a blank white wall, wearing t-shirts that said "undocumented and unafraid" and "The dream is coming." The videos explained why they were taking the actions they planned in downtown Charlotte, and that if you were watching the video, then that meant they had been arrested and someone in the group had posted it. Also, a student filmmaker, Joshua Davis, filmed the protest as he created a documentary about undocumented youth in North Carolina, *The Undocumentary*.

The actual event happened in downtown Charlotte on September 6, 2011. Besides asserting students' right to an education, this pro-immigrant rally took place exactly one year before the Democratic National Convention when President Obama was to be nominated for a second term in downtown Charlotte. The event's timing wasn't by chance. On that same day in 2011, three thousand Democrats came to an event celebrating the upcoming 2012 Democratic National Convention just a mile away (Gutierrez). At Central Piedmont Community College (CPCC), the students started with a rally in favor of student rights and undocumented students' access to education and a response to the anti-immigrant climate in North Carolina. It also was a "coming-out rally" as students announced their undocumented status. CPCC had banned undocumented students and then they reversed the ban. Then they said that undocumented students could take classes, but they would have to be the last ones to register.

The students marched with other supporters—an estimated two hundred people (Benitez-Hernandez)—from the campus to the intersection of Fourth Street and Kings Drive, where I was told to be in my car. "Education not deportation" was one of the main refrains. Then a sit-in started with a group of students sitting around the edges of a huge banner draped on the ground that read, "We will no longer remain in the shadows" (Benitez-Hernandez). Other drivers and I were to stop our cars at the intersection so that other cars wouldn't try to pass and disrupt the protest. At this busy intersection, there was a line of cars behind me and on the other three corners honking their horns.

Organizers were practicing civil disobedience to highlight the need for immigration reform and to bring attention to laws that were exploiting immigrants. In one year, President Obama would be nominated for a second term; however, his administration continued to deport immigrants at a high rate even though his party had a stated pro-immigrant platform. And if organizers were arrested and sent to a detention center, then they planned to challenge their status through immigration court. It was a risky move, but they had consulted with lawyers and other organizers and were prepared.

This event brought together students, faculty, and community members at this downtown intersection. The job of the driver, for example, raised questions about the writing teacher's role both in this action and in the writing classroom. This effort was planned and organized by student organizers; however, a successful event required the participation of other communities of people, including faculty and community members not directly affected by im-

migration policy. The drivers' role did not require much risk, but it did require being present and being part of the overall action. At this intersection, as over two hundred people gathered, a public was constructed. Some members of the public were random people driving through this part of downtown who were inconvenienced by the sit-in. But for that moment, a public heard the demonstrators' demands for immigrant rights, and more people outside that intersection heard them, as it was covered by newspaper, radio, television news, and social media. Then the arrests of the first seven protesters (the NC7) started:

> After [the protesters had stopped] traffic for nearly half an hour, the police arrived and began to arrest the demonstrators. After handcuffing the NC7, the police began arresting others wearing DREAM Team t-shirts who were involved with the action.
>
> Besides criminal charges, the undocumented students were to be processed through the 287g program, which local law enforcement uses to transfer undocumented people to Immigration and Customs Enforcement (ICE) in order to

begin deportation proceedings. (Hutchinson, "A Quick Look at the Arrests in North Carolina")

In addition to the seven people who had planned to practice civil disobedience, the police arrested three more undocumented people and five others for a total of fifteen people. The five additional people arrested were citizens, so they were "released immediately after processing" (Coscia). However, the other ten undocumented youth, including Angelica, Mohammad, and Viridiana, were put in jail and awaited being sent to a detention center because they were not citizens.

Although this action had been planned and organized, the next three days were anxious ones. The house was quiet except for a couple of people who were not arrested. A mother flew to Charlotte from out of state once she learned her son was arrested. And the students then had their hearings in court, which I attended as a supportive witness. Because of all the media exposure, three organizers were released on Wednesday, and the remaining seven were released on Thursday after spending three days in jail. As they exited, they stood all in a line for a photo in front of the downtown jail dressed in their "The Dream is Coming" t-shirts.

The protest in Charlotte didn't immediately create any change to the law, but there were additional protests around the country as part of a longer campaign for immigrant rights. The following year, protests and marches continued in different states, which pressured the Obama administration to act before the November presidential election. May 12, 2012, was a national day of action organized by United We Dream, and people marched in the streets around the country (Khan). Also, there were sit-ins in campaign offices, including by two students from the National Immigrant Youth Alliance (NIYA) who went on a hunger strike inside the Obama campaign office in Denver ("DREAM Act Protesters"). All of these events helped convince the president to make an important announcement that summer before the November election. On June 15, 2012, Obama issued a directive called DACA (Deferred Action for Childhood Arrivals), which allowed more young people to apply for "deferred status" and a work permit (Artze-Vega and

Hutchinson 26). If students received DACA, they would not be deported for at least two years. The requirements for those applying for DACA included the following:

1. Were under the age of 31 as of June 15, 2012;
2. Came to the United States before reaching your 16th birthday;
3. Have continuously resided in the United States since June 15, 2007, up to the present time;
4. Were physically present in the United States on June 15, 2012, and at the time of making your request for consideration of deferred action with USCIS;
5. Had no lawful status on June 15, 2012;
6. Are currently in school, have graduated or obtained a certificate of completion from high school, have obtained a general education development (GED) certificate, or are an honorably discharged veteran of the Coast Guard or Armed Forces of the United States; and
7. Have not been convicted of a felony, significant misdemeanor, or three or more other misdemeanors, and do not otherwise pose a threat to national security or public safety. ("Consideration")

DACA started in 2012, a year after the campaign to stop Erick's deportation as discussed in Chapter 2 (when the Morton Memo instructed ICE to make certain groups low priorities for deportation but this practice was not regularly enforced). Advocacy groups like Students Working for Equal Rights (SWER) at Florida International University organized legal clinics to help people apply for DACA, and as Nicolas, a student at FIU, explains, "I wouldn't be sitting here" in the college classroom without DACA. Because of DACA, Nicolas points out, he was able to get a job with a work permit (he became a receptionist in our writing center), obtain a driver's license, buy his first car, pay for his education, and graduate. He is able to "have a more regular life" even if he can't be a citizen. In 2017, the number of people who had received DACA grew to 790,000 (Krogstad). DACA was possible because student organizers successfully used their rhetorical skills and organizing to pressure politicians to take action. And as the Trump administration has worked to stop the continuation of DACA, these skills continue to be valuable ones to examine and learn from in the community-writing classroom.

The "temporary public" formed during the protest at this downtown intersection was part of both a short-term and a long-term campaign. Short-term, students, faculty, and community members came together to show support for the right to an education. When people were arrested, greater attention was given to the policies of the community college trying to exclude undocumented students from the school. For the long-term movement, the Charlotte protest was part of many others. The rally was timed one year before the Democratic convention and pointed out the anti-immigrant policies being carried out by the Obama administration. After demonstrators were arrested, their individual videos were posted on YouTube. In each video, participants discuss why they took part in the civil disobedience. For example, in her 1-minute 41-second video, Angelica comments that she is "tired of the lies" and says, "Because unless we are seen, we are heard, we are going to continue to be ignored, we are going to continue to be oppressed. And this is an opportunity. If we speak out, they are going to know that we are here and we have a chance to unite, to encourage others and to do more for our community" (Velazquillo, "Angelica V_____ North Carolina").

The Charlotte protest is one example of how groups excluded from mainstream public discourse must create their own space for public discourse. As Nancy Welch points out, for example, there is a decreasing amount of physical public space for people to gather and express themselves with the "steady conversion of public spaces and resources into private, for-profit property" ("Living Room" 474). And in forming publics, Nancy Fraser discusses the importance of having "a multiplicity of publics" (77): In "[s]ubaltern counterpublics . . . members of subordinated social groups invent and circulate counterdiscourses, which in turn permit them to formulate oppositional interpretations of their identities, interests, and needs" (67). A downtown intersection, for example, becomes a place for pro-immigrant discourse in a city, state, and country rife with anti-immigrant policies. These alternative publics, or what Elenore Long calls "local publics" rooted in "time and place" (3), also reflect the intersectionality of social movements. In a campaign for immigrant rights, participants are also concerned with racism, sexism, workers' rights, and other issues that affect one another.

In these multiple public spheres, organizers often link an action to a longer organizing effort. For example, Mohammad distinguishes between an activism that reacts only to something in the moment and organizing that is more systematic and long-term:

> An activist is just someone who is very reactionary. Who acts on different issues that pop up and can apply the theories of organizing to issues. But an organizer is more someone who works with an affected community to empower the community to create long-lasting change. . . .

Similarly, Viridiana comments on the power of organizing:

> For me, honestly, as much as I would like to see immigration reform, comprehensive immigration reform, that's not the most important thing for me. The most important thing is organizing[,] . . . creating new strategies. And the fact that years ago, when an attorney told somebody there's nothing we can do on your case . . . we went from people being heartbroken to . . . we're going to organize and pressure ICE and stop your deportation, we're going to keep you united with your family. The fact we can do that . . . is the most important thing. . . . For me the most important thing is organize, organize, organize. Because the community needs to know the power is within us. As corny or cliché or whatever as that sounds, at the end of the day, we are going to be the people that are going to be holding our elected officials accountable. . . .

Instead of focusing on just one issue, groups organize to address multiple issues affecting their communities. The Charlotte protest was about the local policies of students being unable to attend college, and it also addressed the national policies set by the Obama administration. Also, even if pro-immigrant legislation is passed, that accomplishment doesn't stop the organizing—communities need to organize and use "new strategies," as Viridiana says. Changing one policy is not the goal; organizing the community is a more important goal. Also, such an organizing approach doesn't divide the community by suggesting that some deserve justice more than others. As Helge Schwiertz comments, "This new orientation of the undocumented youth movement deeply challenges the 'antimigrant hegemony' in the US by favoring the organizing of directly impacted diverse communities over short-term activism and by rejecting the criminalization of certain undocumented youth and the resulting 'good immigrant' versus 'bad immigrant' divide" (611).

Although some might object to civil disobedience and prefer a dialogue with lawmakers about immigration policy, such direct actions are often necessary for advocacy work. Dialogue is not possible if lawmakers do not listen and invite these points of view into the conversation. As Welch argues, attempting to participate in what is often described as a "civil" manner and discourse often perpetuates the status quo, and those advocating for social change are often deemed "uncivil":

> These collectivist, populist, and emancipatory movements have brought measurable expansions of who is included in the political sphere and what democratic rights and social justice oversight can be exercised in the economic domain. But these collectivist, populist, and emancipatory movements were also widely denounced in their moments as uncivil and violent. In fact, such movements were widely denounced as uncivil and violent even though their major rhetorical legacies—for instance, soapboxing, sitdowns, boycotts, and the persuasive tactic of folding the arms or withholding labor—are ones we think of today as staples of nonviolent resistance. ("Informed" 112–13)

Although civil dialogue may be valued both inside and outside the classroom, often change requires disruption with actions like sit-ins and demonstrations. The history of social movements shows the power of such actions; however, opponents have regularly labeled such work "uncivil."

In these campaigns, however, organizing is not a partisan activity. Both major political parties reflect a political system that has exploited immigrants and profited from the incarceration of immigrants and people of color. The use of civil disobedience is often directed at those "supportive" politicians whose speeches and platforms contrast with their actions on an issue. Such an approach requires a sophisticated understanding of arguments that appease constituents with language but frustrate with inaction. For example, as the Obama administration deported over three million people, they continued to have a pro-immigrant tone. To explain why deportations continued, one argument was that the president did not have the power to issue an executive memorandum to stop deportations. However, after the collective action of organizers, that viewpoint changed and DACA was signed. In order to be heard in the public sphere, Claudia Anguiano points out, undocumented organizers protest and do sit-ins in the offices of politicians who profess their support for them: "The protestors in attendance noted that they would no longer accept mild support and instead required accountability from those not intently working to enact the bill" (188). Therefore, even though President Obama stated his support for immigration reform, the absence of any action and the continued deportations of immigrants prompted a need for more direct action like the Charlotte protest: "[T]hese numerous examples of civil disobedience were an interventional strategy that showed youth making a move towards escalation, and they worked to force more attention on the issue" (Anguiano 190).

A *NEW* PUBLIC-WRITING CLASSROOM

The community-writing classroom can be a place where many visions of a more inclusive, democratic public sphere can meet. Our field has emphasized how the public sphere is fragmented and excludes others. This public sphere is often a place that has been privatized or monopolized by dominant neoliberal ideologies. For example, both political parties have supported the profit-driven incarceration of immigrants. And even if a political party adopts pro-immigrant discourse, the actions of mass deportations and expanding detention centers reflects an anti-immigrant policy. In this fractured public space, where it is difficult for the majority of people to express their viewpoints, a top rhetorical goal for the community-writing classroom may not be to persuade others, but to organize with others. As Seth Kahn notes, we need to "[reframe] our audiences as people we're organizing with instead of people we're persuading to agree with us . . ." (123). Instead of focusing only on persuading others, writing, then, becomes a tool to mobilize people as it attempts to construct a public sphere. As Lee Artz argues, the task is not to speak truth to power, but to solidify the power of the majority:

> The ideal speech situation, the democratic sphere, imagined by rhetorical theorists can only be realized within and among democratic social movements that challenge existing power—not by speaking truth to that power—but by speaking the power of our new truth: we are the majority, we must collectively argue, debate, and decide how to save humanity. (159–60)

In constructing publics that advocate for change, a combination of organizing and writing can be part of both short-term and long-term campaigns.

In these campaigns, the rhetoric is often direct and focused on galvanizing support rather than engaging in dialogue. In *Youth Activism in an Era of Education Inequality,* Ben Kirshner contrasts "procedural" and "issue-based" approaches (80–82). A procedural approach is a dialogue where participants "[c]ome together and, under well-facilitated conditions, talk, listen, revise beliefs, and develop solutions to problems" (80). In contrast, an issue-based approach is one with "clear objectives that [are] not up for negotiation" (81). If participants are arguing for the right to exist and basic human rights, then there is not much room for compromise. A procedural approach with good conditions for dialogue would not work. As Kirshner comments, "[T]here are certain issues about which it does not make sense for people to 'listen to' or respect other people's arguments, such as perspectives that are dehumanizing or racist" (81).

This organizing framework for the community-writing classroom speaks to a political turn for the field. For example, Carmen Kynard calls on scholars to consider how their work responds to social injustice, including the continued violence against people of color: "What do your research and scholarship—RIGHT NOW—challenge and remake? What do your institutional practices—RIGHT NOW—challenge and remake?" ("All I Need Is One Mic"). This political turn, then, is a chance for writing teachers to examine and work toward a more "[t]rue democracy, equality, and freedom in light of the embeddedness of racism, sexism, heterosexism, xenophobia, and other forms of oppression . . ." (Mutnick et al. 269).

In this challenging pedagogical shift, student organizers have valuable rhetorical skills to share. There is a rich history of student activism, including students from HBCUs protesting for civil rights (Kynard), and Black Lives Matter activists campaigning for racial justice (Richardson and Ragland). In "Taking a Lead from Student Movements in a 'Political Turn,'" Vani Kannan reflects upon her own activism as a student and how it informs her work as a professor:

> My own experience as a student and teacher continue to remind me of the centrality of student movements and student activists' analyses to our "political turn" in this era. Students are often on the front lines. It is up to us to figure out how to take their lead, offering the histories, frameworks, analyses, and experiences we can. (135–36)

This kind of work, then, is not just a spontaneous moment of activism. It is deep, reflective organizing that requires addressing multiple publics. For example, Jonathan Alexander and Susan C. Jarratt discuss how student activists protested against the occupation of Palestinian territory during an event on their college campus. In their interviews of those students who were arrested and part of a longer campaign, they highlight their rhetorical skills:

> [T]hese students seemed to challenge a simplistic framing of rhetoric as a simple, intentional stream flowing from rhetor to audience to effect. Indeed, when we asked our participants about the intended effects of their protest, they answered variously, underscoring the complexity of the protest as an event that could—and would—be interpreted in multiple ways by different publics. (537)

This sophisticated understanding of audience and organizing was not learned from their writing classes, and in fact, Alexander and Jarratt point out the disconnect between these students' education and their organizing work. This chasm between student activism and classroom practices provides an opportunity for a new pedagogical framework to foreground the voices, ideas, and skills of students who write to organize. Also, such a framework emphasizes the collective effort often required for both writers and organizers to enact change. To return to the opening concern of this chapter and Arthur Colbert's complaint to the police, twenty-two other complaints and a growing awareness about police brutality preceded his writing (Wells). When students compose an op-ed or another piece of public writing, they can reflect upon how writing often requires multiple writings by multiple authors and multiple actions organized by a group to work for change. Writing to organize focuses on solidifying support for an issue.

These kinds of writing assignments are not partisan endeavors even if they raise important political questions about writing and change. Interviews with organizers regularly emphasize that they do not see their work as partisan. In the examples of this chapter, organizers are addressing an audience that already supports their policy but is not acting upon that policy. Their tactics, then, tend not to be framed with partisan categories. In addition, it would follow that not everyone in a classroom would have the same viewpoints or issues that engage them. However, foregrounding student voices and actions can be an effective pedagogy for other students to learn valuable writing and organizing skills that they could apply to their own issues and concerns.

A focus on student voices can also diversify public discourse. For instance, besides being part of a coordinated campaign, op-eds can be one way to diversify the media. Op-eds can reach a large audience even with a decline in newspaper subscriptions. The number of people reading a print newspaper is declining but reading online is increasing. A 2017 report from the PEW Research Center shows that 35 million people read a weekly paper (online/print) and 38 million read a Sunday paper (online/print) (Barthel). In addition, when you consider those who read and share articles online, writing op-eds is a way for writers to share their views with many people. For example, in a study of thirty news sites in September 2015, 74,840 articles were accessed by 71 million visitors on cell phones (Mitchell, Stocking, and Matsa). These student organizers' use of op-eds gives writing teachers a new way of talking about public writing in the classroom. Also, newspapers, like many of the media, lack great diversity in who writes the news. In the newsroom of large daily papers, only one in five workers is not white, and that statistic decreases to less than 10 percent at smaller papers ("2015 Census"; Barthel). And if we consider some of the sources often quoted in newspapers, including well-funded anti-immigrant organizations like the Federation for American Immigration Reform (FAIR), we can benefit from more diverse, informed views.

Student organizers can discuss their rhetorical and advocacy work when they are invited to visit classes. Classroom visits/activities can address the ways certain groups can be marginalized by the public sphere. For example, one organizer who was coordinating the social media aspect of the campaign during the Charlotte protest visited my writing class at Johnson C. Smith University, an HBCU, located a few miles from the action. During the class visit, he did an icebreaker with students as they physically moved around the classroom and considered questions of identity and marginalization. In another presentation, students from Howard University visited and discussed their journey to Arizona to learn about anti-immigrant legislation and discussed the racism behind such laws. Their presentation discussed the network of anti-immigrant groups created by the late John Tanton that masquerades white-supremacist ideas as immigration restrictions.

For the class to learn how writing can be part of a network of action, not only can student organizers attend and discuss their work, but, as I have been suggesting, there may be student organizers already enrolled in the class. When sharing an op-ed like Angelica's with a class and discussing their own assignments, we can also emphasize how an op-ed can be part of a coordinated campaign to change something. In her op-ed about the protest that begins this chapter, Angelica tells her story with a lede (twenty words or fewer that summarizes her main point), at least three main points, a response to a counterargument, and a conclusion that appeals to readers' values. This op-ed highlights why many undocumented students risk being arrested through direct action, because, as Angelica puts it, there are those who "want to pretend nothing happened," and students do not want to wait any more for change.

What helps even more is when representatives from SWER or other groups can visit the class to talk about how public writing is part of a campaign, a network of action, and show that students can be experts too. For example, Nicolas and other undocumented students were actively lobbying the administration for in-state tuition. Nicolas published a syndicated op-ed about the need for in-state tuition as they were talking to university administrators, conducting press conferences, and speaking with lawmakers. That semester, Nicolas received an in-state tuition waiver, which helped him continue his education at FIU. Soon after that semester, in-state tuition became official policy for the school, and FIU became the first public institution in the state of Florida to offer in-state tuition for undocumented students who qualify for DACA. In 2014, these same students, along with other concerned activists, successfully lobbied the state legislature in Tallahassee to make this a statewide policy, and Governor Rick Scott signed it into law that same election year. Of course, Nicolas's one op-ed did not cause a Republican governor to sign a bill to grant in-state tuition for undocumented students. It was part of a larger movement that students led, including petitions, demonstrations, and conversations with elected representatives. But Nicolas's op-ed in 2012, which was syndicated in newspapers across Florida and the country, shows how writing can be a tool in a campaign.

Undocumented Students Seek In-State Tuition
By Nicolas Wulff

I'm an undocumented student who wants to be in the college classroom.

I've lived in Miami for 17 years and am attending Florida International University. But because I'm undocumented, my tuition was supposed to cost $1,239 more per class than a "regular" student.

My mom always stressed how vital an education is. I followed her advice and I graduated from high school with a 3.8 GPA and received a Florida Bright Futures Scholarship.

However, Florida revoked my scholarship because of my undocumented status, and I can't afford the out-of-state tuition. I am also denied federal financial aid.

Some other students and I applied for a waiver from Florida International. If it doesn't go through, we will be out of luck.

I'm by no means alone in this predicament. Only 5 percent of the 65,000 graduating undocumented high school seniors in the United States each year can go to college.

Undocumented students should not be charged higher tuition for college.

Our broken immigration system prevents undocumented youth from reaching their potential and categorizes us as second-class citizens.

Some argue in-state tuition should be for only tax-paying citizens, but many don't realize that undocumented people pay taxes too. According to the Institute for Taxation and

Economic Policy, undocumented families paid an estimated $11.2 billion in taxes last year.

Thirteen states offer in-state tuition for undocumented students, and some colleges, like Florida International, sometimes grant in-state tuition waivers or help find private scholarships.

But most states and most colleges do not. They are wasting the talent of so many young people.

All we want is a chance. We want the same opportunities given to everyone else. We want the chance to better not only ourselves, but America too.

Nicolas Wulff is a 21-year-old undocumented student who has lived in Miami since the age of 5. He wants to major in International Relations and Economics at Florida International University.

When discussing their work in class, student organizers can share their thinking about the risks and rewards of going public. Nicolas wanted to publish his work, and at the time, we were able to work with the Progressive Media Project, which helped syndicate op-eds throughout the country using the McClatchy news service. However, mandating that all students submit their writing does not seem practical or advisable since students will have varying willingness to go public. As Brian Gogan notes about his public-writing project, most of his students didn't get their letters published in his "letters-to-the editor" assignment, so publication cannot be the only measure of success for this kind of assignment in the classroom. At the same time, we can discuss how op-eds can be part of a larger network of action to promote change. This op-ed assignment, which at first is a rhetorical exercise, can also be a chance for students to reflect upon their roles as public rhetoricians.

THE WORK CONTINUES

Civil disobedience is one method student organizers use to create publics. Using a collective voice both in their rhetoric and in their actions, they organize both short-term and long-term campaigns. This work is not partisan, as it acts upon the belief that politicians need to hear from their constituents, and as Claudio, former president of SWER, comments, "These politicians usually don't do things unless they are pressured, so we need to build this pressure." In addition, these specific actions of civil disobedience are part of a longer organizing effort. Mohammad points out the power of working with others:

> I've created long-lasting change in myself. I've already gotten a victory. And I think that's sort of the difference as an affected population organizing[,] that you're past the point where you're fighting for yourself and you're fighting for a collective.

This approach is not just about one issue but an effort to voice community concerns and organize for change. This kind of work offers a new lens for the public-writing classroom. More emphasis is needed on listening to how students organize and solidify support. Although dialogue and persuading other people to change their point of view is an important skill, the work of student organizers points us in a different direction: organizing so that their communities can be better represented by laws and policies. Such a framework foregrounds student voices: inviting them as guest speakers, including their published work on the course syllabus, and expanding the possibilities for public writing that focuses on organizing. Listening to students who understand the risks of public writing and action can become a primary focus of a course.

This chapter begins with Angelica's op-ed about why she and nine others decided to protest and go to jail in response to anti-immigrant policies. Discussing this writing and other work of student organizers in the classroom reframes the common "writing-to-change" essay assignment and has changed my pedagogy. This chapter's exploration of pedagogy, though, is shaped and limited by my own positionality as a teacher who is white, male, and a citizen. Writing teachers are not a monolithic group, and other writing teachers can understand and speak to student concerns differently and perhaps more directly. For example, some undocumented students are graduating and leading classrooms themselves. The Migration Policy Institute estimates over 20,000 DREAMers are working as teachers in the US school system (Capps et al. 6). My goal, then, in discussing my shift in pedagogy for the writing classroom is not to create a general pedagogy for all writing teachers—that seems impossible and counterproductive. I hope that discussing how student organizers have impacted my pedagogy will connect to a larger movement for our field to invite more student organizing voices into the public-writing classroom. Besides benefiting the writing classroom, restructuring our courses can also support the work of student organizers.

I also don't intend to argue for some kind of easy answer and suggest some kind of utopia for public writing. Participating in the public sphere is a challenging act, particularly for those, such as undocumented students, whose very existence is challenged. The difficult work of public writing and social change continues to be a struggle. For example, although many positive changes have happened based on the work of student organizers, anti-immigrant rhetoric and policies continue. Although traditional service-learning courses and assignments that ask students to write for, about, and with the community can be useful, the community-writing classroom can place more emphasis upon students' perspectives and the work of student organizers. What actions are people taking on campus to address inequities in access to the college classroom? What examples of systemic racism are affecting students on campus and in their communities? How can writing be part of a network of action to address such issues of social justice? The classroom writing teacher can take an intersectional approach to the classroom, value student voices, and—particularly in my case, given my identity as a white male citizen—follow rather than lead. In this climate of anti-immigrant activity, we need more space for students to lead in the classroom. The op-ed is one example in a network of action as students organize. The op-ed emphasizes that student voices matter, and teachers can see this assignment and other public writing through a new lens with the help of student organizers. Our words are constrained by an oppressive legal and political framework, and change often requires taking risks.

4

Detention/Writing Center Campaigns for Freedom

> I deal with cases. I'm also part of the Education, Not Deportation Team. . . . You get a case and then we have to help the families try and get out from the detention center. . . . He was a parent, a dad from Arizona. We heard about the case because . . . the daughter was an activist in Arizona, but for some reason they sent [him] to Miami. When we heard about the case, we did everything we could. We did vigils. We went to Krome detention center. I believe he was in Krome and then in Broward as well, in the BTC. And even though I did not know the guy, I had only seen him through fliers and pictures, and people had just talked to me about him, we were able to win his case. He came out of the detention center. When I finally saw him, I had never even met the guy, he just gave me a hug, a handshake, and telling me how proud he was of us, he felt like we were his kids and we were his family, when he saw us and then I noticed that he was skinnier; I guess he wasn't eating as well, they don't really eat much or like rice and beans, I think that's it. So the first thing we did was we went to go eat, and so he was telling us about it. Like that got to me. It could be my dad or my mom too that could be detained. Somebody hopefully helps them out like I did. . . . So that's something that I learned from that. . . .
>
> —Francis

Portions of Chapter 4 were published in "Detention/Writing Center Campaigns for Freedom," *Community-Engaged Writing and Literacy Centers: A Critical Field Scan of Theory and History, Practice and Place,* edited by Mark Latta, Chris Giroux, and Helen Raica-Klotz, spec. issue of *Community Literacy Journal,* vol. 15, no. 1, Fall 2020, pp. 7–27.

I really enjoyed the Broward campaign because that's the first time we put Immigration on the defensive. They had to react to our allegations. They had to tell people that they're doing their job instead of us having to say you know it was a whole different spin and I think it's very rare that you're going to find any press release from ICE that mentions an organization and responds to their allegations and that's something we were able to do that was very—I mean it comes I think back to the thing of writing to an extent of, you know, we did our own internal investigation and put out the facts as to what they're doing. In their response, I think that gave a lot of credibility to our allegations and that would not have happened if it wasn't for us sort of manipulating the power of the press and our stories and using it for a greater goal beyond. . . .

—Mohammad

This was about families this whole time. This wasn't about what political party. This wasn't about any of that. It was always about the families—our community, the kids, the parents—that's what it's always about.

—Viridiana

FRANCIS, MOHAMMAD, AND VIRIDIANA, like organizers around the country, work on campaigns to get people out of detention centers. And as depicted in the documentary *The Infiltrators,* Mohammad worked with Viridiana and Marco to infiltrate the Broward Detention Center (BTC), located a few miles north of Miami (Rivera and Ibarra). The documentary shows how they presented themselves to immigration authorities and purposely tried to get arrested. Since they were community organizers with the National Immigrant Youth Alliance, they wanted to get inside BTC and find out who was being held. Once inside BTC, both Viridiana and Marco collected stories and then did media interviews over the phone. They called for a full review of the cases at BTC. They discovered that there were hundreds of people being held without a criminal record, including people eligible for DACA. Most likely, no one would have known about these cases unless they had been publicized. A day after their media interviews, Viridiana and Marco were suddenly released (Sweeney). Because they were able to publicize their story and the stories of other people who were being held in a detention center, they gained a power through their actions. Once they were no longer invisible, the detention center released them. Mohammad helped with the organization of this project from outside the detention center and continues to work on campaigns for immigrant rights. As Mohammad notes, the rhetorical moves of "manipulating the power of the press and our stories" help people gain freedom.

These young organizers' work at detention centers shows that the struggle for immigrant rights isn't just about the right to an education. These leaders were addressing issues of mass incarceration and assisting other immigrants, some of whom were not receiving adequate medical care, including "a woman taken for ovarian surgery and returned the same day, still bleeding, to her cell, and a man who urinated blood for days but wasn't taken to see a doctor" (O'Matz). Therefore, this work with imprisoned immigrants contrasts with some of the traditional work of providing literacy classes inside prisons.

Immigrant rights organizers challenge the incarceration of immigrants and use complex rhetorical moves to work within a system to challenge it. Such advocacy speaks to a need for community-writing projects that do more than provide a writing class/tutoring session or express solidarity with someone. Although there is a growing body of scholarship about teaching writing in prison (Jacobi, "Austerity" and "Speaking Out"; Berry; Cavallaro et al.), these initiatives often struggle between focusing on individual rehabilitation and working toward changing the incarceration system (Plemons). The advocacy work of student organizers highlights the need for writing to make visible what the public sphere has left invisible. For those incarcerated in detention centers, their stories and cases are often silenced by an immigration system that does not provide them legal representation and limits their communication with the outside world. In essence, their imprisonment presumes their guilt and creates an almost impossible rhetorical situation, particularly for the majority who do not have access to legal resources. Such imprisonment has a direct impact on students, their families, and their community. In addition, their imprisonment reflects a fractured democracy wherein millions are disenfranchised from the political process and lack the same legal rights because of their status.

This chapter first discusses how neoliberal policies limit the public sphere and help to create a system of mass incarceration. In response, the dominant models of prison literacy classes are often marketed to the prison as rehabilitation for participants, which can sometimes conflict with goals to challenge a system of mass incarceration. In contrast to traditional prison literacy classes, student advocacy campaigns focus on stopping deportations and releasing people from detention centers. The chapter focuses on Education Not Deportation (END) campaigns at Krome Detention Center between 2013 and 2017 and how this advocacy work shaped a letter-writing project started between my university writing center and a detention center. Writing in this context, then, is not just a personal note expressing sympathy or support; this writing is a collective act, challenging a prison-industrial complex that impacts both the classroom and the community. The work of student organizers can challenge our field to work beyond our disciplinary boundaries and help us find new possibilities for community writing in the classroom and writing centers.

PUBLIC IMPRISONED

Neoliberal policies have changed our relationship with the public sphere and placed limits on participation in it. As Tony Scott and Nancy Welch argue in *Composition in the Age of Austerity*, "From schools to garbage pickup to prisons, we have seen over the past forty years a sea change toward privatization and the economization of public services, and this change is often called neoliberalism" (7). This emphasis upon private enterprise is guided by a belief that "[g]overnment best achieves the greater public good by serving private interests and privatizing government functions" (7). Examples of such policies include legislatures diverting funding from public schools to private charter schools and Congress hiring private corporations to run detention centers. And this movement affects academia with a growing market-like emphasis upon rankings and performance even as government funding decreases. And as support for social programs decreases, government policies favor corporations, contributing to a shrinking of the public sphere. The political system, then, becomes more of a place for private-sector economic policies and less of a place for representative democracy. With unrestricted campaign contributions to candidates from corporations, it seems, super PACs control the discourse on media channels in support of certain policies.

It is difficult, then, to enter the public sphere when both the physical space and media are controlled by a few corporations. As Welch argues, many public spaces have become private spaces, and free-speech zones limit when and where people can share their ideas: "From the malling of suburbia to the vertical integration of radio, television, cable, film, music, and print outlets into a few media monopolies—we face dramatically shrinking material and virtual space . . ." ("Living Room" 474). Susan Wells discusses this broken public sphere as a "prison visiting room," a metaphor she draws from German scholars Oskar Negt and Alexander Kluge: "The visiting room allows communication between inside and out. It represents the prisoner's participation in both worlds" ("Rogue Cops" 335). Therefore, when we write, it is an "exchange between the private, the domain of production, and some approximations of the public sphere" (335). And in this prison visiting room for communication, "[b]oundaries are put in play for both prisoner and guest" (335).

And in the context of immigrant rights and the writing classroom, this prison visiting room is more than just a metaphor. As more people are placed in prisons/detention centers, immigrants are physically restricted in their communications with the outside world. Visitation is closely monitored and regulated, and private corporations charge fees for the use of telephones. In addition, raids on immigrant communities and imprisoning people in detention centers reflects neoliberalism's "reliance on crisis" (Scott and Welch 8). As the state and private corporations place immigrants behind bars, immigrants' rights are taken away as they are criminalized. As Jennifer Wingard notes, "[I]CE has developed an evolving threat matrix where anyone can move from a misdemeanor to [being branded as] a felon in one step" (54). In addition, as Tobi Jacobi points out, "Many universities are inextricably tied to the prison industrial complex through everything from investment in Corrections Corporation of America (CCA) market shares to UNICOR (Bureau of Prisons) dorm furniture contracts" ("Austerity" 108).

The prison-industrial complex's restrictions on communication are significant, particularly since the United States has the highest rate of imprisoning its people in the world. Starting in 1972, the US prison population has increased from 350,000 people to more than 2 million (M. Alexander 8). In *The New Jim Crow: Mass Incarceration in the Age of Colorblindness,* Michelle Alexander emphasizes the problems with the system:

> One way of understanding our current system of mass incarceration is to think of it as a birdcage with a locked door. It is a set of structural arrangements that locks a racially distinct group into a subordinate political, social, and economic position, effectively creating a second-class citizenship. Those trapped within the system are not merely disadvantaged, in the sense that they are competing on an unequal playing field or face additional hurdles to political or economic success; rather, the system itself is structured to lock them into a subordinate position. (185)

Similarly, the immigration system reflects this "birdcage with a locked door" that puts people in "a subordinate position" (185). As Patrisia Macías-Rojas argues in *From Deportation to Prison: The Politics of Immigration Enforcement in Post–Civil Rights America,* the system profits off criminalizing immigrants: "Immigration has surpassed drug violations as the leading charge that sends people to prison . . ." (18). Detention centers have a long but changing history in the United States. Ellis Island in 1892 was the first detention center that kept immigrants "between a few days and several weeks" (Americans for Immigrant Justice and the Southern Poverty

Law Center 5); however, the United States "largely did not detain immigrants in the past" (5) compared to the practices now. Detention started to grow with legislation like the 1996 Illegal Immigration Reform and Immigration Responsibility Act (IIRIRA) and the Department of Homeland Security Appropriations Act, 2010 (United States, Congress). As noted earlier, this bipartisan 2010 bill requires that at least 33,400 beds be maintained for detention at all times, which in practice has meant often using private prison companies like the GEO Group and filling these beds with immigrants.

This system has been supported by administrations from both sides of the aisle, and when Donald Trump became president, prison companies CoreCivic's and GEO's stock prices soared. In 2017, GEO gave $1.7 million to politicians in their lobbying efforts (Americans for Immigrant Justice and the Southern Poverty Law Center 6), and the number of immigrants imprisoned increased:

> On a given day in August 2019, U.S. Immigration and Customs Enforcement (ICE) held over 55,000 people in detention—a massive increase from five years ago when ICE held fewer than 30,000 people. Unsurprisingly, the United States has the largest immigration incarceration system in the world. (2)

The mass incarceration of immigrants was a three-billion-dollar industry in 2018, and Florida, where my university resides, has a large number of immigrants imprisoned. According to Americans for Immigrant Justice, "As of April 2019, Florida had the sixth-largest population of people detained by ICE in the United States" (2). The conditions of detention centers are dangerous, including "inadequate medical and mental health care, lack of accommodations for and discrimination against individuals with disabilities, and overuse of solitary confinement" (2). In addition, imprisoning children is part of this system. For example, there is an immigrant prison for children in Homestead, about thirty miles from FIU, which can imprison over two thousand immigrant children requesting asylum (Kennedy, "Homestead"). And as children are separated from their families, "The trauma that unaccompanied children experience pre-migration, during migration, upon arrival to the US, and within communities can threaten their short- and long-term health and well-being" (Linton et al. 129). Incarceration can affect an entire family. Immigrants imprisoned in detention centers do not have the right to an attorney and have limited communication with the outside world.

As a result of neoliberal economic policies, the detention center is a space often regulated by private prison companies. Visitors must be approved for their visits, arrive at least an hour or more before the scheduled times, go through security, and place all personal belongings in lockers. A visitor may not even have a pencil or piece of paper for fear it could be used as a dangerous tool. The conversation between the visitor and the imprisoned immigrant is through a telephone as they see each other only through a protective glass. And, of course, anything they say can be monitored and perhaps recorded by guards. Immigrants must pay fees to use the phone to call someone outside the center and can only earn money—one dollar a day at Krome and other centers—by working and doing various jobs at the center. In this space, the public sphere has no freedom, and immigrants' ability to see other people, communicate, and work is controlled by a private company or ICE.

In response to this mass incarceration and neoliberal environment, writing teachers have often focused on prison education, including writing courses/writing centers (Jacobi, "Austerity" and "Speaking Out"; Berry; Cavallaro; Hinshaw; Plemons). Over the past decade, the Prison Studies Project has created a directory of prison education programs even though Pell grants for prison education programs ended under the Clinton administration in 1994 (Pettit, "Ending Ban"), making sustaining such programs difficult. In *Beyond Progress in the Prison Classroom: Options and Opportunities,* Anna Plemons discusses how the "liberatory" goals of education can contrast with the realities of a prison system, showing "[t]he tension between complicity and confrontation" in prison education programs (10). A prison writing course, for example, often includes the transformational narrative whereby a writer talks about how they have worked to become a better person. However, as Plemons notes, there are problems with such an assignment: "A program that presumes a writer's highest goal to be individual transformation requires incarcerated scholars to produce texts that exemplify individual meaning-making, thereby foreclosing a critical examination of the wider enterprise" (Plemons 49–50). Although there are different approaches to teaching writing classes in prisons, this dominant model of a writing assignment places blame and emphasis upon the individual writer for self-transformation and ignores the larger social factors of the prison-industrial complex. Our writing assignments, then, can be shaped by neoliberal policies and replicate an ideology of individual responsibility rather than an examination of the private sector's profit motive in criminalizing more and more people.

Prison writing scholarship explores that tension between how to teach a course justified as rehabilitative by the prison system and how to challenge neoliberal incarceration itself. For instance, Jacobi sees such writing as "[p]art of a collective voice and social movement that demands viable alternatives to incarceration" ("Speaking Out" 52). Cavallaro et al. "[r]eject the idea that our work in the prison classroom is aimed at reforming or saving our students." And Patrick W. Berry questions when people turn to "[e]ducation and literacy as the answer to a myriad of social problems" such as mass incarceration (11). However, Plemons argues that we need a shift in our thinking about prison education, favoring a decolonizing approach and pointing out, "Much of the scholarship on prison education highlights the struggle among academics to transcend colonial logics when describing the value of literacy in prison" (52).

Similarly, university/community writing centers also have engaged with prisons, focusing often on educational initiatives of individual writers. In *Rhetoric of Respect: Recognizing Change at a Community Writing Center,* Tiffany Rousculp discusses how community writing centers can consider a mission of "change" (91). Rousculp's Salt Lake Community College Community Writing Center, for example, includes writing projects inside jails. In addition, the University of Miami's and Goucher College's prison initiatives have featured a writing center where university tutors give individual writing consultations inside the prison. Some of these projects are started by nonprofits like Exchange for Change in Miami, where faculty from FIU and other schools volunteer to teach creative writing courses (Hinshaw). Like the writing classes critiqued by Plemons, such projects are constrained by a neoliberal system that continues to place more and more people behind bars for profit and restricts their ability to communicate beyond the prison yard other than within these educational initiatives.

What's even more striking is that such educational initiatives are not even allowed in a detention center like Krome, located near my university in Miami. First, a writing class or writing center partnership with a detention center is not allowed by ICE. Theoretically, a detention center is supposed to be a temporary imprisonment for immigrants as they resolve their immigration cases, so authorities deny education even though many immigrants are imprisoned for years as they challenge their deportations. Krome detention center offers detainees only the ability to watch anger-management videos or attend religious meetings.

Writing classes as described by Jacobi, Berry, and others might find some interested participants in detention centers, but the political/economic reality of such centers complicates such a pedagogy. Unlike a prison, where people have received their sentences, immigrants in a detention center are stuck in a legal limbo as they await decisions on their ability to stay in the country. They often lack legal representation and have few rights. There is no pretense that the detention center is striving to be rehabilitative like a prison. There are no positive public relations and news stories, as there can be about prison education; instead, detention centers want to make immigrants less visible to the public. As Wingard comments on this strategy of creating fear from perceived threats: "Therefore all citizens of the United States must be aware that there are invisible enemies who are waging invisible wars against us who must be stopped, even though we cannot see them" (59). Making immigrants invisible reflects neoliberalism's emphasis upon crisis grounded in fear. A traditional prison literacy initiative conflicts with such neoliberal policies and doesn't address the immediate needs of immigrants contesting their deportations.

NINE MILES TO KROME

Calle Ocho is a street in Little Havana, where Cuban immigrants made their home after escaping the communist Castro regime in the 1960s. From Little Havana, go further west and there's Florida International University. Started in 1972, FIU was built on what was once an airport and now has become the university that awards the most bachelors' and masters' degrees to Latinx students in the country. There are over fifty thousand students representing at least one hundred countries. Fifteen minutes further down Eighth Street, before the alligators of the Everglades, there's the Krome North Service Processing Center, where immigrants are detained (imprisoned) for weeks, months, and years. Only nine miles separate Krome detention center from FIU, and there's no sign telling you to turn onto a long gravel road leading to a giant prison security gate there in the Everglades. Inside there are often five to six hundred immigrants imprisoned because of their citizenship status. The name of this place has so much negative power. In a conference with one of my students, the word *Krome* is mentioned, and my student starts to cry because she remembers a family member's prolonged stay there.

The placement of Krome—both its physical location and its historical context—reflects policies that attempt to make foreign policy and immigrants invisible to the public. First, Krome was a nuclear missile base during the Cold War. According to Jana K. Lipman's historical account, residents of Miami were largely unaware at the time that there were nuclear missiles within a few miles of downtown (119–20). After the 1962 Cuban Missile Crisis, the United States installed a missile launch center in South Florida ("HM69 Nike Missile Base"). At first, the missiles were conventional weapons, but they were replaced with nuclear missiles in 1965 (Lipman 118). Because the missile site was in the Everglades, a swamp, it was built above ground. The soldiers guarding the base experienced tough living conditions, particularly because of the plentiful mosquitoes that persist today. After the last missiles were removed in 1979, the military base became a place for refugees (Lipman 118–19). According to Lipman, there was not much public discussion about transforming a nuclear base into a camp (prison) for refugees, but when thousands of Cubans and Haitians fled persecution in their home countries, the United States government decided to use Krome as one of the places to house them.

The 1980 Mariel boatlift had brought Cuban immigrants wanting to leave Castro's regime, and at the same time, thousands of Haitian immigrants were escaping the Duvalier regime in Haiti. Cubans were treated mostly as political "refugees" because of the United States' Cold War relationship with Cuba. However, Haitians making the journey to the United States often were treated as if they were only leaving the island because of economic reasons even though the brutal Duvalier killed and tortured many Haitians. Edwidge Danticat's powerful memoir *Brother, I'm Dying* tells the story of her elderly uncle traveling to Miami because of the violence in Haiti. Her uncle had a travel visa, but because he mentioned the desire for temporary asylum at the airport, he was arrested and sent to Krome. Without his proper medication, he died a few days later. This harsh treatment has continued. In 1982, thirty-three Haitian women held a hunger strike to protest their conditions, and Krome force-fed some of them (Jaynes). In the 1980s and 1990s, there were widespread reports of guards physically abusing and raping detainees at Krome (Bach). Now an all-male facility, Krome continues to have problems.

Besides refugees seeking asylum, Krome is a place where a resident without the right papers can end up. A boy arrives here when he is four years old, grows up and graduates, gets a job, but is never able to become a citizen. He's now forty-something years old, and at a traffic stop, or some other run-in with the law, he is arrested. Or it could be someone who graduated from high school, wants to attend college, but isn't able to become a citizen. When it's discovered that they are undocumented, they can be given an order of deportation and sent to a detention center like Krome.

A visitation project was started in 2013, affiliated with a national group called CIVIC (now named Freedom for Immigrants), with a goal of ending the isolation at this all-male detention center by talking to detainees for an hour at a time. The local group organizing the visitations is called Friends of Miami-Dade Detainees. Such a project requires approval by the detention center, and it always has the threat of being ended or suspended. The initial tour of the facility took place in October 2013. As volunteers walked from the parking lot to the entrance, we could hear the sound of gunshots in the air from the nearby firing range. Then inside, we got to see where the men—usually five to six hundred—slept and ate. There was a room with padded walls where they could lock people up when they had mental breakdowns. Men were dressed in different color prison uniforms: blue, orange, or red. The color indicates how serious the offense is. Of course, the offense that everyone has committed is not having the right papers. Although a blue uniform is supposed to represent someone whose only offense is not having the right papers, and someone dressed in red committed a felony, the colors aren't always accurate. Some men at Krome had lived in the United States for many years but their countries of birth included Cuba, Ethiopia, Eritrea, Bangladesh, Brazil, Colombia, Honduras, El Salvador, England, Mexico, Jamaica, the Bahamas, and Haiti. During weekly visitations from 2013 to 2017, detainees discussed participating in hunger strikes and other forms of civil disobedience at Krome. Similar to what happened in the 1980s, a judge ruled in 2015 that Krome officials could use "nasal-gastric tubes" to force-feed refugees from Bangladesh who had gone on a hunger strike to protest being held for years in detention (Alexandra Martinez).

Usually all communication is through a glass barrier and phone, but on that first tour, as we walked through the facility, a man wearing red handed us a letter and asked for help. Wally was born in Mexico but had lived in the United States since he was fourteen years old. He had an eleven-year-old son who was a citizen. In February 2012, Wally was arrested at his house in Bradenton (near Tampa) because he was undocumented. He had no criminal record. The only reason he was being detained was that he had overstayed his visa and then reentered the country four times to be with his son. He had crossed the desert in Texas, near Brownsville, and spent four days and four nights trying to get back to his eleven-year-old boy. Wally nearly died from lack of water and exhaustion.

Even though he didn't have a lawyer, he was fighting his case and representing himself. He read up on immigration law with whatever resources they had at the detention center, and he was doing everything he could to stop his deportation so he could return to his son. He said the men called him the "jailhouse lawyer," as he helped them with their cases too. He wanted the help of a student organizing group like SWER (Students Working for Equal Rights), DreamActivist, or United We Dream who conduct END campaigns to stop deportations.

Along with other students, SWER member Francis, whose words begin this chapter, agreed to help, because Wally wanted to go public and use the press to share his story and connect with the community. Students spoke with Wally's family to implement an END campaign that included a call-in campaign, social media, press releases, rallies outside the detention center, and an op-ed. SWER leaders planned and held a rally outside a detention center where Wally's brother made a speech in front of the media. Wally wanted a petition, and he asked his brother to send a photograph that could be used. In this collective effort, student organizers and I worked on drafting an online petition and posting it on change.org. We collaborated online and composed the following:

> Petition:
> Please stop the deportation of Wally, a father who wants to take care of his eleven-year-old son.
> Wally is currently being held in the Krome detention center in Miami.
> Wally came to this country for a better life. In 1990, Wally left Guanajuato, Mexico, when he was fourteen years old. He earned his GED and studied air-conditioning repair at Manatee Technical Institute in Bradenton, Florida. He has worked in construction. He is a Christian and a member of Vida Nueva Church in Bradenton.

Wally has spent fourteen months in two different detention centers and fears he will be deported soon. Wally has no criminal record. The only reason he is being detained is that he overstayed his visa and then reentered the country four times to be with his son.

Because of the psychological stress of his father being away, Wally's son has gotten sick. Missing his father has affected his son's schoolwork and mental health. He even wrote a letter to the deportation officer asking for help to bring his father home. He goes to sleep at night wanting to see his father again.

In February 2012, Wally was arrested at his house in Bradenton, Florida, because he was undocumented. And the last time he saw his son was July 24, 2012.

Wally says that the reason he keeps coming back to the United States is to be with his son. He crossed the desert in Texas, near Brownsville, and spent four days and four nights trying to get back to his eleven-year-old. Wally nearly died from lack of water and exhaustion.

Wally wants to become a civil engineer like his brother and father. His son is a US citizen. His brother is a US citizen. Give Wally a chance to be with his son.

Take action: SIGN the petition and call ICE @ 202-732-3000 or 202-732-3100!

Sample Script: *"Hi, I was calling to ask that ICE stop the deportation of Wally: A#XXXXXXXX. Wally has been living in the US since 1990 and has an eleven-year-old son. Please don't deport Wally!"*

As discussed in Chapter 2, this petition has a rhetorical strategy of emphasizing the person's connection to family and the community, invoking Americanisms as part of its argument. Wally is a father, and he wants to pursue his education and career. Also, he is a member of a church. Part of the argument is discussing American ideals and stressing that the person is a valuable member of the community. And besides asking people to sign, the petition encourages them to call ICE and support the person and use their A# (alien

\#). Importantly, Wally's story is not a story of transformation that might take place in a literacy class. The purpose of telling Wally's story is not to share his story with a university class to create an exchange between people on the inside of the prison and on the outside in the classroom. The purpose of the petition is one of action—to raise the profile of a case.

As the campaign progressed, there were conversations among Wally, the pro bono lawyers, the family, and the organizers. In these conversations, the END campaign sets a strategy about how to go public and to what extent it is a private or a public campaign. As Wally appealed his deportation, court dates were set and the call-in campaign intensified. Then in November, he was transferred to another detention center in Wakulla County outside of Tallahassee, as his case/appeal was pending. This move shows how the detention center system continues to disrupt detainees' lives. When people are transferred to a new detention center, they often lose contact with family and friends who are able to visit them. And if they do have a lawyer, that lawyer might not be able to visit them in person. And their court case would likely be conducted through video conferences. In consultation with Wally's family, the SWER group made a plan to call ICE, plan protests, contact representatives, and involve members of Wally's church.

In December, the SWER group's END team sent out this email:

Good Morning everyone,
    A family needs your help!
    Wally came to this country when he was fourteen years old. Harvey, Wally's eleven-year-old US citizen [son,] has become sick waiting for his father, who has spent the past fourteen months at a detention center. Please help us bring Wally back to his son!
    You can take action by:
(1) Calling ICE and asking for Wally to be released and be reunited with his son for the holidays.
    Numbers to call:
    Acting Director, John Sandweg (202) 732-3000
    AND

> Assistant Field Office Director (Detention): Conrad C. Agagan
> Assistant Field Office Director Line: (407) 440-5100
> Script: "Hi, my name is_____. I am calling to ask that ICE stop the deportation of Wally: (A#XXXXXXXXX). Wally has been living in the US since 1990 and has an eleven-year-old son who needs his father. Please don't deport Wally—let him spend the holidays with his eleven-year-old son.
> (2) Posting his picture and script through social media to get the word out.
> Hashtags: #Not1More #ENDOurPain #StopICE
> *Picture attached below
> We thank you for your support!

This call to action includes specific ICE targets and the use of social media hashtags to raise the visibility of Wally's case. In addition, congressional representatives were contacted to see if they could help. In December of 2013, the Progressive Media Project (PMP) welcomed an op-ed to tell Wally's story and how it connected with those of many other immigrant parents. With help from SWER and other groups, the petition gained nearly five thousand signatures, and the op-ed was published in several newspapers around the country. People wrote online comments from different states and countries in support of Wally. After the op-ed was published, the call-in campaign continued in January and February. The campaign reflected a collective effort combining writing and action to advocate for Wally and his family. Because Wally was imprisoned inside the detention center, he lacked the ability to participate in these events of advocacy. Neoliberal policies of incarceration make it extremely difficult for immigrants facing deportation to participate in the public sphere at all.

Then in March, Wally was transferred back to Krome and tried for a final stay of removal. The next week, the online detainee locator (locator.ice.gov/odls/) indicated that Wally was "not in custody." Wally's family members called to confirm what it meant: Wally was deported in March 2014 after being held in detention for two years and one month. Since Wally had reentered the country after being deported, his offense was treated as a felony. He wore the red, not the blue. Wally had not committed a crime other than wanting to be with his son. At the next SWER meeting on campus, students discussed the campaign for Wally and shared their own hardships when deportation affected their own families. One student shared how he and his brother had to live without their mother. He continues to attend college, and he wants to change the laws to make it possible for his mother to return to the United States. Even though the campaign wasn't successful, organizers continue to work on ending deportations.

The project was led by community organizers and did not have any direct link with a particular class or university department. However, student organizers' rhetorical skills combined with action offer a different framework than traditional prison literacy initiatives. Although Berry, Jacobi, and other scholars discuss the tension between teaching a rehabilitative prison literacy course and social activism, this project focused more on organizing and connecting people for campaigns to escape incarceration. Instead of a writing class, this student-led project challenges neoliberal incarceration policies. The goal for such a project is to make visible what the public sphere makes invisible: the incarceration and deportation of immigrants. Although the campaign to stop Wally's deportation wasn't successful, student organizers had achieved many victories with other END campaigns throughout the country. These organizing efforts inspired a letter-writing project between our writing center and Krome detention center.

WRITING CENTERS, SOCIAL JUSTICE, AND LETTERS

The letter writing project between our university writing center and Krome focused on connecting imprisoned immigrants to resources and groups that would advocate for their release. In addition, when given permission by incarcerated immigrants, the media could be contacted to profile cases. Instead of organizing a literacy class, which was forbidden by Krome, this project aimed to follow some of the activist rhetorical approaches of student organizers.

In many projects, letter writing with those who are incarcerated begins with a goal of greater understanding and sympathy from those on the outside. Amnesty International has a letter-writing campaign every December to show solidarity with people whose human rights have been violated and who are imprisoned. Wendy Hinshaw discusses letter exchanges between writing classrooms and those incarcerated in prison as part of the Exchange for Change program: students on the inside (the prison) and students on the outside (the university classroom) write about similar topics and have a conversation through writing letters to each other (using pseudonyms). She points out that such exchanges can help "build community through listening" to one another (69). Another example of letter writing with prisons, Detainee Allies, is an organization started by several San Diego State professors. They have created an online collection of letters from immigrant detainees (Pettit). The purpose of the project is not to "solve" the issue, but to "document" what is happening (Pettit). A project called "Vision from The Inside" turns letters written by detained people into art. The goal of their project is to publicize what many immigrants are experiencing inside detention centers and how people are coping. Such projects have value in creating conversation between those incarcerated and those on the outside, a way to end isolation and show solidarity. Some detainees have not had direct contact with family members or friends for years, and several commented how they valued and were thankful for receiving a letter in the mail, including those from the volunteers in the visitation program. In addition, sometimes detainees write back about their desire to go to college and what they would like to study, asking for books that they can read while they are confined. The tutors at the writing center, for example, donated novels, dictionaries, GED preparation books, and atlases. However, besides showing solidarity and responding to these requests, we wanted to add an activist component to this letter-writing project and help challenge incarceration policies. Most letters from the detention center focused on people's frustration as to why they are being imprisoned and also their need for legal help.

The project started with volunteers who visited Krome detention center composing letters to those they had visited. With support from the writing center director, Dr. Paula Gillespie, FIU-affiliated visitors could use the writing center mailbox to send and receive mail to the detention center. More letter writers volunteered to help when the project was discussed during a writing center staff meeting and during my class. The organizers of Friends of Miami Dade Detainees had a list of people who wanted visitations at the detention center, and once we had their A#s we could write letters. Student volunteers and I composed letters in English, Spanish, and French to detainees, telling them about the hotline we had started, a four-digit number they could call that was free so that they wouldn't be charged money that many don't have to call their families. Students would write the letters by hand in the writing center, or I would type them in my office. Also, we created letter writing events to encourage others to correspond, including an action with the Mass Story Lab hosted by the University of Miami in February of 2017. This traveling project aims to raise awareness through featuring five-minute stories from people who are directly affected by mass incarceration. FIU's chapter of the Student Alliance for Prison Reform, which has done a variety of activities on campus to raise awareness about the prison system, also joined the project and set up a letter-writing table in the FIU student center. Here are some sample introductory letters:

Sample Spanish First Letter
El 14 de agosto, 2014
XXXXXXXX (A#XXX-XXX-XXX)
Estimado Señor XXXXXXX ,

Le escribo para mandarle un saludo. Siento mucho que se encuentre en esta situación tan difícil. No soy un abogado. Soy un voluntario para el grupo, "Friends of Miami-Dade Detainees."

Cada semana, nosotros (con "Friends of Miami-Dade Detainees") visitamos a los hombres en Krome. Para hacer esto, se necesitaría que usted diera permiso y firmara la lista para aprobar visitantes que Krome le provee ("Friends of

Miami-Dade Detainees"). La lista está en tu pod (donde tú vivas).

Si quisiera, "Friends of Miami-Dade Detainees" provee una línea telefónica en la cual usted se puede comunicar con una amistad o familiar. Es gratis y el número es *9233. También, usted puede escribir una carta a mi dirección.

Le deseamos lo mejor.

Atentamente,

Sample English First Letter
August 8, 2014
Dear XXXX (A#: XXX-XXX-XXX),

Hello. My name is _____. I am not a lawyer, but I am a volunteer for the group, "Friends of Miami-Dade Detainees."

Each week, we visit men in Krome. If you would like for us to visit you, please sign our visitation list. The list is in your pod.

Also, we have a free hotline (*9233) that you can call to leave messages or to connect with family members and friends. The phone call does not cost you anything.

I hope things improve for you, and I hope to talk to you soon.

Sincerely,

Students and I then followed up these introductory letters with more personal letters based on the responses. Also, some men would share their stories when people would visit them at the detention center. But in the process of writing letters, there's a possibility of not getting a response and the letter could be returned for various reasons—the person could have been transferred to another center or deported.

After these initial letters, we tried to connect detainees with people who could help. The letter writing project became more than just writing to show solidarity; it became part of different kinds of action modeled by student organizers. The FIU law school was one resource, with its immigration clinic, and represents some detainees pro bono as many cannot afford legal representation. In their letters, detainees would sometimes ask someone to attend their court hearing at the detention center. In some hearings, for example, there was no one in the courtroom other than the judge, the prosecution, the defense attorney (if the detainee has one), and the detainee. Having a family member or friend present is a show of support from the community and lets the court know the person is not alone. Also, if family members couldn't be present, the letter-writing project participants sometimes spoke with their family members and passed along or relayed information to them. One man worried about his access to HIV medication if he was deported. Other men feared that if they were deported back to their birthplaces they would be killed because of their political beliefs or other aspects of their identity, including their sexual orientation.

In responding to some of these cases, student organizers from SWER assisted in crafting and sharing petitions about detainees and contacting the media. For example, in July of 2015, Nina Agrawal, a reporter for the local NPR station (WRLN), received permission to bring in a camera and recording equipment, and ICE officials gave consent forms to detainees (three of whom were people we had been visiting for several months) for an interview. There was much concern about the consent forms, because at Krome, signing something can have great significance, including agreeing to one's own deportation. The men signed the forms after analyzing them closely, but right before the interview two of the men who had been held for several months were suddenly released. Therefore, the men were not interviewed, because they were freed from Krome. The power of the press or going public gave them freedom; their stories were no longer invisible. At the interview, several ICE officials, including the director of Krome, greeted us in the lobby. NPR was able to interview two detainees, including a man profiled in the story who was being deported to Brazil after living in the United States for twenty years.

Arranging such media visits is a bureaucratic challenge, and so student organizers and I drafted petitions for other men, including those from Bangladesh and Ethiopia requesting asylum, who waited sometimes years in the detention center for a decision on their cases. For example, in January 2017, Abdul was released after having been incarcerated for fifteen months. We had created a petition for him, telephoned ICE, and connected him to a pro bono attorney. However, the work of student organizers shaped this letter-writing project into something different from many traditional prison literacy efforts. The rhetorical and advocacy work of student organizers in assisting people who are imprisoned in detention centers shows a sophisticated use of media. Such campaigns often require publicizing a case so that people can speak out and pressure ICE and/or their elected representatives to act. This letter-writing project was shaped, then, by the work of student organizers and found a connection with our writing center and other interested student groups on campus.

CONCLUSION

Making visible what the public sphere has made invisible may be a guiding principle for such advocacy work. Instead of being in the shadows, people gain a power through using a public voice. Doing so is difficult, particularly when confronting a neoliberal system of incarceration that profits off of immigrants' being behind bars. In addition, neoliberal policies are often fueled by the fear of the unknown, creating a perpetual sense of crisis and threats with the rhetoric of elected leaders demonizing immigrants as invaders.

Such work raises questions about community-writing projects. Writing partnerships can be effective in showing support for a group and engaging in an educational initiative like teaching a class or conducting a writing center inside a prison. At the same time, though, such partnerships can be limited and sometimes not permitted by a system that incarcerates and exploits immigrants. As Shannon Carter, Deborah Mutnick, Stephen Parks, and Jessica Pauszek comment in their introduction to *Writing Democracy: The Political Turn in and beyond the Trump Era,* "[c]ommunity engagement work—despite the best of intentions—too often underscores the problem of supporting social justice movements absent a critique of systemic inequality, escalating state repression and surveillance, and a rapacious market indifferent to human suffering" (13). A writing project connected to a detention center, then, is encountering a system of mass incarceration that exploits immigrants. Community writing, then, becomes less of an opportunity for participants to become "better" writers; instead, this kind of community writing combined with advocacy has goals that extend beyond our disciplinary boundaries. Letter writing is being guided by community organizers who enact campaigns to challenge deportations. In addition, letter writing can be a way to share the contact information of the law school and other pro bono attorneys that can help navigate this system. Such work pushes us to think beyond our discipline and recognize writing as one tool for community organizing. By foregrounding student voices, the writing classroom becomes a space where students can have a conversation and engage with projects that focus also on organizing rather than just volunteering.

Not all campaigns and petitions succeed, as seen with Wally's case. In addition, some letters didn't lead to an activist campaign, because there wasn't enough time before the person was deported. At one point, the hotline was suspended. These institutional barriers are increased even more by anti-immigrant policies passed by the Trump administration. Although petitions and media campaigns continue to be tools for challenging incarceration, organizers continue to adapt their tactics and strategies. For example, in 2019 *The Infiltrators* received premieres in various film festivals across the country, including Sundance. As the film about how undocumented people organized within a detention center gained notoriety, one of the detainees who helped the youth organizers inside Broward Detention Center, Claudio, was deported to Argentina shortly after the premiere. Such an act by ICE shows the complex and dangerous landscape of immigration in the United States seven years after the action at Broward. Publicity and rhetorical advocacy work can make a big difference in helping to stop deportations; however, the anti-immigrant system continues to marginalize and exploit people, and strategies must adapt as more change is needed. As César Cuauhtémoc García Hernández comments, "The United

States should shut down its immigration prison system. The federal government should redirect the billions of dollars it spends jailing migrants—$2.7 billion alone in 2017 for ICE's detention system—to helping them navigate the labyrinthine legal process."

If universities and writing programs/centers can engage in community-organizing initiatives, we can challenge a system of incarceration that exploits people. This work moves us beyond the prison waiting room metaphor of public discourse and engages with different ways of participating in the public sphere. In addition, this work connects with our mission as educators. This kind of work can represent university-community engagement that challenges incarceration. For instance, the night that Abdul was released, he walked down the isolated road from the detention center, and when he was picked up he asked if he could see FIU. He had heard talk about FIU for several months through visits and letters. That night he was released was rainy, but we drove around the campus and looked at some key buildings, and he commented on the beauty of the campus. We saw the giant palm trees lining the front entrance, the towering library at the center of campus, and all the new buildings built on this place that was once an airport. After gaining freedom and joining his family in the Northeast, Abdul plans to attend college.

5

A Shift toward Being an Accomplice

> We need to raise the level of consciousness of the college campus so that people can make their own decisions and can design activities or organizing, whichever way they want to. As of right now, there's a lot of lobbying going on. I don't advocate for lobbying as much as I advocate for organizing the people and having them lobby themselves. . . .
>
> —Claudio

THE GOAL IN THIS BOOK WAS TO foreground student voices like Claudio's from the prologue and argue that their work as organizers in the immigrant rights movement needs a greater presence in the community-writing classroom. The syllabus that begins this book shows the many assumptions that I made as a new writing teacher and does not include a curriculum inclusive of student organizing against unjust policies affecting their own lives. Student organizers have campaigned to stop deportations, advocated for in-state tuition, and practiced civil disobedience in support of immigration reform. In these efforts, organizers have used a variety of rhetorical skills combined with action: drafting petitions, composing op-eds, and using social media. In doing so, student organizers challenge systemic inequalities in immigration policy, the prison system, and deportations. This organizing work is responding to a neoliberal system that continues to restrain democracy by shrinking the public sphere and favoring policies for the private sector. In addition, the preceding chapters have also explored some of the ways that teachers can act in solidarity with immigrant students on campus and in the community, including making student voices more central to the classroom/curriculum and participating in pro-immigrant actions both on and off campus. If the field of writing studies moves beyond the limits of disciplinarity and takes more of a political turn, then there needs to be a shift in pedagogy.

This shift does not mean a rejection of all community partnerships and service-learning, but it can be a way to bring together and build upon different aspects of the field's scholarship. Scholars have found important organizing principles already from the work of Saul Alinsky (Goldblatt) and the need for more activism within our departments (Parks). Also, an intersectional approach to the work we do raises important questions about our ethical responsibilities as writing teachers in responding to racism, including police violence toward people of color (Kynard, "All I Need"). And as white writing teachers practice critical race education (Baker-Bell et al.), the writing classroom needs to reject the ideas of white supremacy (Inoue). In this racist system, Kate Vieira stresses the important role that immigration papers play in writers' literacies and the opportunities available to them. And as Ana Milena Ribero notes, citizenship excludes many people based on their identities, including some students in the writing classroom. As Sara del Pilar Alvarez discusses the distinctive qualities, or what she calls "conciencia bilingüe," in immigrant rights organizers' writing, she highlights the complex literacies in their activism about these issues.

To build upon the work of this scholarship and the work of student organizers, this final chapter explores some guiding principles for a pedagogical shift. However, teachers will create different pedagogies based on their own positionalities. My identity as a white male citizen shapes and limits my perspective, thereby affecting what a new role for the writing teacher might mean for me. These principles, then, are offered not as an exact model but instead one to encourage more conversation about how we can make student organizing more a focus of what we do: (1) a rethinking of the possible roles and responsibilities of the writing teacher as students respond to systemic inequalities; (2) a greater emphasis upon long-term community organizing led by students and the communities in which they live; and (3) a focus on writing as part of a network of action. In this discussion of principles is a reflection on how such work can start to be applied in revising syllabi, connecting new students to student leaders, and incorporating student activism into creative projects.

ROLES OF THE WRITING TEACHER

And so if we had, like, even one teacher who reached out, like oh, this was amazing, this really affected me, I didn't know this was happening, that would have really, I think, been helpful to us in maybe our future work when trying harder to build alliances with teachers.

—Mohammad

As argued in the previous chapters, and as indicated by Mohammad's comment from the prologue, student organizers have often been ignored by faculty during their campaigns. Shifting from a partnership model of community engagement to one that includes more emphasis upon student organizing can change the writing teacher's role into a more active, listening one. In a community partner model, the teacher often emphasizes that students need to become active citizens in the community and engage in service-learning or other community-minded projects organized by nonprofits. In addition, by volunteering for nonprofits, students can connect their individual projects with larger social issues and consider what it means to be active citizens. In this approach, the teacher coordinates this partnership between the classroom and the community. However, as discussed in the previous chapters, many organizers like Mohammad are confronting systemic inequalities of a neoliberal system that directly impacts their own lives and those of their communities. And the goal of being active citizens is problematic if students are excluded from citizenship based on anti-immigrant and racist laws. If teachers foreground student concerns, listen to student organizers, and include such community organizing in the curriculum, then the roles and responsibilities of the writing teacher can shift too.

First, this changing role reflects an ethical responsibility, or what Leigh Patel calls "answerability." Scholars need to consider the ways they are answerable to learning, knowledge, and context.

Patel writes about the importance of decolonizing our approach to education and points out how "[s]chooling has acted as a conduit for intertwined systems of oppression, including racist capitalism, heteropatriarchy, and ableism" (80). Patel discusses her reaction to the George Zimmerman verdict's being announced at the same time she was at an academic conference. She reflects upon the "disconnect" (67) between what was discussed at the conference and a court decision that found Zimmerman innocent of shooting Trayvon Martin:

> Schooling is one of the key locations of social reproduction in society. That means, put less academically, that schools are one of the core spaces where some are privileged and others are marginalized. It is where standards of competency and images of intellect are conveyed, all culturally based and, typically, biased. Schools, as a part of a nation built on white supremacy, reflect this culture. From pedagogy and curriculum to policy and private interests, schools do the bidding of a nation constructed to eradicate Indigenous populations, ensure that populations of color are trained to populate low-income home, work, and incarceration spaces, and maintain property rights for European Americans. (67)

Education, then, can replicate social inequalities, including the ways that white supremacy sustains social hierarchies and institutional racism. And a community-writing course could also reinscribe the very inequalities that it aims to change. For example, the writing teacher could ignore the fact that some students are excluded from citizenship and marginalized by anti-immigrant and white supremacist laws. A community-writing pedagogy needs to make more central the voices of students confronting an oppressive neoliberal system. In community projects, we need to reflect upon the context of the work that we are doing as scholars and teachers: "Projects of systemic social change cannot pursue knowledge without regard to the context they are trying to change" (Patel 81). In the context of immigrant rights, students and their families are resisting a system that dehumanizes and deports.

Also, teachers like me have an ethical obligation to consider how teaching practices can reinforce or challenge institutional racism. Past scholarship often includes pedagogical assumptions about citizenship, identity, and privilege that are unchallenged. In other words, my beginning years as a teacher assumed that student experiences were similar to my own, thereby reinforcing a white gaze. My first community-writing course, for example, often explored questions about voting and citizenship; however, my curriculum design did not acknowledge the reality that many students were prevented from becoming citizens because of their status. In discussing culturally sustaining pedagogies, Django Paris and H. Samy Alim discuss the prevalence of this white gaze:

> What would our pedagogies look like if this gaze weren't the dominant one? What would liberating ourselves from this gaze and the educational expectations it forwards mean for our abilities to envision new forms of teaching and learning? What if, indeed, the goal of teaching and learning with youth of color was not ultimately to see how closely students could perform White middle-class norms but to explore, honor, extend, and, at times, problematize their heritage and community practices? (86)

Writing teachers can attempt to avoid acting on and through this white gaze by listening more to their students and considering how their classroom practices can be complicit in a system of inequality. Asao B. Inoue challenges white teachers to change the way they teach and end "White language supremacy" in the classroom. Carmen Kynard urges scholars and teachers to ask how their work responds to injustices like the violence against people of color ("All I Need Is One Mic"). In addition, for those teachers like me who may never have questioned their own assumptions about citizenship, identity, and the American dream, it is important to decenter our own perspectives in designing the curriculum for a community-writing course and reimagine what our roles can be.

These new roles for writing teachers mean more than being allies, and require a deeper commitment. The word *ally* might be used for a partnership model; for example, Anne Bishop defines an *ally* as someone "who works to end a form of oppression which gives her or him privilege" (152). However, the role of an ally is often one that can be seen as distant and separate and does not require much risk. As Aja Martinez points out, sometimes people call themselves allies, but it is merely an empty "gesture of allyship through the wearing of safety pins" (230). This allyship lacks action; just saying you're an ally—or wearing some symbol to represent that—isn't sufficient. In addition, as Martinez notes, it may be problematic for teachers to label themselves as allies (228–29). It can sound self-aggrandizing and lack substance without any action. Martinez prefers a different term that is "[t]rue allyship—an allyship that ventures into what others have aptly characterized instead as being an accomplice—whereas allies are viewed as those who identify as helpers to the oppressed, accomplices are those who will bear the risk of consequences . . . " (231). Other scholars in education and social work, including Jessica Powell and Amber Kelly, also prefer *accomplice* and stress the need for more teachers to be "risk-takers who aim to destabilize white supremacy in ourselves, families, schools, communities, and within the judicial system" (43). In her keynote speech to the International Writing Center Association, Neisha-Anne Green explains, "Accomplices actively demonstrate allyship" (29). She emphasizes the importance for accomplices to take risks and follow the lead of others:

> Titles are overrated. If you have to say that you're against oppression, then chances are you're probably really not. If you have to announce that you're an accomplice, then I already don't trust you. All I really wanna see is that WERK. (32)

Being an accomplice is more than stating your support; it means taking an active role and doing something. Such work requires taking a risk and acknowledges the ways in which some laws and policies commit violence toward people's identity and existence, including laws that exploit marginalized groups through travel bans on certain ethnic groups, laws that discriminate because of a person's sexual orientation, or policies that treat people as "illegal" because of their national origin. At the campus level, when universities implement anti-immigrant and racist policies, faculty may need to help challenge these policies as accomplices. In the community, when detention centers are incarcerating students and their families, then teachers can work with student organizers in finding ways together to use rhetorical skills to challenge anti-immigrant laws.

This role of the writing teacher as an accomplice, one that takes more risks, is one that listens more to student expertise. Paul Feigenbaum notes that many faculty often move to "[u]nfamiliar geographic regions, which is particularly problematic for scholars who place engagement at the core of their academic identities" (*Collaborative Imagination* 119). However, student organizers can help teachers learn more about their communities. Romeo García, for instance, discusses the importance of community listening but comments on how many of his teachers ignored his point of view in the classroom. García advises writing teachers to listen to the "lived experience" of the community (13). And most students attending public four-year institutions like mine reside in the local community. A study by the American Council on Education shows that 57 percent of first-year students studying at public institutions are less than fifty miles from home (Hillman and Weichman 2). And students' homes are an average distance of eighteen miles from the public university they attend; forty-six miles from their private school; and eight miles from their two-year institution (3).

Implementing this principle of a revised teacher's role in the classroom benefits from student input. The syllabus for my first community writing/service-learning course precedes the first chapter, and the revised version follows this final chapter. This new version is not a model but a work-in-progress, an attempt to address some of the gaps in my own pedagogy. My initial syllabus lacked readings about a number of topics, including intersectionality and racism. There were no texts authored by student organizers. Guest speakers tended to be only representatives of nonprofits, professors, or politicians. In addition, the structure of the assignments focused on volunteering a set number of hours for a nonprofit and encouraging students to define what being an active citizen is.

In addition to the inclusion of scholarship that focuses on identity and intersectionality, students in my classes have helped to critique and shape this new syllabus into something more responsive to student needs. In contrast with the original syllabus, there isn't a specific number of hours that a student needs to volunteer. In this newer version, students work individually or in groups to address a community project that interests them and, based on that project, determine what kind of writing might be appropriate. Some students may join the organizing efforts discussed by guest speakers and may work with organizers to help them recruit new members as they prepare to graduate. Others may work together to be part of new projects. This syllabus continues to be modified based on student concerns and input.

In this revised syllabus, published writings by undocumented organizers such as Prerna Lal and Tania Unzueta, Angelica Velazquillo, Nicolas Wulff, Thomas Kennedy, and Gaby Pacheco play a central role. Guest speakers include leaders of undocumented immigrant rights organizations, the Student Alliance for Prison Reform, environmental-rights groups, the campus voting-engagement project, the Student Government Association president, and students from previous semesters who share what they have accomplished with their community-writing projects. In addition, readings include perspectives from the field on immigration (Ribero), the Black Lives Matter movement (Richardson and Ragland), and community listening (García). The course readings address intersectionality (Crenshaw) as well as Asao Inoue's 2019 CCCC keynote on white supremacy and language. Also, the syllabus is a working document that invites student input for guest speakers and readings. Student suggestions are added to the syllabus with a note about the authors of the suggestion, including student Danielle's recommendation of Keeanga-Yamahtta Taylor's *From #BlackLivesMatter to Black Liberation*. Also, I share excerpts of my own scholarship where I am working through the idea of what role the writing teacher should play, drawing upon the work of Aja Martinez in defining allies and accomplices. We have a conversation about how community-writing scholarship has engaged in service-learning and community organizing, and students and I discuss possible roles for the writing teacher in the classroom. As teachers share the disciplinary expertise of our field with students, can we also be followers of student organizers and find ways of being more than allies and something more like accomplices?

LONG-TERM COMMUNITY ORGANIZING

This was about families this whole time. This wasn't about what political party. This wasn't about any of that. It was always about the families—our community, the kids, the parents—that's what it's always about. For me, honestly, as much as I would like to see immigration reform, comprehensive immigration reform, that's not the most important thing for me. The most important thing is organizing . . . creating new strategies.

—Viridiana

That's when I decided to step back and I started doing activism more with the criminalization of people of color. And that really opened my mind to realize that the whole system was created that way just to criminalize people. . . .

—Julio

Viridiana and Julio, like the other organizers quoted in the prologue, stress the importance of community organizing as a long-term project. The projects discussed in this book are not tied to a political party or about only one particular piece of legislation. Even if there are short-term goals, organizing is a way for communities to be better represented by elected politicians. In addition, such organizing is confronting a neoliberal system that exploits marginalized groups, including "the criminalization of people of color," as Julio points out.

Organizing tactics, then, must change and adapt based on the context. As discussed in Chapter 3, because of the shrinking public sphere organizers must sometimes use civil disobedience to create publics so their perspectives can be heard. Many media outlets are controlled by a handful of corporations, and neoliberal policies shrink the availability for public spaces (Welch, *Living Room*). In addition, as anti-immigrant policies continue, groups must adjust their tactics and strategies. At the state level in 2019, the ACLU issued a travel advisory for immigrants in Florida because of recent anti-immigrant legislation that bans sanctuary cities and requires all state agencies, including universities, to comply with ICE. The Florida Immigrant Coalition and other groups have filed a lawsuit against the state (Boryga). And nationally there continue to be numerous stories about ICE detaining and deporting immigrants, the political fight about the border wall, and more restrictions on asylum claims. There have been thousands of immigrant children held in a detention center in Homestead, Florida, located less than an hour away from my campus. In response, some groups have focused more on registering voters and supporting political candidates who will better represent pro-immigrant views.

Organizing is nonpartisan even if it focuses on voting and elections, because both political parties have exploited immigrants. In an interview about the documentary *The Infiltrators,* youth organizer Mohammad comments that President Trump is continuing the deportation machine that was present before he took office:

> We always joke that people finally care about us as immigrants under the Trump administration because he's so vocal about what they're doing. He's so vocal about separating children. These are all things that we witnessed under the Obama administration and we were screaming into the void. We had to literally send ourselves into detention centers to be able to show people the type of people getting deported and now under the Trump administration, people actually care. They're actually listening and they're looking for the information. Our communities can remain safe if we're at the forefront. ("*The Infiltrators* Film").

Mohammad argues that more people started to discuss deportation policies during the Trump administration. Indeed, if it is true, then we can ask why this is the case. Perhaps it's more convenient to think in partisan terms, because it creates a political world that is easier to understand, assuming that one party is pro-immigrant and the other is not. However, this partisan thinking ignores the neoliberal policies supported by both parties, such as privatizing detention centers and devoting more and more tax money to the incarceration of immigrants.

Partisan thinking also often justifies such exploitation by creating an *other*. For example, the keynote speaker for the CCCC 2016 Convention in Portland, Jose Antonio Vargas, a Pulitzer Prize–winning journalist who also is undocumented, gave a powerful speech that emphasized how a good-versus-bad discourse often afflicts the conversation about immigration. This discourse labels people "illegal," and, as Amanda Espinosa-Aguilar comments, it is "the language of dehumanization" (165). And if policies and rhetoric specify that one is the good group of immigrants deserving citizenship and status, another group is inevitably excluded. In *Against Citizenship: The Violence of the Normative,* Amy L. Brandzel argues that "whenever we work on behalf of citizenship, whenever we strive to [include] more types of peoples under its reign, we inevitably reify the violence of citizenship against nonnormative others." Although anti-Trump sentiment has motivated more people not directly affected by such policies to become interested in immigration, people may believe in a problematic narrative that justifies past immigration policies by believing only "bad" immigrants were deported by previous presidents.

Long-term organizing must avoid partisan thinking that demonizes one group. In this citizen/noncitizen framework, we can challenge partisan explanations for deportations. We can avoid categorizing stories of migration as "the story of the other" (Powell 318). As Katrina M. Powell comments on stories requesting asylum: "if the story is good enough, they can come to the United States for an education" (307). In the petitions to stop deportations discussed in Chapters 2 and 4, there is a similar rhetorical act involved when trying to stop deportations; however, immigrant rights organizers avoid a good-bad dichotomy by writing from a place where everyone is exceptional and deserves rights.

Considering such work as long-term organizing challenges some assumptions about the single-issue approach of some community engagement. When I first started teaching, we would often discuss one particular anecdote from Chapter 6 in Paul Loeb's *Soul of a Citizen*. It is about a classroom where a college student shares a great volunteering experience he had at a homeless shelter. The student adds that he learned more from his volunteer work than all of his college courses, and he hopes that his grandchildren will be able someday to volunteer at such a shelter. According to Loeb's chapter, classmates pointed out that they were working toward a day without the need for homeless shelters. As Loeb concludes, "The student meant no harm, but his words raised a question about the relationship between long-term change and the volunteer work that so many of us do in our communities" (144). In my classroom, I would often focus on the student who makes the comment about his grandkids volunteering at the shelter and his assumption that homelessness was inevitable. Then we considered the thoughtful comments of his classmates, encouraging him to think more critically about long-term change and whether homelessness can end. Another point, though, that student organizers often make in their meetings and presentations is how their work is not about one issue; it's an ongoing campaign for people to organize. These issues of homelessness and economic inequality intersect with institutional racism, gender discrimination, workers' rights, and many other concerns.

It is not only about solving one particular issue like homelessness and anti-immigrant policies; it's an ongoing movement. For example, even if comprehensive immigration reform were passed, there still is a need for community organizing and placing pressure on elected leaders to represent the community's best interests. As former SWER president Claudio comments, "I don't advocate for lobbying as much as I advocate for organizing the people and having them lobby themselves." This framework based on organizing for a public-writing course, then, could intersect with multiple issues that are affecting students and their communities. For example, many students are facing financial obstacles to attending college and sometimes work full-time as they take their classes. Although undocumented students are not eligible under current law, 58 percent of FIU students received Pell grants in 2016 (*Fulfilling the Promise* 7). Some students and their families are encountering issues of homelessness and food insecurity. In discussing and addressing these kinds of issues, students can help lead in the classroom.

Long-term organizing also is global and crosses borders. For example, 1.4 million young people, sometimes called "los otros DREAMers," were deported to Mexico in the last decade (Linthicum). At their university located an hour and a half south of the US border, faculty from Universidad Autónoma de Baja California focus on helping los otros DREAMers who are having challenges—linguistically, academically, and culturally—as the students are now attending school in Mexico after being deported (De los Santos et al.). In addition, student organizers cross borders, as in 2013 when three members of NIYA (the National Immigrant Youth Alliance) returned to Mexico and then came to the border with six other DREAMers who had been forced to leave the United States. At the border entry in Nogales, Arizona, they requested asylum (Carcamo). The action was to raise awareness of los otros DREAMers who have been deported even though they have spent most of their lives in the United States. This ongoing organizing of transnational people crosses borders and connects people globally.

One way faculty can help all the work above is to consistently connect new students in their classes with leaders before they graduate, because organizing requires the training of new leaders. As Gaby Pacheco, one of the leaders of the Trail of Dreams walk from Miami to Washington, DC, writes, student organizers "[w]ill have to pass on the baton. This is important not just for the continuity of a movement but also for the sanity of the individuals within it" ("What the Dreamers Can Teach the Parkland Kids"). After gaining DACA, some SWER members were able to focus more of their time on school, family, and work once they had work permits and the ability to take more than one class per term since they no longer had to pay out-of-state tuition. Because of these changes, some SWER members have less time for organizing, and when they graduate there is a growing need to train new organizers. Faculty who are involved with such groups can share information with new students and connect them with student organizers who are graduating.

For example, at a weekend training during the summer of 2017, veteran SWER members (some of whom had graduated and some of whom were finishing up their degrees) helped to guide younger members on how to organize. The group that came to the training included high school students, many of whom were unaware about the history of the movement and the principles of organizing. Some were reluctant to go public with their stories and so there was a need for veteran SWER members to discuss what the movement's refrain "come out of the shadows" means. One high school participant wanted to know what ICE was. The training covered an entire weekend: the history of the movement, mass incarceration, the root causes of migration, how to talk to the media, direct action, canvassing, and a workshop on the op-ed. Like most trainings, there were icebreaker activities and efforts to build community among the group. There was also a direct action (a rally against detention centers) at the nearby Broward Transitional Center, the detention center that Viridiana and Marco infiltrated in 2012, as discussed in Chapter 4. Some of the new participants were unaware of the detention center—some were coming from nearby towns and communities—and a crowd of about eighty people gathered and protested outside the pinkish walls of what looks like an elementary school. Thus, for a movement to continue, new students need to become leaders, and faculty can play a role in helping connect students to existing organizations.

WRITING AS PART OF A NETWORK OF ACTION

[T]he op-ed was the first one I had ever written. . . . It felt very empowering. . . . It still feels like a tool that we can use to share our thoughts and hopefully to reach a sector of the public that we're not always in contact with, that we're not aware of. And yet they're still interested in our stories, they're still interested in hearing our thoughts. It was very exciting and humbling to see how far that op-ed actually ended up being published and imagining the people it reached. I avoided

seeing the negative comments . . . but I think it's so refreshing to have something, some medium available to you where you can share your thoughts. At least for me and my generation, you grow up in silence, and not wanting to share, and not wanting to bring attention to yourself, and so it's such a different approach that it's sometimes less intimidating than being in public and sharing your story. And you have a bit more control, how you write it, what it's about. And then just letting it go and seeing where it takes you. I think that's something that I'm very proud of that we collaborated on. . . .
—Angelica

As Angelica discusses in the above quotation from the epilogue, writing is an effective tool in going public, but doing so requires action, too. As discussed in Chapter 3, Angelica's op-ed was written after an act of civil disobedience for immigrant rights and part of a long-term campaign that resulted in DACA. For the writing classroom, then, student organizers can help students see writing as part of a network of action. For example, the op-ed is a popular assignment in many writing courses; however, student organizers can offer a new way of looking at composing them. Besides the basic structure of how to write an op-ed, they can discuss how an op-ed can be part of a campaign to change something, including to stop deportations. In addition, like many op-ed writers, immigrant rights organizers appeal to their readers' sense of shared values, but when they invoke Americanisms, they do so in a nuanced way. As S. P. Alvarez notes, writers are negotiating a complex sense of belonging and not belonging in the United States. When writing a petition that will be circulated online or in person and also sent to different political leaders, the argument is often how that one individual represents the best of the community and America. However, in this writing of Americanisms, everyone can be exceptional, and even if someone doesn't identify as American, everyone belongs. And such writings are often part of a larger campaign that often includes an action—like a rally outside the detention center, visiting politicians' offices, sit-in demonstrations, and other forms of civil disobedience to raise the visibility of a person's case or a law.

Writing combined with action is also a method to create publics. As the private sector expands its control in a neoliberal economy, the public sphere becomes even more confined. We communicate in a "prison visiting room," in Oskar Negt and Alexander Kluge's metaphor, and this metaphor points to the restrictions on the public sphere. In addition, there is a physical reality that the United States has the highest rate of imprisoning its people in the world (Alexander). Therefore, a system of mass incarceration attempts to silence people being imprisoned, including immigrants. Student organizers must find ways, then, of creating publics where their views and perspectives can be voiced. As when SWER students blocked a bus leaving the detention center so that they couldn't take immigrants to the airport for their deportations. Or, as depicted in *The Infiltrators* in 2019, all the planning, long hours, and courage displayed by Viridiana, Marco, and others in going inside a detention center so they could help to free people. Or when students were arrested for protesting in downtown Charlotte, a year before the Democratic convention was held there. In all of these cases, writing took on an urgency because it was linked to a network of action. That urgency can give the community-writing classroom a needed change that can be led by students.

In their community work outside the classroom, faculty can apply these ideas by finding connections between student organizing and creative projects. For example, theater both inside the proscenium and outside on the streets can connect with the work of student organizers. In Charlotte in 2008, organizers, actors, and I produced a play based on the activism of Marie Gonzalez, a Missouri college student. Her parents had been deported to Costa Rica, and she had become a public activist for the DREAM Act. To encourage more conversation about this issue and make more of these stories known, several groups came together to collaborate. We connected leaders from the theater and the Hispanic Cultural Center, and in these conversations we started to imagine a project that would dramatize the issues affecting undocumented students. I emailed Marie and proposed the idea of interviewing her and writing a play called *Limbo*. She agreed, and so in the summer of 2008 we performed a play that focused on the story of Marie and others criminalized by immigration laws. The story is framed by two student filmmakers who want to make a documentary about Marie and other students in their communities. In this collaborative effort, we worked and revised scenes during the rehearsal process as we dramatized how agents of ICE could arrest people who were undocumented and imprison them in a detention center. The play also showed how Marie became part of a group of young people, DREAMers, who were campaigning for immigrant rights. Marie was able to stay in the country because of a temporary bill sponsored by Senator Richard Durbin of Illinois. Marie even testified before Congress and shared her story. The first weekend of the production, Marie came to Charlotte and held talkbacks with the audience after each performance. She discussed her reaction to the play and also her thoughts about immigration reform. With her consent, the theater videotaped these talkbacks and posted them online.

Theatrical projects also provide an opportunity for petition signings and other kinds of actions led by student organizers. *The Pot* was inspired in part by what happened to Angelica's brother, Erick (as discussed in Chapter 2). Narrated by an adopted son, a college student, the story takes place at Thanksgiving as a family reacts when a daughter's boyfriend is arrested and placed in a detention center. I shared my draft with Angelica and others for feedback as we developed it into a play for readings in various locations and performances in North Carolina, Florida, and Alabama (2011 to 2017). We organized talkbacks and petition signings following the performances and provided an opportunity for student organizers to speak and invite people to join campaigns. Before rehearsals started at FIU, we had a design presentation for the show, a read-through, and a conversation with the cast about the play. For the conversation, five student organizers who were active in the immigrant rights movement visited with the cast. They talked about their own personal experiences with being undocumented. The five student leaders also showed a video about how the detention center system is a profit-driven business that makes money from criminalizing immigrants.

Besides productions inside theaters, the street can become a public space for organizing through invisible theater (Boal). For example, in 2010 local immigrant rights groups planned a rally in response to Arizona's SB1070 bill. This anti-immigrant law gave greater power to local police to stop people and ask for their papers, and we saw the emergence of copycat bills in states around the country, including North Carolina. To advertise the pro-immigrant rally, organizers liked the idea of a street theater piece that could be performed throughout the city. A cast of community actors and I collaborated on a script, and we performed it on Davidson Street in the arts district, downtown in front of Bank America, and in front of Senator Kay Hagan's office on the other side of town. We dressed up as Lady Liberty, and three people played the Bill of Rights, arrested by two people dressed up as Arizona. At the end of the scene, we carried Lady Liberty on a stretcher down the street and handed out fliers for a rally. At US Senator Hagan's office, we performed the scene and delivered and recorded a formal invitation for her to come to our rally. She didn't come to the rally, but the purpose of such performances was to practice invisible theater, where the performance becomes part of the public space as random people encounter it.

These creative projects are an extension of the classroom work discussed and offer an opportunity for faculty to engage with students through creative work. The work can be collaborative and receive input from students and other community members. In addition, creative projects can provide an opportunity for other actions such as petitions and demonstrations in the streets like invisible theater.

FUTURE DIRECTIONS

This pedagogical shift toward student organizing is not an abandonment of the social-justice work of service-learning and community partnerships. For the revised syllabus of the community-writing course, some students continue to choose traditional community projects like helping with Meals on Wheels for senior citizens, volunteering with clothing drives for immigrants newly arrived in Miami, or tutoring children. The course, then, needs to include the ideas and scholarship of the field addressing university-community relationships (Cushman; Mathieu) and the ways students can engage in inquiry (Flower, *Community Literacy*) and writing partnerships (Deans, *Writing Partnerships*).

However, with greater disparities of wealth, the continued assault on immigrant rights, and the increased control of the public sphere by corporations, we also need change. In the conclusion of *Writing Democracy*, the editors urge us to consider how we can be part of efforts "[t]o achieve true democracy, equality, and freedom" (Carter et al. 269) in response to the systemic inequalities of neoliberalism. This trend toward restraining democracy makes it even more evident that a radical shift in thinking is required.

Politically, more students are advocating for change as they respond to social inequities. Besides anti-immigrant legislation and institutional racism, students are going into greater and greater debt to attend school, and face an economy that does not give them hope. Responding to these concerns in the classroom is a political turn for the field, but, as repeated throughout this book, organizing is not necessarily partisan. In fact, recognizing that systemic problems are not easily solved from a partisan perspective creates a freedom for deeper conversations and possibilities. Our classrooms must be part of that change. Although "apathy" is a label often given to each generation, there is a rich history of students organizing for change (Kirshner; Richardson and Ragland). There are many examples of how the education system and the culture tell us that change isn't really possible. And even though many of our students may appear to practice what Paul Feigenbaum calls "passive progressivism" ("Nudging" 143), that perception of disengagement may change as teachers listen more to their students' concerns.

Scholarship that raises important questions, including those about identity (S. P. Alvarez; Vieira; Ribero), intersectionality (Crenshaw), and institutional racism must be central to the field (Kynard; Inoue; Young). And the work of student organizers needs to be more central to what we do inside and outside the classroom. In addition to service-learning projects, we need a radical shift as we listen more to our students and give space in the classroom for them to lead.

In this shift, the writing teacher may adopt a different role. Rather than just being an ally with others, the writing teacher may need to take more risks, or be what Aja Martinez and others call an accomplice. It is not enough just to wear a pin on one's shirt to indicate support; teachers have an ethical responsibility to stand in solidarity with students working for equal rights. This is not an easy role to define, and it may vary depending on a teacher's positionality. Such work requires considering the question, To what are we answerable in learning, knowledge, and context (Patel)? And what do our scholarly work and pedagogies "challenge and remake" (Kynard, "All I Need")?

This framework isn't based on one single issue; it's a process of long-term organizing. This approach moves past an individualistic mindset that all we need are more individual volunteers to solve a particular social issue. Service-learning has long challenged such individualism (Herzberg), and long-term organizing recognizes the need for communities of people to come together, organize, and put pressure on elected representatives to vote for their best interests. On campus, faculty can help connect new students with student leaders before they graduate to help sustain such movements. At a moment when democracy faces even more challenges with a shrinking public sphere, organizing offers possibilities for a better future when more people's voices are heard.

Finally, writing is part of a network of action to create change. Writing assignments, then, become more than individual pieces written for one particular moment. Writing for change requires collaborating with others and coordinating with other actions. Such an approach is based upon the belief that students have important things to say, and that as they practice and learn new rhetorical skills, they can work with others to make a difference in their own communities.

Our field has a wealth of scholarship about community engagement, and student organizers' input can build upon this work. This chapter concludes, then, with an observation about community work by Mohammad. One popular story about community service is the story of the starfish: a boy throws back one starfish after another into the ocean to save it even though there are countless more scattered across the beach. The moral often told is the importance of each individual doing something to help that one starfish even if there are many more that can't be saved. In a different version, Mohammad shares the story about his tattoo of a starfish and how it represents something different from what he calls that "corny starfish story." Instead of a story that focuses on someone helping someone else—much like a charity or community service model—Mohammad's version focuses on giving power to the starfish:

> [T]he other story that [Rev. McDonald] told us is that he's from the beaches of Georgia. And so for him, the starfish means justice, because it's unlimited. Because if you break off one of its feet, it grows a new one. And so he said he always sees justice as a starfish, because it's not like a pie; it's not a limited number of slices. There's enough to go around for everyone. . . . Just empower the starfish, and it will grow one more.

Community Accomplice Syllabus Spring 2020

ENC 4331 U01 Writing, Rhetoric, and Community Spring 2020 T/R 11am–12:15pm
Classroom: GC 278A

Dr. Glenn Hutchinson, Director, Center for Excellence in Writing	gchutchi@fiu.edu Office Phone: (305) 348-6671 Cell: (305) 857-8372
Offices: GL 124D (MMC) & HL212 (BBC)	Office Hours: Tuesday/Thursday 10–10:45am, 2–3pm, or by appointment.

Texts: Available on Canvas.

Course Goals: The theme of this course is #studentorganizing—how students organize to address issues of #socialjustice on and off campus. You will be invited to write about a project that interests you. Below are goals for this #writingand rhetoric course:

- Community Literacy: Students will be able to develop best practices for participating in community-writing and service-learning projects in and beyond the South Florida community that work toward community engagement and social action.
- Personally Meaningful Writing: Students will be able to produce rigorous, personally meaningful writing projects that draw on their own experiences and demonstrate both flexibility and a willingness to take creative risks.
- Textual Analysis: Students will be able to analyze a variety of everyday and academic texts for their strengths and weaknesses according to rhetorical, contextual, and cultural criteria.

- Audience: Students will be able to analyze various audiences' needs and adapt writing to the expectations of those audiences.
- Ethics: Students will be able to analyze the ethical implications of writing situations and practices. They will know how to take appropriate ethical action when faced with complex communication situations.
- Writing Process: Students will be able to employ a flexible writing process. They will be able to invent rhetorically appropriate content; provide and incorporate constructive feedback; proofread, revise, and edit their own and others' work; and address stylistic preferences of various audiences.
- Collaborative Writing: Students will be able to work on complex projects with team members. They will be able to employ a range of strategies for managing projects and negotiating team dynamics.
- Research: Students will be able to conduct primary and secondary research. They will be able to analyze sources for credibility, biases, accuracy, depth, and sophistication. And they will be able to professionally integrate research and sources in ways that support their project's goals.
- Cross-Cultural Communication: Students will demonstrate respect for others' views. They will be able to craft communications for members of other cultures and to bring their own resources to writing practices, including their multilingual and multicultural resources. Students will be able to work within and across language standards and conventions and the cultural and political values associated with them.

Course Assignments:

1. In-Class and Weekly Writings 20%
Each week you will write about the readings and questions that emerge in class. Please see the assignment calendar for the specific assignments.

> Grading = 20%. Full, regular, and thoughtful participation means that 20 percent of your grade is an A.

2. Community-Writing Project 30%
Explore a question/community issue related to the theme of the course: student organizing, writing/rhetoric, and community. Your community writing project could include one or more of the following: an op-ed, a letter to the editor, a press release, a petition, or a combination of texts. These writings can be part of a network of action that you complete throughout the term. Your community writing project topic will include primary and secondary research. In addition to writing a proposal, you'll submit drafts for review and submit a final revised version at the end of the semester. More details on assignment handout.

3. Midterm/Final Portfolio 30% (please see portfolio information below.)

4. Participation 20%
Active participation in class, including helping to lead the discussion on at least one of the readings for class.

Expectations:
1. ATTENDANCE: Your presence is essential to this class. Its format is primarily discussion; rarely will I lecture on any topic. So please be present and punctual. If you miss more than three classes, then we will need to discuss your options for dropping the course.

2. ACTIVE PARTICIPATION: For our discussions and activities to be successful, we all need to be active participants in class. Please consider Emerson's advice: "Trust thyself. Every heart vibrates to that iron string." Therefore, please refrain from any behavior that prevents you and other students from being active participants in class. Avoid cell phone use in class. Also, laptops may be used for writing, but please do not use them for nonclassroom activities.

3. RESPECT: We need to be respectful of our classmates, instructors, and speakers and their ideas; let us create an atmosphere in which we all feel comfortable expressing our viewpoints. When we have different opinions or outlooks, we need to express them to one another in a respectful language and tone. Hateful language will not be tolerated in this classroom.

4. DIVERSITY: We want to create an academic climate in which the dignity of all individuals is respected and maintained. Therefore, we celebrate diversity that includes, but is not limited to, ability/disability, age, culture, ethnicity, gender, language, race, religion, sexual orientation, and socioeconomic status. *Use inclusive language.* There are many techniques to avoid sexist language. We will discuss them.

5. WORK REQUIREMENTS: Please complete assignments by their due date. Late work will receive a penalty. Completion of all work is necessary to pass the course. Also, it is your responsibility to keep a copy of all writings submitted.

6. PLAGIARISM: Plagiarism is cheating and stealing. Plagiarism is the use of the words and ideas of others without giving them credit, such as submitting an assignment that is not the result of the student's own thinking and effort. Students who plagiarize assignments, including using work of their own that they have written for high school or previous courses, will receive a zero for that assignment

and may face further consequences, from receiving a failing grade for the course to dismissal from the university. The university's code of academic integrity is found in the Student Handbook (undergrad.fiu.edu/academic-misconduct/pdfs/code-of-academic-integrity.pdf). The FIU library has also created a resource for understanding and avoiding plagiarism at libguides.fiu.edu/plagiarism.

7. DISABILITY SERVICES: Students requiring special accommodations and/or assistance are encouraged to register with the Disability Resource Center:
MMC: 11200 SW 8th Street - GC 190 Phone: (305) 348-3532
BBC: 3000 NE 151st Street - WUC 131 BBC Phone: (305) 919-5345

8. FUN: And finally . . . think, learn, and have fun.

Other Resources:
The mission of Counseling and Psychological Services (CAPS) is to provide mental health services to students that will facilitate and enhance their personal learning, emotional well-being, and academic skills development.
    MMC: LOCATION: SHC 210 PHONE: (305) 348-2277
    BBC: LOCATION: WUC 320 PHONE: (305) 919-5305

"Staying Safe and Healthy" videos available on FIU Canvas.

Assignment Calendar (subject to change)

Week 1
T 1-7   Course Introduction
R 1-9   Read Joe Fassler interview with Edwidge Danticat, "All Immigrants Are Artists"
    (1) Weekly Writing #1 due: Letter to Glenn
    (2) Due: 25 interview questions on separate notecards/pieces of paper.

Week 2
T 1-14   Weekly Writing #2 due: Write profile of partner.
R 1-16   Read Romeo Garcia, "Creating Presence from Absence and Sound from Silence."
    Guest Speakers: Former Students from ENC4331 (Fall 2019)

Week 3
T 1-21   Read Elaine Richardson and Alice Ragland, "#StayWoke: The Language and Literacies of the #BlackLivesMatter Movement"
    Read Ellen Cushman, "The Rhetorician as an Agent of Social Change"

Read Asao B. Inoue, #4C19 Chair's Address (RECOMMENDED)
Weekly Writing #3 due: Write down your reactions to the readings. Also, what's a question/community project that you would like to explore this semester?

R 1-23   Read Chapter 2, Glenn Hutchinson
Guest Speaker: Nery Lopez, Florida Student Power Network

Week 4

T 1-28   Read Prerna Lal and Tania Unzueta, "How Queer Undocumented Youth Built the Immigrant Rights Movement," and Ana Milena Ribero, "Citizenship," from *Decolonizing Rhetoric and Composition Studies: New Latinx Keywords for Theory and Pedagogy*
"Breaking the Ice," by Michael May (from "The One Thing You're Not Supposed to Do," *This American Life*) (Optional)
Weekly Writing #4 due: What did you notice about how the guest speakers discussed community organizing and writing? What connections can you make between the readings for today? What questions do you have?
Guest Speaker: Monica Matteo Salinas, Florida/Georgia Director Campus Election Engagement Project

R 1-30   Read Alex Harris, "'I'm Terrified about Our Future': Zero Hour Youth Summit Brings Teen Activists to Miami."
Guest Speaker: Kendall Kieras (TBA), Zero Hour

Week 5

T 2-4   Weekly Writing #5 due: Review the op-ed packet from class and write a draft for your own op-ed.
Read Thomas Kennedy, "Homestead Detention Center Is No Kids' Summer Camp."
Read Angelica Velazquillo, "An Undocumented Immigrant Speaks Out."
Read Nicolas Wulff, "Undocumented Student Wants Change."

R 2-6   Read Corinne Segal, "In a Florida Prison, a Poet Grapples with Power and Oppression."
Guest Speaker: Elimelech Risse, former President of Student Alliance for Prison Reform

Week 6

T 2-11   Weekly Writing #6 due: Proposal for Community-Writing Project
Readings about wealth (topic suggested by Nicole, ENC4331 Fall 2019)

R 2-13   Conversation with students in Algeria about social activism (online)

Week 7
T 2-18 Weekly Writing #7 due: draft of midterm reflection
R 2-20 Midterm Portfolio due

Week 8
T 2-25 * NO CLASS * SPRING BREAK
R 2-27 * NO CLASS * SPRING BREAK

Week 9
T 3-3 Read Kimberlé Crenshaw, "Mapping the Margins: Intersectionality, Identity Politics, and Violence against Women of Color."
R 3-5 Weekly Writing #8 due: First draft of Community Writing Project

Week 10
T 3-10 Weekly Writing #9 due: Open Topic
Read Aja Martinez, "The Responsibility of Privilege: A Critical Race Counterstory Conversation" *or* Keeanga-Yamahtta Taylor's *From #BlackLivesMatter to Black Liberation,* Chapter 6 (suggestion from Danielle, Fall 2019 class)
R 3-12 Read excerpt from Ben Kirshner's *Youth Activism in an Era of Education Inequality*

Week 11
T 3-17 Read Jeff Amy, "Author's Speech Cancelled after Georgia Students Burn Book" and Amy Binder and Jeffrey L. Kidder, "Student Activism Is Often Uncivil. We Can Change That."
Weekly Writing #10 due: Please write a response to this article about student activism from the *Chronicle of Higher Education.* Do you think a more diverse set of viewpoints are needed in higher education? Please explain. For example, when you are writing an op-ed or another persuasive piece of writing, how important is it to respond to different points of view?
R 3-19 TBA

Week 12
T 3-24 Zoom class discussion
R 3-26 Revision of Community-Writing Project due

Week 13
T 3-31 SGA President Sabrina Leeloo Rosell/Writing Workshop
Read Gaby Pacheco, "What the Dreamers Can Teach the Parkland Kids"

Weekly Writing #11 due: Open Topic
R 4-2   Writing Workshop

Week 14
T 4-7   Weekly Writing #12 due: Draft of Final Reflection
         Read excerpt from Paul Loeb's *Soul of a Citizen*
R 4-9   TBA

Week 15
T 4-14   Portfolio Workshop
R 4-16   FINAL PORTFOLIO DUE * LAST DAY OF REGULAR CLASS *

Final Exam Meeting Time: no final exam

ENC4331 Portfolio Information
A portfolio? A portfolio is both a selection from and a reflection upon your writing and learning. Think of it as a snapshot of you as a writer, student, and peer tutor. How?
(1) COLLECT: Save everything that you write this semester. This collection will be the source for your portfolio.
(2) SELECT: The next step is to select certain pieces (see below). Choose pieces that you particularly liked and also pieces that represent your experience. Explain why you chose certain writings and not others.
(3) REFLECT: At the midterm and end of the semester, write an introduction or reflection for your portfolio. This reflection (approximately three typed double-spaced pages) is your chance to look back and think about your writing and the class.

What should it look like and what's in it?
1) Table of Contents: List what you've included and in what order.
2) Midterm/Final Reflection (three to four typed double-spaced pages): At the beginning of your portfolio, reflect upon what you've learned, your writing, the readings, guest speakers, and community involvement.
3) In-Class Writings: Choose two or three and include an introduction that explains why you chose them.
4) Weekly Writings: Choose two to three and include an introduction that explains why you chose them.
5) Community Writing Project: Include at least one draft and the final revision.

6) Other: Anything else you want to include.

When is it due? The midterm portfolio is due at midterm. The final portfolio is due on the last day of class. (See assignment calendar for dates.)

Expectations:

It's important that

* you've done all the writing assignments and attended class;

*you've taken the time to revise and improve your writing based on feedback; and

* you've written an introduction/reflection that comments on what you've learned from your community involvement, the readings, and your writing.

Epilogue: Reflections from Student Organizer-Writers

[T]he op-ed was the first one I had ever written. . . . It felt very empowering. . . . It still feels like a tool that we can use to share our thoughts and hopefully to reach a sector of the public that we're not always in contact with, that we're not aware of. And yet they're still interested in our stories, they're still interested in hearing our thoughts. It was very exciting and humbling to see how far that op-ed actually ended up being published and imagining the people it reached. I avoided seeing the negative comments . . . but I think it's so refreshing to have something, some medium available to you where you can share your thoughts. At least for me and my generation, you grow up in silence, and not wanting to share, and not wanting to bring attention to yourself, and so it's such a different approach. That it's sometimes less intimidating than being in public and sharing your story. And you have a bit more control, how you write it, what it's about. And then just letting it go and seeing where it takes you. I think that's something that I'm very proud of that we collaborated on. . . .
—Angelica

And after a long year of fighting and struggling, it was going to pass through . . . late April. Things were going smooth, there was lots of pressure happening, lots of actions leading up to May first. And there was enough support from the community and politicians who were being lobbied pretty hard. So on the last day of April, I rented a van with some of the folks from Students Working for Equal Rights. And we gathered eight or nine people who were able to get in this van and we all drove up to Tallahassee, Florida's capital, and we sat there in the session where they discussed whether in-state tuition was going to be passed or not. There were maybe thirty or forty DREAMers sitting there in the chambers wearing orange graduation caps. And we all were there expecting and watching and wanting this to happen. I think it was really romantic in a sense for it to have passed on May Day. I thought it was really great. I think that's why I remember it the most. Because it was May Day when we passed in-state tuition for undocumented students. . . .

—Claudio

I wouldn't be sitting here talking to you if I didn't have DACA. Because of DACA, I've had—I was able to buy my first car . . . and my brother's car. We both put in money for it. I'm paying for my education here at FIU, where I'm graduating next semester. Which I wouldn't have been able to do because the money that I had paying for it before . . . it had already run out. So if DACA hadn't passed, exactly when it had passed, I would have taken off time from school. And also, a driver's license, a work permit, so basically having the ability to work, having the ability to drive, I can now drive my mom around so that she doesn't have to drive and risk being stopped for a broken taillight. And just being able to have a more regular life. Live like a regular resident or US citizen. Having some restrictions because you still can't—I still can't qualify for federal loans, financial aid, all that stuff, but this is something that helps me out right now.

—Nicolas

Back in 2009, that's when I started doing activism . . . I started sharing my story on TV . . . and then I became the organizer at one of the campuses and we were able to stop deportations, so many activities . . . awareness for the DREAM Act. I think one of the most important actions was one of the billboards in 2010 when we were asking former Senator George

LeMieux to vote for the DREAM Act, we had a huge human billboard on the beach saying DREAM Act Now 2010. That was the best action that I remember.

—Julio

I learned from my family. . . . I was the first one to get more involved, then my brother, my mom and my dad. And so now we're all working together. The advice that I would give them is always first thing should be school. Of course, your family as well. But activism, I think, comes from whether you want to stand up for something that's right.

—Francis

About immigration reform . . . there's a lot of false information going on around this. Immigrants are coming in, getting free laptops, getting their bills paid. Getting all this and that. And none of that is true. You should do some research about what's really happening. And go and do your part. Whether it's by voting, whether it's by inviting others to go, whether it's by joining local organizations, you should be involved in politics because they really affect us. And it's really comfortable to just sit home and read a magazine and think that's what's really going on, but unless you go to your community and you experience the needs and the reality of the people in it, you won't really know what's going on. And based on that, I think you could make a really conscious decision. . . .

—Claudio

So the conservative argument was that you would be giving in-state tuition to people who don't deserve it or . . . how are you going to give in-state tuition to undocumented students and not give it to US citizens from other states? But they can get in-state tuition in their own states. If they go to another state, they just have to wait a year. We've been waiting for years and finally it just passed in the last legislature, so that enabled a lot more students to attend universities like FIU and continue their education, not being stuck in that limbo stage after graduating from high school. . . . Let's say if a kid grew up here his whole life—he went to elementary, middle, and high school, the state has already invested all that money and these resources in that student. So why would you create a barrier for him to go to the next level? . . .

I don't think it would have passed without the activism aspect into it. Because you had to hit it from all sides. It's the businesses, it's the government, it's the Democrats and Republicans, but it's also the organizations, the nonprofits, unions all that pushing for it. You have to have a message and put it out there. . . .

—Nicolas

We confronted Senator Rubio here. . . . I knew that he was doing a class that day. . . . We had this big check for six billion dollars—the tax cut for the wealthy that was included in the ACA package. So I went with these Obamacare recipients and basically waited until the class was over—we wanted to be respectful. And then when he was leaving the class, we went in and gave him the check. It went really viral—because when Rafael, who was one of the Obamacare constituents, was talking to him, he asked him why he wouldn't hold a town hall to share his reasoning with the public, he said, "I don't do town halls because they get rude and stupid." . . . That got over 10,000 retweets and then I wrote an op-ed about it (Kennedy, "The Florida Legislators"). That was a fiasco for him; . . . the whole episode was embarrassing. They tried to bring in the police to escort us out. And I had an FIU ID and everybody that was with me was an FIU alumni. I was like, you literally can't kick me out of here. You're going to have to arrest me, and I'll see you in court if you kick me out of here. Because I'm not in the classroom, I have my student ID, and I'm in the hallway, and he has to step into the hallway to leave. . . .

—Thomas

And we had grown as a movement. We are able to stop deportations now. We've grown a lot. And so I knew that I believed that we had what it took to hold Senator Hagan accountable at both a state scale and a national scale. So that's why I really wanted to make sure a campaign like that took place. Understanding that we don't have the ability to vote but that doesn't mean that we don't have a say or can't participate in some way in the election process.

—Viridiana

Nelson Mandela spent like thirty years in jail. I'm not in jail. People have it really bad out there. Most movements for social change have taken decades. I'm not one of those people that think three years from now, we are going to take back the government. It's going to take a long-ass time.

—Thomas

WORKS CITED

"2015 Census." *News Leaders Association,* members.newsleaders.org/diversity-survey-2015. Accessed 29 Oct. 2020.

Abdollahi, Mohammad. Personal interview. 28 July 2016.

Adler-Kassner, Linda, et al., editors. *Writing the Community: Concepts and Models for Service-Learning in Composition.* Stylus Publishing in cooperation with the National Council of Teachers of English, 1996.

Agrawal, Nina. "Krome Corps: Volunteers Reach Out to Immigrants in Detention." *WLRN,* 27 July 2015, wlrn.org/post/krome-corps-volunteers-reach-out-immigrants-detention. Accessed 30 Oct. 2020.

Ahmed, Sara. *On Being Included: Racism and Diversity in Institutional Life.* Duke UP, 2012.

Albert, Gail, editor. *Service-Learning Reader: Reflections and Perspectives on Service.* National Society for Experiential Education, 1994.

Alexander, Jonathan, and Susan C. Jarratt. "Rhetorical Education and Student Activism." *College English*, vol. 76, no. 6, July 2014, pp. 525–44.

Alexander, Michelle. *The New Jim Crow: Mass Incarceration in the Age of Colorblindness.* New Press, 2010.

Alinsky, Saul D. *Rules for Radicals: A Practical Primer for Realistic Radicals.* Random House, 1971.

Alvarez, Sara del Pilar. *Conciencia Bilingüe: The Multilingual and Academic Writing Practices of Undocumented Immigrant Activists.* 2018. U of Louisville, PhD dissertation, doi:10.18297/etd/2930.

Alvarez, Sara P., and Amy J. Wan. "Global Citizenship as Literacy: A Critical Reflection for Teaching Multilingual Writers." *Journal of Adolescent & Adult Literacy,* vol. 63, no. 2, pp. 213–16.

Alvarez, Steven. *Community Literacies* en Confianza: *Learning from Bilingual After-School Programs.* NCTE, 2017.

Americans for Immigrant Justice and the Southern Poverty Law Center. "Prison by Any Other Name: A Report on South Florida Detention Facilities." 9 Dec. 2019, default.salsalabs.org/T496d6c3b-c165-4e00-b387-a1f2f862b192/0db04647-2409-4192-ab6a-1a686fd093a1. Accessed 29 Oct. 2020.

Amy, Jeff. "Author's Speech Cancelled after Georgia Students Burn Book." *Tuscaloosa News,* 23 Oct. 2019, www.tuscaloosanews.com/news/20191023/authors-speech-cancelled-after-georgia-students-burn-book. Accessed 17 Nov. 2020.

Anders, Tisa. "Combahee River Collective (1974–1980)." *Black Past,* 23 Apr. 2012, www.blackpast.org/african-american-history/combahee-river-collective-1974-1980/. Accessed 18 May 2020.

Anguiano, Claudia Alejandra. *Undocumented, Unapologetic, and Unafraid: Discursive Strategies of the Immigrant Youth Dream Social Movement.* 2011. U of New Mexico, PhD dissertation, digitalrepository.unm.edu/cj_etds/24.

"Arizona's Immigration Enforcement Laws." *National Conference on State Legislatures,* 28 July 2011, www.ncsl.org/research/immigration/analysis-of-arizonas-immigration-law.aspx. Accessed 4 Dec 2020.

Artz, Lee. "Speaking the Power of Truth: Rhetoric and Action for Our Times." *Activism and Rhetoric: Theories and Contexts for Political Engagement,* 2d ed., edited by JongHwa Lee and Seth Kahn, Routledge, 2020, pp. 159–72.

Artze-Vega, Isis, and Glenn Hutchinson. "Small Step Forward yet Uncertain Future for the DREAMers." *Hispanic Outlook in Higher Education,* vol. 23, no. 2, 15 Oct. 2012, pp. 26–28.

Bach, Trevor. "Guards and Immigration Detainees Describe Widespread Abuse at Krome Processing Center." *Miami New Times,* 18 Aug. 2015, miaminewtimes.com/news/guards-and-immigration-detainees-describe-widespread-abuse-at-krome-processing-center-7829882. Accessed 29 Oct. 2020.

Baker-Bell, April, et al. "Editorial: The Pain and the Wounds: A Call for Critical Race English Education in the Wake of Racial Violence." *English Education,* vol. 49, no. 2, Jan. 2017, pp. 116–29.

Barthel, Michael. "In the News Industry, Diversity Is Lowest at Smaller Outlets." *PEW Research Center,* 4 Aug. 2015, www.pewresearch.org/fact-tank/2015/08/04/in-the-news-industry-diversity-is-lowest-at-smaller-outlets/. Accessed 27 Oct. 2020.

Benitez-Hernandez, Elisa. "Undocumented Youth Block Intersection for College Access." *Workers World,* 29 Sept. 2011, www.workers.org/2011/us/undocumented_youth_1006/. Accessed 29 Oct. 2020.

Berry, Patrick W. *Doing Time, Writing Lives: Refiguring Literacy and Higher Education in Prison.* Southern Illinois UP, 2018.

Binder, Amy, and Jeffrey L. Kidder. "Student Activism Is Often Uncivil. We Can Change That." *The Chronicle of Higher Education,* 22 Sept. 2019,

www.chronicle.com/article/student-activism-is-often-uncivil-we-can-change-that/. Accessed 17 Nov. 2020.
Bishop, Anne. *Becoming an Ally: Breaking the Cycle of Oppression in People.* Zed Books, 2002.
Boal, Augusto. *Theatre of the Oppressed.* Theatre Communications Group, 1979.
Boone, Mario. "Durham High School Sees Attendance Drop after Immigration Raid." *WCNC,* 11 Feb. 2016, www.cbs17.com. Accessed 29 Oct. 2020.
Boryga, Andrew. "Immigrant Groups Sue over Florida's Sanctuary Cities Ban." *South Florida Sun Sentinel,* 16 July 2019, www.sun-sentinel.com/news/fl-ne-immigrant-rights-group-challenge-sanctuary-cities-ban-20190716-shjy7ba6vjeonfekq3s756i5ou-story.html. Accessed 29 Oct. 2020.
Boyle-Baise, Marilynne, and Christine E. Sleeter. "Community-Based Service Learning for Multicultural Teacher Education." *Educational Foundations,* vol. 14, no. 2, Spring 2000, 33–50.
Brandzel, Amy L. *Against Citizenship: The Violence of the Normative.* Kindle ed., U of Illinois P, 2016. Dissident Feminisms.
Cambria, Bridget. "FREE Alisson a 7 Year Old Girl Trapped in Family Detention." *Change.org,* n.d., www.change.org/p/sarah-saldana-free-alisson-7-year-old-girl-trapped-in-family-detention. Accessed 29 Oct. 2020.
Capps, Randy, et al. "The Education and Work Profiles of the DACA Population." *Migration Policy Institute,* Aug. 2017, www.migrationpolicy.org/research/education-and-work-profiles-daca-population. Accessed 29 Oct. 2020.
Carcamo, Cindy. "Officials Mulling Deportation, Release of 'Dream 9' in Arizona." *Los Angeles Times,* 1 Aug.2013, articles.latimes.com/2013/aug/01/nation/la-na-nn-ff-immigration-dreamers-deportation-20130731. Accessed 27 Oct. 2020.
Carter, Shannon, et al. "Introduction: What *Does* Democracy Look Like?" Carter et al., 1–24.
———, eds. *Writing Democracy: The Political Turn in and beyond the Trump Era,* Kindle ed., Routledge, 2020. Research in Writing Studies.
Cavallaro, Alexandra J., et al. "Inside Voices: Collaborative Writing in a Prison Environment." *Harlot: A Revealing Look at the Arts of Persuasion,* no. 15, 2016, harlotofthearts.org/index.php/harlot/article/view/323/188. Accessed 29 Oct. 2020.
Collins, Patricia Hill, and Sirma Bilge. *Intersectionality.* Polity Press, 2016.

"Consideration of Deferred Action for Childhood Arrivals (DACA)." *US Citizen and Immigration Services,* www.uscis.gov/archive/consideration-deferred-action-childhood-arrivals-daca. Accessed 29 Oct. 2020.

Cooper, David D., and Laura Julier. "Democratic Conversations: Civil Literacy and Service-Learning in the American Grains." Adler-Kassner et al., pp. 79–94.

Coscia, Jessica. "NC Judge Grants Reprieve to Student Who Is Facing Deportation." *Fox News Latino,* 19 July 2011, www.foxnews.com/world/nc-judge-grants-reprieve-to-student-who-is-facing-deportation. Accessed 28 July 2014.

Crenshaw, Kimberlé. "Mapping the Margins: Intersectionality, Identity Politics, and Violence against Women of Color." *Stanford Law Review,* vol. 43, no. 6, 1991, pp. 1241–99.

"Criminal Justice Fact Sheet." *National Association for the Advancement of Colored People,* www.naacp.org/criminal-justice-fact-sheet/. Accessed 27 Oct. 2020.

Cushman, Ellen. "The Rhetorician as an Agent of Social Change." *College Composition and Communication,* vol. 47, no. 1, Feb. 1996, pp. 7–28.

Danticat, Edwidge. *Brother, I'm Dying.* Vintage Books, 2008.

Davis, Joshua. *The Undocumentary,* www.joshdavis.org/undocumentary. Accessed 2 Nov. 2020.

Deans, Thomas. "Writing Across the Curriculum and Community Service Learning: Correspondences, Cautions, and Futures." Adler-Kassler et al., pp. 29–38.

———. *Writing Partnerships: Service-Learning in Composition.* NCTE, 2000.

De los Santos, René, et al. "Revealing the Educational Experiences and Needs of Los Otros DREAMers." Conference on College Composition and Communication, 15–18 Mar. 2017, Portland.

Dewey, John. *Democracy and Education: An Introduction to the Philosophy of Education.* 1916. Free Press, 1967.

"DREAM Act Protesters Who Staged Sit-In at Obama's Denver Campaign Office, Call Off Hunger Strike, Vow More Actions to Come." *Huffington Post,* 13 June 2012, www.huffpost.com/entry/dream-act-protesters-who_n_1593739. Accessed 2 Nov. 2020.

Espinosa-Aguilar, Amanda. "Illegal." Ruiz and Sánchez, pp. 155–67.

Fassler, Joe. "All Immigrants Are Artists." *The Atlantic,* 27 Aug. 2013, www.theatlantic.com/entertainment/archive/2013/08/all-immigrants-are-artists/279087/. Accessed 28 Oct. 2020.

Feigenbaum, Paul. *Collaborative Imagination: Earning Activism through Literacy Education.* Southern Illinois UP, 2015.

———. "Nudging Ourselves toward a Political Turn." Carter et al., pp. 138–49.
Flores, Nelson, and Jonathan Rosa. "Undoing Appropriateness: Raciolinguistic Ideologies and Language Diversity in Education." *Harvard Educational Review,* vol. 85, no. 2, Summer 2015, pp. 149–71.
Flower, Linda. *Community Literacy and the Rhetoric of Public Engagement.* Southern Illinois UP, 2008.
———. "Intercultural Inquiry and the Transformation of Service." *College English,* vol. 65, no. 2, Nov. 2002, pp. 181–201.
Fraser, Nancy. "Rethinking the Public Sphere: A Contribution to the Critique of Actually Existing Democracy." *Social Text,* no. 25/26, 1990, pp. 56–80.
Freire, Paulo. *Pedagogy of the Oppressed.* Translated by Myra Bergman Ramos, Herder and Herder, 1970.
Fulfilling the Promise, Serving the Need: Advancing College Opportunity for Low-Income Students. United States Dept. of Education, Mar. 2016, www2.ed.gov/about/overview/focus/advancing-college-opportunity.pdf. Accessed 28 Oct. 2020.
"FY 2016 ICE Immigration Removals." *United States Immigration and Customs Enforcement,* www.ice.gov/ removal-statistics/2016. Accessed 28 Oct. 2020.
Galindo, René. "Undocumented and Unafraid: The DREAM Act 5 and the Public Disclosure of Undocumented Status as a Political Act." *The Urban Review,* vol. 44, no. 5, 2012, pp. 589–611.
Gamber-Thompson, Liana, and Arely M. Zimmerman. "DREAMing Citizenship: Undocumented Youth, Coming Out, and Pathways to Participation." *By Any Media Necessary: The New Youth Activism,* by Henry Jenkins, et al., New York UP, 2016, pp. 186–218. opensquare.nyupress.org/books/9781479899982/read/.
García, Romeo. "Creating Presence from Absence and Sound from Silence." *Community Literacy Journal,* vol. 13, no. 1, 2018, pp. 7–15.
García Hernández, César Cuauhtémoc. "Abolish Immigrant Prisons." *The New York Times,* 2 Dec. 2019, www.nytimes.com/2019/12/02/opinion/immigration-detention-prison.html. Accessed 15 Mar. 2020.
Gee, Lisa Christensen, Matthew Gardner, and Meg Wiche. *Undocumented Immigrants' State and Local Tax Contributions. Institute on Taxation and Economic Policy,* 2016, itep.org/wp-content/uploads/immigration2016.pdf. Accessed 29 Oct. 2020.
Gelb, Adam, and Phillip Stevenson. "US Adult Incarceration Rate Declines 13 Percent in Eight Years." *PEW,* 12 Jan. 2017, https://www.pewtrusts.org/en/research-and-analysis/articles/2017/01/12/us-adult-incarceration-rate-declines-13-percent-in-8-years. Accessed 2 Nov. 2020.

Gogan, Brian. "Expanding the Aims of Public Rhetoric and Writing Pedagogy: Writing Letters to Editors." *College Composition and Communication,* vol. 65, no. 4, June 2014, pp. 534–59.

Goldblatt, Eli. "Alinsky's Reveille: A Community-Organizing Model for Neighborhood-Based Literacy Projects." *College English,* vol. 67, no. 3, Jan. 2005, pp. 274–95.

Gonzales, Roberto G. *Lives in Limbo: Undocumented and Coming of Age in America.* U of California P, 2016.

Gonzales, Roberto G., and Leo R. Chavez. "'Awakening to a Nightmare': Abjectivity and Illegality in the Lives of Undocumented 1.5-Generation Latino Immigrants in the United States." *Current Anthropology,* vol. 53, no. 3, 2012, pp. 255–81.

Gonzales, Roberto G., and Veronica Terriquez. *How DACA Is Impacting the Lives of Those Who Are Now DACAmented: Preliminary Findings from the National UnDACAmented Research Project. Immigration Policy Center of the American Immigration Council, in collaboration with the Center for the Study of Immigrant Integration, U of Southern California,* Aug. 2013, http://americanimmigrationcouncil.org/sites/default/files/research/daca_final_ipc_csii_1.pdf. Accessed 27 Oct. 2020.

Gonzales, Roberto G., et al. "No Place to Belong: Contextualizing Concepts of Mental Health among Undocumented Immigrant Youth in the United States." *American Behavioral Scientist,* vol. 57, no. 8, Aug. 2013, pp. 1174–99.

Goss, Stephen, et al. "Effects of Unauthorized Immigration on the Actuarial Status of the Social Security Trust Funds." Actuarial Note no. 151, Apr. 2013, *Social Security Administration,* www.ssa.gov/oact/NOTES/pdf_notes/note151.pdf. Accessed 29 Oct. 2020.

Green, Neisha-Anne. "Moving beyond Alright: And the Emotional Toll of This, My Life Matters Too, in the Writing Center Work," *The Writing Center Journal,* vol. 37, no. 1, 2018, pp. 15–34.

Gries, Laurie E. "Writing to Assemble Publics: Making Writing Activate, Making Writing Matter." *College Composition and Communication,* vol. 70, no. 3, Feb. 2019, pp. 327–55.

Gutierrez, Bertrand M. "Young Immigrants Arrested during Charlotte Protest." *Winston-Salem Journal,* 6 Sept. 2011, www.journalnow.com/news/local/young-immigrants-arrested-during-charlotte-protest/article_139bc926-665f-5159-a64f-71ba3a4f2e94.html. Accessed 28 Oct. 2020.

Harris, Alex. "'I'm Terrified about Our Future': Zero Hour Youth Summit Brings Teen Activists to Miami." *Miami Herald,* 12 July 2019.

Herzberg, Bruce. "Community Service and Critical Teaching." *College Composition and Communication,* vol. 45, no. 3, Oct. 1994, pp. 307–19.

Hillman, Nicholas, and Taylor Weichman. *Education Deserts: The Continued Significance of "Place" in the Twenty-First Century.* American Council on Education, 2016, www.acenet.edu/news-room/Documents/Education-Deserts-The-Continued-Significance-of-Place-in-the-Twenty-First-Century.pdf. Accessed 28 Oct. 2020.

Hinshaw, Wendy Wolters. "Writing to Listen: Why I Write across Prison Walls." *Community Literacy Journal,* vol. 13, no. 1, 2018: pp. 55–70.

"HM69 Nike Missile Base." *National Park Service,* www.nps.gov/ever/learn/historyculture/hm69.htm. Accessed 29 Oct. 2020.

Hutchinson, Glenn. "Charlotte, NC: Community Rallies, Rodrigo Cruz Ambrocio Saved from Deportation." *Imagine 2050,* 18 Oct. 2011, newcomm.com. Accessed 28 July 2014.

———. "The Dream Generation." *Imagine 2050,* 16 Dec. 2010, newcomm.com. Accessed 28 July 2014.

———. "Help Students and the American Dream." *Imagine 2050,* 29 July 2011, newcomm.com. Accessed 28 July 2014.

———. "LIMBO: Marie Gonzalez and The Dream Act." *Reflections on Community-Based Writing Instruction,* vol. 8, no. 2, Mar. 2009, pp. 62–93.

———. "Please Don't Cite Hate Groups in Articles." Letter to the editor, *The Chronicle of Higher Education,* 31 May 2011, www.chronicle.com/article/Please-Dont-Cite-Hate-Groups/127723. Accessed 29 Oct. 2020.

———. "A Quick Look at the Arrests in North Carolina." *Imagine 2050,* 9 Sept. 2011, newcomm.webfactional.com/2011/09/09/a-quick-look-at-the-arrests-in-north-carolina/nc-dream-team-1/). Accessed 28 July 2014.

———. "Stop Separating Families This Holiday Season." *The Progressive,* 12 Dec. 2013, progressive.org/op-eds/stop-separating-families-holiday-season/. Accessed 29 Oct. 2020.

———. "Story Time in Arizona: Four Heroes and You." *Imagine 2050,* 4 June 2010, newcomm.com. Accessed 1 Sept. 2014.

"Immigration Detention 101." *Detention Watch Network,* www.detentionwatchnetwork.org/issues/detention-101. Accessed 29 Oct. 2020.

"*The Infiltrators* Film Aims to Open Americans' Eyes to the Reality of Deportation." *PRI's The World,* 18 Mar. 2019, www.pri.org/stories/2019-03-18/infiltrators-film-aims-open-americans-eyes-reality-deportation. Accessed 29 Oct. 2020.

"Influence and Lobbying." *Open Secrets,* opensecrets.org/influence/. Accessed 29 Oct. 2020.

Inoue, Asao B. "#4C19 Chair's Address." *YouTube,* uploaded by NCTE, 4 Apr. 2019, www.youtube.com/watch?v=brPGTewcDYY&feature=youtu.be. Accessed 29 Oct. 2020.

Jacobi, Tobi. "Austerity behind Bars: The 'Cost' of Prison College Programs." *Composition in the Age of Austerity,* edited by Nancy Welch and Tony Scott, UP of Colorado, 2016, pp. 106–19. *JSTOR,* www.jstor.org/stable/j.ctt1b3h9ts.10. Accessed 17 Apr. 2020.

———. "Speaking Out for Social Justice: The Problems and Possibilities of US Women's Prison and Jail Writing Workshops." *Critical Survey,* vol. 23, no. 3, Sept. 2011, pp. 40–54.

Jaynes, Gregory. "US Is Remaining Adamant as Detained Haitians Press Appeals for Asylum." *The New York Times,* 24 Apr. 1982, www.nytimes.com/1982/04/24/us/us-is-remaining-adamant-as-detained-haitians-press-appeals-for-asylum.html. Accessed 29 Oct. 2020.

Kahn, Seth. "Audience Addressed? Audience Invoked? Audience Organized!" Carter et al., pp. 123–29.

Kannan, Vani. "Taking a Lead from Student Movements in a 'Political Turn.'" Carter et al., pp. 130–37.

Kazin, Michael, and Joseph A. McCartin. Introduction. *Americanism: New Perspectives on the History of an Ideal,* U of North Carolina P, 2006, pp.1–21. www.jstor.org/stable/10.5149/9780807869710_kazin.3.

Kennedy, Thomas. "The Florida Legislators Who'd Rather Hide than Talk with You." *Huffington Post,* 2 Mar. 2017, www.huffpost.com/entry/the-florida-legislators-whod-rather-hide-than-talk_b_58b8b3aee4b0fa65b844b173?guccounter=1. Accessed 16 Nov. 2020.

———. "Homestead Detention Center Is No Kids' Summer Camp." *Miami Herald,* 14 June 2019, www.miamiherald.com/opinion/op-ed/article231550468.html. Accessed 29 Oct. 2020.

———. Personal interview. 12 June 2017.

Khan, Mahwish. "May 17, 2012: DREAMers Launch 'Right to DREAM' Campaign with National Day of Action." *America's Voice,* 16 May 2012, americasvoice.org/blog/dreamers-demand-protection-and-launch-right-to-dream-campaign-with-national-day-of-action/. Accessed 29 Oct. 2020.

Kirshner, Ben. *Youth Activism in an Era of Education Inequality.* New York UP, 2015.

Kluge, Alexander, and Oskar Negt. *History and Obstinacy.* Translated by Richard Langston et al., Zone Books, 2014.

Kochhar, Rakesh, et al. *The New Latino South: The Context and Consequences of Rapid Population Growth.* Pew Research Center, 26 July 2005, https://www.pewresearch.org/hispanic/2005/07/26/the-new-latino-south/.

Krogstad, Jens Manuel. "DACA Has Shielded Nearly 790,000 Young Unauthorized Immigrants from Deportation." *Pew Research Center,* 1 Sept. 2017, www.pewresearch.org/fact-tank/2017/09/01/unauthorized-immigrants-covered-by-daca-face-uncertain-future/. Accessed 29 Oct. 2020.

Krogstad, Jens Manuel, et al. "Five Facts about Illegal Immigration in the US." *Pew Research Center,* 12 June 2019, www.pewresearch.org/fact-tank/2019/06/12/5-facts-about-illegal-immigration-in-the-u-s/. Accessed 30 Oct. 2020.

Kynard, Carmen. "'All I Need Is One Mic': A Black Feminist Community Meditation on the Work, the Job, and the Hustle (and Why So Many of Yall Confuse This Stuff)." Keynote Address. Conference on Community Writing, 18 Oct. 2019, U of Pennsylvania, Philadelphia.

———. "From Candy Girls to Cyber Sista-Cipher: Narrating Black Females' Color-Consciousness and Counterstories in and out of School." *Harvard Educational Review,* vol. 80, no. 1, 2010, pp. 30–52.

———. *Vernacular Insurrections: Race, Black Protest, and the New Century in Composition-Literacies Studies.* State U of New York P, 2013.

Lal, Prerna, with Tania Unzueta. "How Queer Undocumented Youth Built the Immigrant Rights Movement." *Huffington Post,* 28 Mar. 2013, www.huffpost.com/entry/how-queer-undocumented_b_2973670. Accessed 29 Oct. 2020.

Lee, Eunjeong, and Sara P. Alvarez. "World Englishes, Translingualism, and Racialization in the US College Composition Classroom." *WorldEnglishes,* 20 Feb. 2020, pp. 1–12.

Leon, Kendall. "Chicanas Making Change: Institutional Rhetoric and the Comisión Femenil Mexicana Nacional." *Reflections,* vol. 13, no. 1, Fall 2013, pp. 165–94.

Linthicum, Kate. "US-Raised Dreamers Are Building New Lives—Back in Mexico." *Los Angeles Times,* 4 Nov. 2014, www.latimes.com/world/la-fg-c1-mexico-dreamers-20141104-story.html. Accessed 27 Oct. 2020.

Linton, Julie M., et al. "Unaccompanied Children Seeking Safe Haven: Providing Care and Supporting Well-Being of a Vulnerable Population." *Children and Youth Services Review,* vol. 92, Sept. 2018, pp. 122–32.

Lipman, Jana K. "'The Fish Trusts the Water, and It Is in the Water That It Is Cooked': The Caribbean Origins of the Krome Detention Center," *Radical History Review,* vol. 115, 2013, pp. 115–41.

Loeb, Paul Rogat. *Soul of a Citizen: Living with Conviction in a Cynical Time.* St. Martin's Griffin, 1999.

Logan, Rebeca. "Could the DREAM Act Have Saved Joaquin Luna's Life?" *NEA Today,* 12 Dec. 2011, neaedjustice.org/2011/12/21/could-the-dream-act-have-saved-joaquin-lunas-life/. Accessed 29 Oct. 2020.

Long, Elenore. *Community Literacy and the Rhetoric of the Local Publics.* Parlor Press, 2008.

"'Love Not Raids': A Webinar for Educators and Students' Support Staff." *United We Dream,* 17 Mar. 2016, unitedwedream.org/wp-content/uploads/2016/03/March-17-2016_final.pptx.pdf. Accessed 27 Oct. 2020.

Macías-Rojas, Patrisia. *From Deportation to Prison: The Politics of Immigration Enforcement in Post–Civil Rights America.* New York UP, 2016.

Mahendra, Jacquelyn. "DREAM Now Series Launch: Letter from Mohammad Abdollahi to President Barack Obama." *America's Voice,* 19 July 2010, americasvoice.org/blog/dream_now_letters_mo/. Accessed 2 Mar. 2020.

"Major US Immigration Laws 1790–Present." *Migration Policy Institute,* Mar. 2013, www.migrationpolicy.org/research/timeline-1790. Accessed 29 Oct. 2020.

Martinez, Aja Y. "The Responsibility of Privilege: A Critical Race Counterstory Conversation." *Peitho Journal,* vol. 21, no. 1, 2018, 212–33.

Martinez, Alexandra. "Judge's Order to Force-Feed Ten Hunger-Strikers at Krome Sparks Immigration Protest." *Miami New Times,* 28 Dec. 2015, www.miaminewtimes.com/news/judges-order-to-force-feed-ten-hunger-strikers-at-krome-sparks-immigration-protest-8138104. Accessed 28 Oct. 2020.

Martinez, Viridiana. Personal interview. 17 Nov. 2014.

Mathieu, Paula. *Tactics of Hope: The Public Turn in English Composition.* Boynton/Cook, 2005.

Mitchell, Amy, Galen Stocking, and Katerina Eva Matsa. "Digital Readership Data and What It Can Tell Us." Part 1 of *Long-Form Reading Shows Signs of Life in Our Mobile News World. Pew Research Center,* 5 May 2016, www.journalism.org/2016/05/05/1-digital-readership-data-and-what-it-can-tell-us/. Accessed 29 Oct. 2020.

Monberg, Terese Guinsatao. "Writing Home or Writing *as* the Community: Toward a Theory of Recursive Spatial Movement for Students of Color in Service-Learning Courses." *Reflections,* vol. 8, no. 3, Spring 2009, pp. 21–51.

Morton, John. Memorandum. 17 June 2011, *United States Customs and Immigration Enforcement,* www.ice.gov/doclib/secure-communities/pdf/prosecutorial-discretion-memo.pdf. Accessed 29 Oct. 2020.

Muñoz, Susana M. *Identity, Social Activism, and the Pursuit of Higher Education: The Journey Stories of Undocumented and Unafraid Community Activists.* Peter Lang Publishing, 2015.

Mutnick, Deborah, et al. "Conclusion: Further Notes on the Political Turn." Carter et al., pp. 261–72.

Negrón-Gonzales, Genevieve. "Undocumented, Unafraid and Unapologetic: Re-Articulatory Practices and Migrant Youth 'Illegality.'" *Latino Studies,* vol. 12, no. 2, Summer 2014, pp. 259–78.

———. "Undocumented Youth Activism as Counter-Spectacle: Civil Disobedience and Testimonio in the Battle around Immigration Reform." *AZTLÁN: A Journal of Chicano Studies,* no. 1, 2015, pp. 87–112.

"North Carolina Job Loss during the NAFTA-WTO Period." *Public Citizen,* www.citizen.org/article/north-carolina-job-loss-during-the-nafta-wto-period/. Accessed 29 Oct. 2020.

O'Matz, Megan. "Immigrants with No Criminal History Get Lengthy Stays at Little-Known Jail." *South Florida Sun Sentinel,* 5 Jan. 2013, articles.sun-sentinel.com/2013-01-05/news/fl-private-immigration-jail-20130105_1_illegal-immigrants-deutch-human-rights-abuses. Accessed 28 Oct. 2020.

"The One Thing You're Not Supposed to Do." *This American Life,* 21 June 2013, www.thisamericanlife.org/498/the-one-thing-youre-not-supposed-to-do. Accessed 27 Oct. 2020.

Ordoñez, Frank. "CPCC Student's Deportation Dropped." *Charlotte Observer,* 30 July 2011, www.charlotteobserver.com/2011/07/30/2491179/students-deportation-dropped.html#ixzz1TyfqQnDz. Accessed 3 May 2018.

Ortiz, Gabe. "Guards Block Children from Delivering Letters of Support to Migrant Kids Jailed at Prison Camp." *Daily Kos,* 28 May 2019, www.dailykos.com/story/2019/5/28/1860903/-Guards-block-children-from-delivering-letters-of-support-to-migrant-kids-jailed-at-prison-camp. Accessed 29 Oct. 2020.

Ortiz Juarez-Paz, Anna V. "Undocumented Identity Storytelling: (Re)framing Public Relations." *International Journal of Media and Cultural Politics,* vol. 13, no. 1, Mar. 2017, pp. 165–78.

Pacheco, Gaby. "Trail of Dreams: A Fifteen-Hundred-Mile Journey to the Nation's Capital." *Undocumented and Unafraid: Tam Tran, Cinthya Felix, and the Immigrant Youth Movement.* Edited by Kent Wong et al., UCLA Center for Labor Research and Education, 2012, pp. 56–68.

———. "What the Dreamers Can Teach the Parkland Kids." *The New York Times,* 17 Mar. 2018, www.nytimes.com/2018/03/17/opinion/dreamers-march-lives-parkland.html. Accessed 13 Nov. 2020.

Paris, Django, and H. Samy Alim. "What Are We Seeking to Sustain through Culturally Sustaining Pedagogy? A Loving Critique Forward." *Harvard Educational Review,* vol. 84, no. 1, Spring 2014, pp. 85–100.

Parks, Steve. "Sinners Welcome: The Limits of Rhetorical Agency." *Reimagining the Social Turn.* Spec. issue of *College English,* vol. 76, no. 6, July 2014, pp. 506–24.

Patel, Leigh. *Decolonizing Educational Research: From Ownership to Answerability.* Routledge, Kindle ed., 2016.

———. "Immigrant Populations and Sanctuary Schools." *Journal of Literacy Research,* vol. 50, no. 4, 2018, pp. 524–29.

Pettit, Emma. "'Begging to Have Their Stories Told': San Diego State Professors Create Living Archive of Migrants' Letters from Detention." *The Chronicle of Higher Education,* 13 Feb. 2019, www.chronicle.com/article/begging-to-have-their-stories-told-san-diego-state-professors-create-living-archive-of-migrants-letters-from-detention/. Accessed 14 July 2019.

———. "Ending Ban on Pell Grants for Prisoners Is Said to Yield 'Cascade' of Benefits." *The Chronicle of Higher Education,* 16 Jan. 2019, www.chronicle.com/article/ending-ban-on-pell-grants-for-prisoners-is-said-to-yield-cascade-of-benefits/. Accessed 15 Mar. 2020.

Plemons, Anna. *Beyond Progress in the Prison Classroom: Options and Opportunities.* NCTE, 2019.

Powell, Jessica, and Amber Kelly. "Accomplices in the Academy in the Age of Black Lives Matter." *Journal of Critical Thought and Praxis,* vol. 6, no. 2, 2017, pp. 42–65.

Powell, Katrina M. "Rhetorics of Displacement: Constructing Identities in Forced Relocations." *College English,* vol. 74, no. 4, 2012, pp. 299–324.

Pritchard, Eric Darnell. *Fashioning Lives: Black Queers and the Politics of Literacy.* Southern Illinois UP, 2017.

"Profile of the Unauthorized Population: United States." *Migration Policy Institute,* 2018, www.migrationpolicy.org. Accessed 4 Apr. 2018.

Ratcliffe, Krista. *Rhetorical Listening: Identification, Gender, Whiteness.* Southern Illinois UP, 2005.

Reno, Janet. "Keynote Address by the Honorable Janet Reno, Attorney General of the United States, Fiftieth Anniversary of UNC–Charlotte." 4 Oct. 1996, www.justice.gov/ag/speeches-7. Accessed 28 Oct. 2020.

Ribero, Ana Milena. "Citizenship." Ruiz and Sánchez, pp. 31–45.

Richardson, Elaine, and Alice Ragland. "#StayWoke: The Language and Literacies of the #BlackLivesMatter Movement." *Community Literacy Journal,* vol. 12, no. 2, Spring 2018, pp. 27–56.

Rivera, Alex, and Cristina Ibarra, directors. *The Infiltrators.* Ion Cinema, 2019.

Rousculp, Tiffany. *Rhetoric of Respect: Recognizing Change at a Community Writing Center.* CCCC/NCTE, 2014.

Ruiz, Iris D., and Raúl Sánchez. *Decolonizing Rhetoric and Composition Studies: New Latinx Keywords for Theory and Pedagogy.* Palgrave Macmillan, 2016. E-book, doi 10.1057/978-1-137-52724-0.

Schutz, Aaron, and Anne Ruggles Gere. "Service Learning and English Studies: Rethinking 'Public' Service." *College English*, vol. 60, no. 2, Feb. 1998, pp. 129–49.

Schwiertz, Helge. "Transformations of the Undocumented Youth Movement and Radical Egalitarian Citizenship." *Citizenship Studies,* vol. 20, no. 5, 2016, pp. 610–28.

Scott, Tony, and Nancy Welch. Introduction. *Composition in the Age of Austerity,* edited by Welch and Scott, UP of Colorado, 2016, pp. 3–18. *JSTOR,* www.jstor.org/stable/j.ctt1b3h9ts.3. Accessed 17 Apr. 2020.

Segal, Corinne. "In a Florida Prison, a Poet Grapples with Power and Oppression." *PBS NewsHour,* 16 Apr. 2018, www.pbs.org/newshour/arts/florida-prison-poet-power-exchange-for-change. Accessed 18 Nov. 2020.

Sundvall, Scott, and Katherine Fredlund. "The Writing on the Wall: Activist Rhetorics, Public Writing, and Responsible Pedagogy." *Composition Forum,* vol. 36, 2017.

Sweeney, Chris. "Two Activists Infiltrate a Center Where Illegal Immigrants Are Held." *Miami New Times,* 25 Oct. 2012, www.miaminewtimes.com/news/two-activists-infiltrate-a-center-where-illegal-immigrants-are-held-6389574. Accessed 29 Oct. 2020.

Taylor, Keeanga-Yamahtta. *From #BlackLivesMatter to Black Liberation.* Haymarket Books, 2016.

Thompson, Ginger, and Sarah Cohen. "More Deportations Follow Minor Crimes, Records Show." *The New York Times,* 6 Apr. 2014, www.nytimes.com/2014/04/07/us/more-deportations-follow-minor-crimes-data-shows.html. Accessed 28 Oct. 2020.

"Trends in US Corrections." *The Sentencing Project,* 22 June 2018, www.sentencingproject.org/publications/trends-in-u-s-corrections/. Accessed 14 August 2019.

Tuck, Eve. "Suspending Damage: A Letter to Communities." *Harvard Educational Review,* vol. 79, no. 3, Fall 2009, pp. 409–28.

"Undocumented Student Tuition: Overview." *National Conference of State Legislatures,* 29 Oct. 2015, www.ncsl.org/research/education/undocumented-student-tuition-overview.aspx. Accessed 29 Oct. 2020.

United States, Congress. PL 111–83, Department of Homeland Security Appropriations Act, 2010. 28 Oct. 2009. 123 Stat. 2149, www.govinfo.gov/app/details/PLAW-111publ83. Accessed 2 Nov. 2020.

———. House. *Hearing before the Subcommittee on Immigration, Citizenship, Refugees, Border Security, and International Law of the Committee on the Judiciary*, 18 May 2007, www.govinfo.gov/content/pkg/CHRG-110hhrg35453/html/CHRG-110hhrg35453.htm. Text transcription of hearing. Accessed 6 Dec. 2020.

Vargas, Jose Antonio. *Dear America: Notes of an Undocumented Citizen*. William Morrow, 2018.

———. "Define American." *DefineAmerican.com*, www.defineamerican.com/stories/view/josesstory. Accessed 13 Aug. 2019.

———. Keynote Address. Conference on College Composition and Communication. 18 Mar. 2017, Portland.

Velazquillo, Angelica. "Angelica V_____ North Carolina: We Will No Longer Remain in the Shadows!" *DREAMTeamNC*, 6 Sept. 2011, www.youtube.com/watch?v=HuqoGX8hP20. Accessed 2 Mar. 2020.

———. "Fighting Together: Angelica's Story." NC DREAM Team, 4 July 2011, ncdreamteam.wordpress.com/2011/07/04/fighting-together-angelicas-story/. Accessed 24 Jan. 2020.

———. "An Undocumented Immigrant Speaks Out." *Philadelphia Inquirer*, 26 Sept. 2011, www.inquirer.com/philly/opinion/20110926_An_undocumented_immigrant_speaks_out.html. Accessed 4 Nov. 2020.

Vieira, Kate. *American by Paper: How Documents Matter in Immigrant Literacy*. U of Minnesota P, 2016.

Welch, Nancy. "Informed, Passionate, and Disorderly: Uncivil Rhetoric in a New Gilded Age." *Unruly Rhetorics: Protest, Persuasion, and Publics*, edited by Jonathan Alexander et al., U of Pittsburgh P, Kindle ed., 2018, pp. 107–27.

———. "Living Room: Teaching Public Writing in a Post-Publicity Era." *College Composition and Communication*, vol. 56, no. 3, Feb. 2005, pp. 470–92.

———. *Living Room: Teaching Public Writing in a Privatized World*. Boynton/Cook Heinemann, 2008.

Wells, Susan. "Rogue Cops and Health Care: What Do We Want from Public Writing?" *College Composition and Communication*, vol. 47, no. 3, Oct. 1996, pp. 325–41.

Who Makes the News? Global Media Monitoring Project, 2015, whomakesthenews.org/gmmp/gmmp-reports/gmmp-2015-reports. Accessed 29 Oct. 2020.

Wildes-Muñoz, Laura. *The Making of a Dream: How a Group of Young Undocumented Immigrants Helped Change What It Means to Be American.* HarperCollins Publishers, 2018.

Wingard, Jennifer. *Branded Bodies, Rhetoric, and the Neoliberal Nation-State.* Lexington Books, 2013.

Wulff, Nicolas. Personal interview. 12 Nov. 2014.

———. "Undocumented Student Wants Change." *Lansing Journal.* 26 August 2012, p. 5.

Ybarra, Maggie. "Experts Say Changing Trade Pacts Could Hurt North Carolina." *Charlotte Observer,* 21 July 2016, www.charlotteobserver.com/news/politics-government/election/article91085177.html. Accessed 12 August 2019.

Yee, Allie. "Asian Americans in North Carolina." *North Carolina Justice Center,* Mar. 2016, www.ncjustice.org/wp-content/uploads/2018/11/IRRP_Asian-Americans-in-NC-2016.pdf. Accessed 13 August 2019.

Young, Vershawn Ashanti. "Momma's Memories and the New Equality." *Present Tense: A Journal of Rhetoric in Society,* vol. 1, no. 1, 2010, pp. 1–6.

———. "Should Writers Use They Own English?" *Writing Centers and the New Racism: A Call for Sustainable Dialogue and Change,* edited by Laura Greenfield and Karen Rowan, UP of Colorado, 2011, pp. 61–72.

Zong, Jie, and Jeanne Batalova. "How Many Unauthorized Immigrants Graduate from US High Schools Annually?" *Migration Policy Institute,* April 2019, www.migrationpolicy.org/research/unauthorized-immigrants-graduate-us-high-schools. Accessed 22 Apr. 2020.

INDEX

Abdollahi, Mohammad, 1, 3, 5, 6, 13–14, 27, 37, 43–44, 50, 53–54, 67, 75–76, 81, 84, 94, 97, 98, 123, 130, 141
accomplice, becoming an, 126–27
Acosta, Wildin, 38
activism, rhetorical
    deportation petitions, 43–49, 59–60
    detention center petitions, 109–10
    DREAMer movement, 45–46
    ethical dimension in, 59
    framing with Americanism, 43–49, 59–60, 110
    home, identification of, 60
    learning, 86–93
    power of, 72–73
    procedural vs. issue-based approach, 87–88
    in the public sphere, 70, 77
    responsibility of, 73
    successful, 72
    teaching, responsibility for, 74
activists. *See* organizers
Adler-Kassner, Linda, 17
advocacy
    asking for what is promised, 5, 44
    coming-out rallies, 3–4
    detention releases, 5–6
    student stories of, 3–4
Agagan, Conrad C., 112
Against Citizenship: The Violence of the Normative (Brandzel), 131
Agrawal, Nina, 117

Ahmed, Sara, 29
Albert, Gail, 24
Alexander, Jonathan, 88
Alexander, Michelle, 35, 89, 101
Alim, H. Samy, 21, 125
Alinsky, Saul, 20, 122
ally vs. accomplice, 126
Alvarez, Sara del Pilar, 16, 27–28, 43, 46, 62, 122, 135
Alvarez, Steven, 37
Amerasian Immigration Act, 26
American, meaning of, 62
American by Paper: How Documents Matter in Immigrant Literacy (Vieira), 28, 61
American dream, 47, 48, 49, 53, 54, 60, 125
American identity, challenging, 49–50
Americanisms, framing petitions with, 43–49, 62, 135
Americanness, 28
Angelica. *See* Velazquillo, Angelica
Anguiano, Claudia, 45, 55, 86
answerability, 65, 123
anti-immigrant policies, risks of challenging, 74–75
Arizona SB1070 law, 31, 43, 55, 75, 138
Artz, Lee, 87
asking for what is promised, 5, 44

Baker-Bell, April, 28
Batalova, Jeanne, 13
Berry, Patrick W., 104, 105, 113

173

Beyond Progress in the Prison Classroom: Options and Opportunities (Plemons), 103
Bilge, Sirma, 32, 34
Birthright Citizenship Act, 30
Bishop, Anne, 126
Black queers, 21
Brandzel, Amy L., 131
Brother, I'm Dying (Danticat), 107
Broward Detention Center (BTC), 5, 96–97, 119
Bush (George W.) administration, 68
Butler, Tamara, 28
Byrd, Robert, 35

campaigns, email, 2–3
Carter, Shannon, 118
Castro, Fidel, 107
Cavallaro, Alexandra J., 104
change
    civil disobedience for, 75
    forcing, 67, 68, 85–86, 94
Charlotte, NC, 22–23, 77–86
Chicana organizers, 20–21
"Chicanas Making Change: Institutional Rhetoric and the Comisión Femenil Mexicana Nacional" (Leon), 20
children, imprisoning undocumented, 38, 102–3, 130
children of undocumented parents, 30–31
Chinese Exclusion Act, 31
citizen, term use, 44
citizenship
    children of undocumented parents, 30–31
    as exclusion, 30–31
    legislating, 31
    marked on the body, 32
    teaching, 22–26
    white supremacist ideas embedded, 44
citizenship policy, 45

civil disobedience
    Americanness of, 69–70
    for change, 75
    change, forcing, 86
    Charlotte protest, 77–86
    counter-spectacle of, 76–77
    documenting, 78
    learning about, 67
    media and, 76, 81, 83
    network of actions in, 76
    power of, 94
    reasons for, 68–70, 83, 85–86
    risk of, 76–77, 80–81
    risks taken, x, 74
    in theory vs. implementation, 74
    timing, 75, 78
Clinton (Bill) administration, 103
Colbert, Arthur, 72, 76, 89
collective action, power of, 72–73
Collins, Patricia Hill, 32, 34
coming out, 49–54
coming-out rallies, 3–4, 51–53, 78
community, building through listening, 66–67, 114
Community Accomplice Syllabus, Spring 2020, 143–50
Community Literacies en Confianza: *Learning from Bilingual After-School Programs* (Alvarez), 37
community partnerships
    graduate school training in, 15–16
    with universities, 17–20
Community Partner Syllabus, Fall 1997, 7–12
community relations, role in deportations, 58–59
"Community Service and Critical Teaching" (Herzberg), 16
community work
    graduate school training in, 20–22
    models for, 16–19
community writing, 113–19
community writing centers, 104
community-writing projects, 18

community-writing/service-learning courses
  assignments, 71
  beginnings, 23–24
  focus of, 66–67
  goal of, 25, 64, 87–88
  organizing framework for, 64–65, 87–89
  overview, 24
  requirements, 25–26, 128
  revising, 86–93, 94–95, 123–29
  student advocates, contributions of, 26–27
  syllabi
    Community Accomplice Syllabus, Spring 2020, 143–50
    Community Partner Syllabus, Fall 1997, 7–12
    first, 127
    revised, 127–28
  topics, 24–25
  transforming pedagogy, 64–67, 94–95, 122
  white gaze in, 125
Composition in the Age of Austerity (Scott & Welch), 99
conciencia bilingüe, 46
Conciencia Bilingüe: The Multilingual and Academic Writing Practices of Undocumented Immigrant Activists (Pilar Alvarez), 27
confianza, 37
Congress, risks of testifying before, 52
Cooper, David, 17
corporations, power of, 34–35, 100–101, 129
Corrections Corporation of America (CCA), 101
Crenshaw, Kimberlé, 32
Crooks, Robert, 17
Cuban refugees, 107
Cushman, Ellen, 17

DACA (Deferred Action for Childhood Arrivals) directive, 81–83, 86
DACA (Deferred Action for Childhood Arrivals) eligible
  assistance in applying for, 82
  deportations, 81–83, 86
  in detention, 97
  statistics on receiving, 83
DACA (Deferred Action for Childhood Arrivals) legislation
  families, effects on, 61
  organizing for passage of, 14, 70, 83, 86, 135
  university commitment to students under, 1–2, 13, 29, 38
DACA (Deferred Action for Childhood Arrivals) program
  eligibility for, 33
  statistics, 34
DACA (Deferred Action for Childhood Arrivals) students
  benefits and risks, 37, 82, 133, 152
  in-state tuition for, 1, 91
  qualifications for, 33, 82
Danticat, Edwidge, 107
Davis, Joshua, 78
Dear America: Notes of an Undocumented Citizen (Vargas), 63
Decolonizing Educational Research: From Ownership to Answerability (Patel), 65
Department of Homeland Security Appropriations Act, 102
deportations
  families, effects on, 113
  low priority, 5, 44, 48, 57–59
  Obama administration, 78, 86
  prioritized, 34
  statistics, 13, 34, 34f, 86, 133
deportations, petitions to stop
  examples, 47–48, 55–58
  media campaigns, 59–60
  reasons to use, 58
  rhetorical strategies, 43–49, 59–60

deportations, stopping
  DACA directive, 81–83, 86
  going public, x
  network of actions required, 64–65
  reasons for, 58–59
  vigils, 60–63
  writing and activism for, 54–63
Detainee Allies, 114
detainees. *See* immigrants, imprisoned
detention centers
  children in, 38, 102–3, 130
  conclusions, 120
  documenting, 97–98
  END campaigns, 109–12
  historically, 101–2
  media access to, 117
  normalization of, 35
  politics of, 35–36
  population statistics, 102, 106
  privatization of, 100–101, 103
  profitability of, 35–36, 102, 120
  statistics, 35, 106
  stories of release from, 96–97
  time spent in, 105, 106, 112, 118
  transfers, results of, 111
  visitation project, 107–8
  Wally's story, 108–13
detention centers, conditions in
  communication restrictions, 100–101, 103
  discrimination, 102
  education denied, 105
  isolation, 102, 107, 114
  medical care, 98, 102, 107
  physical abuse/rape, 107
  protesting, 107–8
  right to an attorney, 103
  visitation monitoring, 100, 103
detention centers, petitions for release
  purpose of, 111
  rhetorical strategies, 109–11
  social media/media in, 111–12
Dewey, John, 20
DREAM Act
  expansion of, 50
  organizing for passage of, 54, 62, 75–76, 81, 136–37, 152–53
  passage of the, ix
DREAM Act-eligible youth
  advocates, stories of, 52
  assumptions about, 62
  low priority for deportation, 48, 57–59
DREAMActivist, 43, 54, 109
DREAMer movement, 45–46, 75
DREAMers, 61, 62, 65
"DREAMing Citizenship" (Gamber-Thompson & Zimmerman), 53–54
DREAM Team, 42–43, 46, 54–63, 77–86
drivers' licenses, ix, 57, 63
Durbin, Richard, 53, 137
Duvalier, Jean-Claude ("Baby Doc"), 107

education. *See* community-writing/service-learning courses; higher education; students, undocumented
Education, Not Deportation Team, 5, 96
educational change, need for, 65–66
END campaigns, 59–60, 109–12
Erick. *See* Velazquillo, Erick

families
  arrests, effects on, ix–x
  DACA, effect on, 61
  deportations effect on, 113
  immigrant, separating, 38
  risking through coming out, 52–53
Fashioning Lives: Black Queers and the Politics of Literacy (Pritchard), 21
fear, student stories of, 4
Fernald, Denny, 23
"Fighting Together'" (Velazquillo), 42
Flores, Nelson, 21
Florida Immigrant Coalition, 130
Florida International University, 2,

38–39, 101, 105–6, 113–18, 120
Flower, Linda, 18–19, 25, 64
Fourteenth Amendment, 30
Fraser, Nancy, 83
Fredlund, Katherine, 73–74, 76
freedom of speech, 100–101, 103
Freire, Paulo, 20
Friends of Miami-Date Detainees, 108, 115
From #BlackLivesMatter to Black Liberation (Taylor), 128
"From Candy Girls to Cyber Sista-Cipher: Narrating Black Females' Color-Consciousness and Counterstories in and out of School" (Kynard), 29
From Deportation to Prison: The Politics of Immigration Enforcement in Post–Civil Rights America (Macías-Rojas), 101

Galindo, René, 77
Gamber-Thompson, Liana, 53–54
García, Romeo, 66, 127
García Hernández, César Cuauhtémoc, 119
GEO Group, 35–36
Gere, Anne Ruggles, 17
Gillespie, Paula, 115
Gogan, Brian, 93
Goldblatt, Eli, 20, 27
Gonzales, Roberto G., 37, 45–46
Gonzalez, Marie, 52–53, 136–37
government, privatizing, 99–100
graduation protests, 75, 77
Green, Neisha-Anne, 126
Gries, Laurie E., 73

Habermas, Jürgen, 71
Hagan, Kay, 54, 56, 58, 138, 155
Haitian immigrants, 107
Hart-Celler Act, 28, 31
Herzberg, Bruce, 16–17, 23
higher education

anti-immigrant policies, 64, 78
community work, graduate school training in, 15–16, 20
failures in addressing student needs, 13–14, 27, 29
federal aid for, ix
in-state tuition for undocumented students, 13, 91–92, 153–54
policies marginalizing people, 38
prison industrial complex, ties to the, 101
protest for the right to, 78, 83, 85
racism, institutional, 28–29, 39
role in deportations, 58–59
safety in, 38–39
for undocumented students, x–xi, 1–2, 13, 37–38, 91–92, 132–33, 153–54
university-community partnerships, 17–18, 39
whiteness, institutional, 29
white supremacy, effect on, 30
Hinshaw, Wendy, 114
"How Do We Language So People Stop Killing Each Other, or What Do We Do about White Language Supremacy?" (Inoue), 30
"How Queer Undocumented Youth Built the Immigrant Rights Movement" (Lal & Unzueta), 51
Hutchinson, Glenn, xi–xii, 15, 20

ICE threat matrix, 101
identity
American, challenging through storytelling, 49–50
complexity of undocumented activists, 46
complexity of undocumented students, 27, 37–38, 46, 61–63
Identity, Social Activism, and the Pursuit of Higher Education (Muñoz), 50
"Illegal" (Espinosa-Aguilar), 44

illegal, term use, 44
Illegal Immigration Reform and
    Immigrant Responsibility Act
    (IIRIRA), 44–45, 102
immigrant
    as other, 45, 131
    term use, 44
immigrant rights movement
    intersectionality in the, 50–51, 84,
        132–33
    LGBTQ+ experiences and the,
        50–51
    rhetorical strategies in the, 77
    undocumented youth in the, 28,
        70–77
immigrants, imprisoned. *See also*
        detention centers
    children, 102–3
    emotional distress of, 47
    growth in, 102
    invisibility of, 105, 106
    letter-writing project for, 113–19
    profitability, 102
    releases, stories of, 5–6, 96–97
    rights of
        communication restrictions,
            100–101
        visitation monitoring, 100
    silencing, 98, 136
    statistics, 102
    teaching writing to, 98–99
immigrants, undocumented
    coming out, 49–54
    criminalizing, 45, 57, 74–75, 81,
        101, 107–8
    demographics, 33–34
    documentation status, significance
        of, 62
    financial burden on, 36
    generalizations about, 62
    identity question for, 62–63
    statistics, 13, 33–34, 62–63
    storytelling to challenge beliefs
        about, 49–54
immigrants' rights, 36

immigration, divisive rhetoric of,
    44–45
Immigration Act, 33
Immigration and Nationality Act,
    31, 32
immigration legislation, 31, 33
immigration policy, 44
Immigration Reform and Control
    Act, 31
immigration system, 101
income tax, 36
The Infiltrators (documentary film),
    97, 119, 130, 136
injustice, factors shaping, 32
Inoue, Asao B., 30, 39, 125, 128

Jacobi, Tobi, 101, 104, 105, 113
Jarratt, Susan C., 88, 89
Johnson, Lamar, 28
Johnson C. Smith University, 22
Julier, Laura, 17

Kahn, Seth, 87
Kannan, Vani, 88
Kazin, Michael, 45
Kelly, Amber, 126
Kennedy, Thomas, 128
King, Martin Luther Jr., 5
King, Rodney, 72
Kirshner, Ben, 87–88
Kluge, Alexander, 100, 136
Krome North Service Processing
    (detention) Center, 5, 105,
    106–8, 113, 115, 117
Kynard, Carmen, 29, 37, 39, 88, 125

Lal, Prerna, 51, 128
language
    divisive rhetoric of immigration,
        44–45
    linguistic legitimacy, 27–28
    linguistic practices of whiteness, 21
    ownership of, 62
    White language supremacy, 30,
        125

Lee, Eunjeong, 62
LeMieux, George, 152–53
Leon, Kendall, 20
letter-writing project, 113–19
LGBTQ+ population, 50–51
Limbo (Gonzalez), 137
linguistic legitimacy, 27–28
Lipman, Jana K., 106–7
listening
    to build community, 114
    classroom vs. community, 66–67
    rhetorical, 66
literacy, 21, 28
literacy normativity, 21
Loeb, Paul, 26, 132
Long, Elenore, 84
los otros DREAMers, 133
Luna, Joachín, 37–38

Macías-Rojas, Patrisia, 101
The Making of a Dream (Wildes-Muñoz), 74
Mandela, Nelson, 155
Mariel boatlift, 107
Martin, Trayvon, 124
Martinez, Aja, 126, 128, 140
Mass Story Lab, 115
Mathieu, Paula, 18
McCain, John, 75–77
McCartin, Joseph A., 45
McDonald, Tim, 5, 141
media
    civil disobedience and the, 76, 81, 83
    corporate control of the, 100, 129
    detention centers, documenting, 97–98
    diversity in the, 90
    organizers use of the, 59–60, 90, 111–12
    power of the, 117, 134–35
Mohammad. *See* Abdollahi, Mohammad
Monberg, Terese Guinsatao, 21

Morton, John (Morton memorandum), 47, 56–57, 58, 59, 60, 65
Muñoz, Susana M., 50–51, 62
Mutnick, Deborah, 118

Napolitano, Janet, 47–48, 56, 57, 58
National Immigrant Youth Alliance (NIYA), 51, 133
Naturalization Act, 31
Negrón-Gonzales, Genevieve, 49, 75–76
Negt, Oskar, 100, 136
neoliberalism, 99, 103–5, 131
network of actions, 64–65, 76, 134–38, 140
The New Jim Crow: Mass Incarceration in the Age of Colorblindness (Alexander), 35, 101
newspaper readership, 90
North Carolina Community College, 22
North Carolina Driver's License Law, 57–58
nuclear missiles, 106–7

Obama, Barack, x, 48, 57, 58, 70, 78–79, 86
Obama (Barack) administration, 5, 34, 44, 48, 68, 69, 81, 83, 85–86
op-eds, 90, 91–93, 112, 134–35, 151
organizers
    Chicana, 20–21
    media, use of the, 59–60, 76, 81, 83, 90
    risks taken, 74–75
organizers, student
    in the classroom, 90–91
    focus of, 62
    future for, 133–34
    rhetorical strategies, learning, 86–93
    teachers of, 123–29

organizers, undocumented
   beginners, stories of, 5–6
   coming out, risk with, 52–53
   focus of, 62
   identity, complexity of, 46
   writing for activism, 27–28
organizer-writers, reflections from student, 151–55
organizing
   future of, 133–34
   goal of, 129
   importance of, 4
   long-term, 129–34, 140, 155
   partisanship in, 130–31
   requirements for, 133
   strategies, 129–30
Ortiz Juarez-Paz, Anna V., 50
other, immigrant as, 45, 131

Pacheco, Gaby, 51–52, 55, 128, 133
Paris, Django, 21, 125
Parks, Steve (Stephen), 19, 27, 118
Patel, Leigh, 38, 39, 65, 123–24
Pauszek, Jessica, 118
Plemons, Anna, 103–4, 105
policy, risks of challenging, 74–75
The Pot (theater), 137
Powell, Jessica, 126
Powell, Katrina M., 131
prison-industrial complex, 33, 99, 101, 112–13
prison population, 35, 101
prisons
   beds maintained for detention in, 102
   economics of, 33
   education programs, 103–6
   literacy classes in, 98–99
   neoliberal policies of, 103–6, 112, 118
   privatization of, 100–101
Prison Studies Project, 103
prison visiting room, 100, 136
Pritchard, Eric Darnell, 21

privatization, 99–100
Progressive Media Project (PMP), 112
public discourse, participating in, 71
public space
   availability of, 129–30
   constructing a, 76–77
   invisible theater organizing, 138
public sphere
   constructing a, 71–73, 80, 83–84, 87
   control of the, 100
   limits on participation, 99
   rhetorical activism in the, 70, 77
public writing, 70–77, 84–85
public-writing classroom
   conclusions, 93–95
   goals and possibilities, 91
   op-eds, 68–69, 91–93
   revising the, 86–93, 94–95

race education, 29
racial profiling, 31–32
racism
   citizenship policy, 45
   immigration and, 33
   institutional, 28–29, 39, 124–25
   justice system and, 35
   Reagan (Ronald) administration, 31
Reno, Janet, 23
restorative literacies, 21
Rhetoric of Respect: Recognizing Change at a Community Writing Center (Rousculp), 104
Ribero, Ana Milena, 30, 32, 39, 122
risk-taking, 51–53, 55, 73–74
"Rogue Cops and Health Care: What Do We Want from Public Writing?" (Wells), 71
Rosa, Jonathan, 21
Rousculp, Tiffany, 104
Rubio, Marco, 154

Sandweg, John, 111
Schutz, Aaron, 17

Schwiertz, Helge, 85
Scott, Rick, 91
Scott, Tony, 99
self-definition, literary practices of, 21
Sensenbrenner bill, 74
service-learning/community-writing courses
    citizenship, teaching, 22–26, 30–32
    creative projects, 136–38
    goal of, 16–18, 19–20
    intersectionality, 32–37, 132–33
    pedagogical change, need for, 138–40
    student skills, acknowledging, 39
    students of color in, 21
Service-Learning Reader (Albert, ed.), 24
social media, 111–12
Social Security, 36
Soul of a Citizen (Loeb), 26, 132
stories of self
    challenging American identity through, 49–50
    structuring, 49–50
stories of self, sharing
    to build solidarity, 50
    for change, 54
    coming out, 49–54
    to Congress, 52
    to connect with one another, 50
    importance of, 55
    online, 53
    risks with, 51–53, 55
Story of Self activity, 49
storytelling
    to challenge beliefs, 49–54
    silencing, 98
    theater for, 136–37
Student Alliance for Prison Reform (FIU), 115
students, undocumented. *See also* organizers, student; youth, undocumented
    activism, 39–40
    additional worries for, 2, 27, 37–38, 62
    changing viewpoints of, 16–17
    citizenship, desire for, 37
    criminalizing, 80–81, 83
    DACA changes for, 82–83
    documentation status, learning about significance of, 63
    emotional distress of, 37–38, 45, 63
    exclusions for, 63, 71
    higher education, failure of, 13–14, 27, 29
    higher education available to, x–xi, 1–2, 13, 37–38, 91–92, 132–33, 153–54
    high school graduates, 13, 92
    identity, complexity of, 27, 37–38, 46, 61–63
    in-state tuition for, 13, 91–92, 153–54
    listening to, 127
    rhetorical responsibilities, 73
    risks taken, 76–77, 91
Students Working for Equal Rights (SWER), 82, 109, 112, 117, 133–34, 136
Sundvall, Scott, 73–74, 76

tactics of hope, 18
Tactics of Hope (Mathieu), 18
Trail of Dreams walk, 51–52
"Taking a Lead from Student Movements in a 'Political Turn,'" (Kannan), 88
Tanton, John, 91
Taylor, Keeanga-Yamahtta, 128
teacher-student relationships, 37
Temporary Protected Status (TPS), 33
Terriquez, Veronica, 37
testimonio, 49–50
theater, 136–37
"Trail of Dreams" (Pacheco), 51–52

Trump (Donald) administration, 13, 36, 38, 83, 119, 130
Trump, Donald, 102
Tuck, Eve, 14
tuition, in-state, 13, 91–92, 153–54

undocuactivists, 46
The Undocumentary (Davis), 78
undocumented. *See* immigrants, undocumented; students, undocumented
"Undocumented, Unafraid and Unapologetic: Re-articulatory Practices and Migrant Youth 'Illegality'" (Negrón-Gonzales), 75
Undocumented and Unafraid (Negrón-Gonzales), 49
Undocumented and Unafraid: Tam Tran, Cinthya Felix, and the Immigrant Youth Movement (UCLA Center for Labor Research and Education), 52
"Undocumented Identity Storytelling: (Re)framing Public Relations" (Ortiz Juarez-Paz), 50
"An Undocumented Immigrant Speaks Out" (Velazquillo), 68–70
Undocumented Student Movement (USM), 50
"Undocumented Students Seek In-State Tuition" (Wulff), 92–93
undocumented youth movement, 85
undocuqueer, 51
UNICOR (Bureau of Prisons), 101
United We Dream, 81
university-community partnerships, 17–18, 39. *See also* higher education
Unzueta, Tania, 51, 128
U visa, x–xi

Vargas, Jose Antonio, 63, 131
Velazquillo, Angelica, ix–xii, 2, 14, 27, 42–43, 54–60, 61, 68–70, 77, 81, 91, 94, 128, 134–35, 137, 151
Velazquillo, Erick, 42–43, 54–60, 64, 77, 82, 137
Vernacular Insurrections: Race, Black Protest, and the New Century in Composition-Literacies Studies (Kynard), 29
Vieira, Kate, 28, 39, 61, 122
Vision from The Inside project, 114
volunteerism, 19–20, 25
voting, 24–25

Wan, Amy, 16
Welch, Nancy, 83, 85, 99
Wells, Susan, 71–72, 76, 100
whiteness
  institutional, 29
  linguistic practices of, 21
  shaping involvement/limiting perspective, 15, 21
white supremacy, 30, 44, 124
Wildes-Muñoz, Laura, 74
Wingard, Jennifer, 101, 105
women's rights, 32–33
workers rights, 34–35
writing as a network of action, 134–38, 140
Writing Democracy: The Political Turn in and beyond the Trump Era (Carter, et al.), 118, 139
writing for activism
  academic writing vs., 28
  importance of, 27–28
writing partnerships, 103–5, 113–18
writing teachers, roles of, 88, 123–29, 140
Writing the Community: Concepts and Models for Service-Learning in Composition (Adler-Kassner & Crooks, eds.), 17
writing to organize, 86–93
Wulff, Nicolas, 91–93, 128

youth, undocumented. *See also* students, undocumented
  answerability of, 65
  coming out, risk with, 52–53
  criminalizing, 68–69
  desires of, 69
  forming a more inclusive public sphere, 70
  immigrant rights advocacy, 28, 70–77
  pedagogies developed by, 65
  in the public-writing classroom, 70–77
  rhetorical activism, 70
  risks taken, 69, 77
  writing, importance to, 28
  writing for activism, 27–28
Youth Activism in an Era of Education Inequality (Kirshner), 87–88

Zimmerman, Arely, 53–54
Zimmerman, George, 124
Zong, Jie, 13

AUTHOR

Glenn Hutchinson teaches rhetoric/composition and directs the writing center at Florida International University in Miami. Since 2007 he has volunteered with different immigrant rights groups in North Carolina and Florida. He has published articles in *Community Literacy Journal*, *The CEA Critic*, and *Reflections*. Hutchinson also writes plays and op-eds.

BOOKS IN THE CCCC STUDIES IN WRITING & RHETORIC SERIES

Writing Accomplices with Student Immigrant Rights Organizers
Glenn Hutchinson

Counterstory: The Rhetoric and Writing of Critical Race Theory
Aja Y. Martinez

Writing Programs, Veterans Studies, and the Post-9/11 University: A Field Guide
D. Alexis Hart and Roger Thompson

Beyond Progress in the Prison Classroom: Options and Opportunities
Anna Plemons

Rhetorics Elsewhere and Otherwise: Contested Modernities, Decolonial Visions
Edited by Romeo García and Damián Baca

Black Perspectives in Writing Program Administration: From the Margins to the Center
Edited by Staci M. Perryman-Clark and Collin Lamont Craig

Translanguaging outside the Academy: Negotiating Rhetoric and Healthcare in the Spanish Caribbean
Rachel Bloom-Pojar

Collaborative Learning as Democratic Practice: A History
Mara Holt

Reframing the Relational: A Pedagogical Ethic for Cross-Curricular Literacy Work
Sandra L. Tarabochia

Inside the Subject: A Theory of Identity for the Study of Writing
Raúl Sánchez

Genre of Power: Police Report Writers and Readers in the Justice System
Leslie Seawright

Assembling Composition
Edited by Kathleen Blake Yancey and Stephen J. McElroy

Public Pedagogy in Composition Studies
Ashley J. Holmes

From Boys to Men: Rhetorics of Emergent American Masculinity
Leigh Ann Jones

Freedom Writing: African American Civil Rights Literacy Activism, 1955–1967
Rhea Estelle Lathan

The Desire for Literacy: Writing in the Lives of Adult Learners
Lauren Rosenberg

On Multimodality: New Media in Composition Studies
Jonathan Alexander and Jacqueline Rhodes

Toward a New Rhetoric of Difference
Stephanie L. Kerschbaum

Rhetoric of Respect: Recognizing Change at a Community Writing Center
Tiffany Rousculp

After Pedagogy: The Experience of Teaching
Paul Lynch

Redesigning Composition for Multilingual Realities
Jay Jordan

Agency in the Age of Peer Production
Quentin D. Vieregge, Kyle D. Stedman, Taylor Joy Mitchell, and Joseph M. Moxley

Remixing Composition: A History of Multimodal Writing Pedagogy
Jason Palmeri

First Semester: Graduate Students, Teaching Writing, and the Challenge of Middle Ground
Jessica Restaino

Agents of Integration: Understanding Transfer as a Rhetorical Act
Rebecca S. Nowacek

Digital Griots: African American Rhetoric in a Multimedia Age
Adam J. Banks

The Managerial Unconscious in the History of Composition Studies
Donna Strickland

Everyday Genres: Writing Assignments across the Disciplines
Mary Soliday

The Community College Writer: Exceeding Expectations
Howard Tinberg and Jean-Paul Nadeau

A Taste for Language: Literacy, Class, and English Studies
James Ray Watkins

Before Shaughnessy: Basic Writing at Yale and Harvard, 1920–1960
Kelly Ritter

Writer's Block: The Cognitive Dimension
Mike Rose

Teaching/Writing in Thirdspaces: The Studio Approach
Rhonda C. Grego and Nancy S. Thompson

Rural Literacies
Kim Donehower, Charlotte Hogg, and Eileen E. Schell

Writing with Authority: Students' Roles as Writers in Cross-National Perspective
David Foster

Whistlin' and Crowin' Women of Appalachia: Literacy Practices since College
Katherine Kelleher Sohn

Sexuality and the Politics of Ethos in the Writing Classroom
Zan Meyer Gonçalves

African American Literacies Unleashed: Vernacular English and the Composition Classroom
Arnetha F. Ball and Ted Lardner

Revisionary Rhetoric, Feminist Pedagogy, and Multigenre Texts
Julie Jung

Archives of Instruction: Nineteenth-Century Rhetorics, Readers, and Composition Books in the United States
Jean Ferguson Carr, Stephen L. Carr, and Lucille M. Schultz

Response to Reform: Composition and the Professionalization of Teaching
Margaret J. Marshall

Multiliteracies for a Digital Age
Stuart A. Selber

Personally Speaking: Experience as Evidence in Academic Discourse
Candace Spigelman

Self-Development and College Writing
Nick Tingle

Minor Re/Visions: Asian American Literacy Narratives as a Rhetoric of Citizenship
Morris Young

A Communion of Friendship: Literacy, Spiritual Practice, and Women in Recovery
Beth Daniell

Embodied Literacies: Imageword and a Poetics of Teaching
Kristie S. Fleckenstein

Language Diversity in the Classroom: From Intention to Practice
Edited by Geneva Smitherman and Victor Villanueva

Rehearsing New Roles: How College Students Develop as Writers
Lee Ann Carroll

Across Property Lines: Textual Ownership in Writing Groups
Candace Spigelman

Mutuality in the Rhetoric and Composition Classroom
David L. Wallace and Helen Rothschild Ewald

The Young Composers: Composition's Beginnings in Nineteenth-Century Schools
Lucille M. Schultz

Technology and Literacy in the Twenty-First Century: The Importance of Paying Attention
Cynthia L. Selfe

Women Writing the Academy: Audience, Authority, and Transformation
Gesa E. Kirsch

Gender Influences: Reading Student Texts
Donnalee Rubin

Something Old, Something New: College Writing Teachers and Classroom Change
Wendy Bishop

Dialogue, Dialectic, and Conversation: A Social Perspective on the Function of Writing
Gregory Clark

Audience Expectations and Teacher Demands
Robert Brooke and John Hendricks

Toward a Grammar of Passages
Richard M. Coe

Rhetoric and Reality: Writing Instruction in American Colleges, 1900–1985
James A. Berlin

Writing Groups: History, Theory, and Implications
Anne Ruggles Gere

Teaching Writing as a Second Language
Alice S. Horning

Invention as a Social Act
Karen Burke LeFevre

The Variables of Composition: Process and Product in a Business Setting
Glenn J. Broadhead and Richard C. Freed

Writing Instruction in Nineteenth-Century American Colleges
James A. Berlin

Computers & Composing: How the New Technologies Are Changing Writing
Jeanne W. Halpern and Sarah Liggett

A New Perspective on Cohesion in Expository Paragraphs
Robin Bell Markels

Evaluating College Writing Programs
Stephen P. Witte and Lester Faigley

In this book, the voices of US transnational students at the intersections and margins of nation, equity, and higher education are loud and vibrant. It is through this very amplification of young adult voices that Glenn Hutchinson richly shares with educators and scholars the paths, limitations, and journeys of writing with and for our students and their communities. The commitment to justice in this book is bound to transform our conceptualization of community writing and immigrant-led activism.

— Sara P. Alvarez, Queens College, City University of New York

Writing Accomplices with Student Immigrant Rights Organizers serves as a model of how white writing teachers (and writing teachers writ large) can support the organizing work of students, specifically by contributing to students' efforts and partaking in the risk-taking that accomplice work entails. By positioning his students' voices and activism as central to, rather than segmented from, his writing classroom, Hutchinson showcases how writing classrooms can provide opportunities for students to do work that matters, to them and the world. Hutchinson engages with tough questions regarding privilege and positionality while making space for his students' perspectives and expertise to shine.

— Laura Gonzales, University of Florida

How might writing instructors dedicated to community-writing or service-learning courses take into account and even mobilize the lived experiences of *all* their students? Veteran community-writing instructor Glenn Hutchinson charts the history of his understanding that the conventional goal of such courses, to engage students in their communities and help them become more active citizens, doesn't acknowledge the reality of the many college students who are prohibited from becoming US citizens, in spite of long years of residence in this country.

Writing Accomplices with Student Immigrant Rights Organizers argues for a pedagogical shift toward centering the public-writing classroom on students' work as organizers and rhetoricians. Instead of focusing only on community partnerships, the writing classroom can foreground the work of student organizers and how they can better inform the field's teaching practices. Each chapter focuses on students' rhetorical skills through petitions, op-eds, and campaigns to stop deportations. Hutchinson emphasizes teachers' responsibility to act in solidarity with immigrant students, pointing to a new role for the writing teacher in changing anti-immigrant and white supremacist laws and policies.

Glenn Hutchinson teaches rhetoric/composition and directs the writing center at Florida International University in Miami.

CONFERENCE ON COLLEGE COMPOSITION AND COMMUNICATION/
NATIONAL COUNCIL OF TEACHERS OF ENGLISH
340 N. Neil St., Suite #104, Champaign, Illinois 61820
800-369-6283 or 217-328-3870
www.ncte.org

ISBN 978-0-8141-5850-0

This book was typeset in Garamond and Frutiger by Barbara Frazier.
Typefaces used on the cover include Garamond and News Gothic.
The book was printed on 50-lb. White Offset paper
by Seaway Printing Company, Inc.

www.ingramcontent.com/pod-product-compliance
Lightning Source LLC
Chambersburg PA
CBHW070401240426
43661CB00056B/2498